HINDUISM

# STUDIES
## IN THE HISTORY OF RELIGIONS

(SUPPLEMENTS TO *NUMEN*)

XXXIII

HINDUISM

NEW ESSAYS IN
THE HISTORY OF RELIGIONS

LEIDEN
E. J. BRILL
1976

# HINDUISM

## NEW ESSAYS IN THE HISTORY OF RELIGIONS

EDITED BY

BARDWELL L. SMITH

LEIDEN
E. J. BRILL
1976

ISBN 90 04 04495 7



PRINTED IN THE NETHERLANDS

# CONTENTS

## RELIGIOUS EXPERIENCE
## AND ITS INSTITUTIONALIZATION

## NEW INTERPRETATIONS IN EPIC MYTHOLOGY

## TRANSCRIPTION OF INDIAN WORDS

In the essays of this volume the transcription of words from various Indian languages have followed the customary scholarly conventions. In general, the system used by A. L. Basham in *The Wonder That Was India* has been employed, but for reasons of simplification certain changes have been made. (1) Well-known place names are without diacritical marks, unless in the case of ones such as Purī and Mathurā and some others it seemed helpful to include them. But, large cities, state names, and their derivatives (e.g., Agra, Bengal, Bengali, etc.) are without diacritical marks. In the case of less familiar regions or names no longer used markings are included. (2) *Varṇa* and *avarṇa* terms (brahman, kshatriya, vaishya, shudra, untouchable, harijan) have no marks on them *in most cases* and are in lower case. *Jāti* names begin with capital letters and have marks. (3) Sanskrit terms are in italics the first time used in each essay (though not caste names, proper names, or place names). If they are frequently used in the essay, they appear in italics the first time used but not thereafter. If not frequently used, they remain italicized. No diacritical system suits all readers; the above merely identifies the system employed for the most part throughout this volume. For various reasons consistency was not always possible or even desirable.

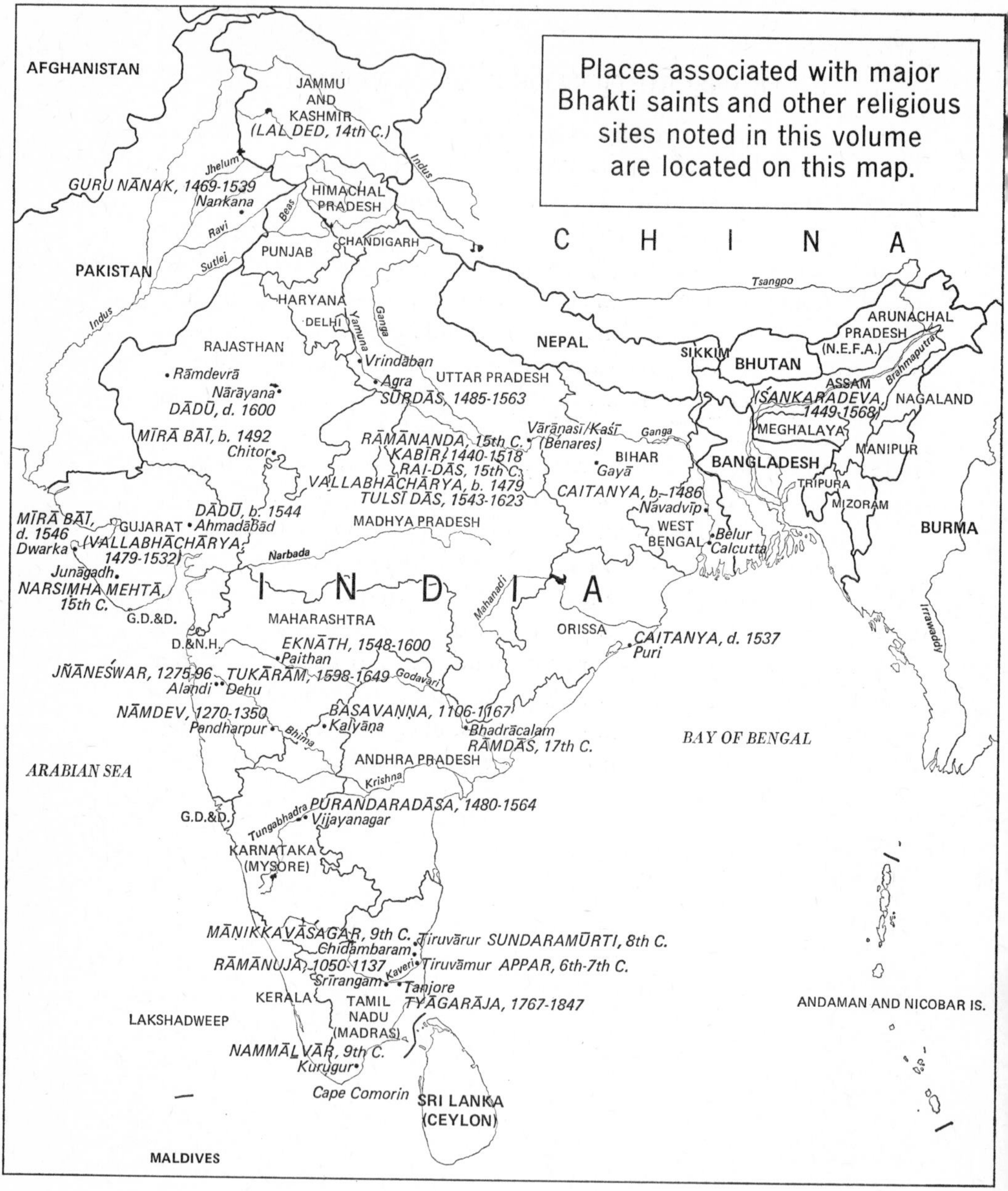
Places associated with major Bhakti saints and other religious sites noted in this volume are located on this map.
AFGHANISTAN
JAMMU AND KASHMIR
(LAL DED, 14th C.)
Jhelum
Indus
GURU NĀNAK, 1469-1539
Nankana
HIMACHAL PRADESH
Beas
Ravi
Sutlej
PAKISTAN
PUNJAB
CHANDIGARH
CHINA
Tsangpo
HARYANA
DELHI
Yamuna
Ganga
RAJASTHAN
NEPAL
SIKKIM
BHUTAN
ARUNACHAL PRADESH (N.E.F.A.)
Brahmaputra
Vrindāban
• Rāmdevrā
Agra
UTTAR PRADESH
Nārāyanā
DĀDŪ, d. 1600
SŪRDĀS, 1485-1563
ASSAM
(SANKARADEVA, 1449-1568)
NAGALAND
MEGHALAYA
MANIPUR
Vārānasī/Kaśī (Benares)
Ganga
MĪRĀ BĀĪ, b. 1492
Chitor
RĀMĀNANDA, 15th C.
KABĪR, 1440-1518
RAI-DĀS, 15th C.
VALLABHĀCHĀRYA, b. 1479
TULSĪ DĀS, 1543-1623
BIHAR
Gayā
BANGLADESH
TRIPURA
MIZORAM
CAITANYA, b. 1486
Navadvīp
MĪRĀ BĀĪ, d. 1546
DĀDŪ, b. 1544
GUJARAT • Ahmadābād
MADHYA PRADESH
WEST BENGAL
Belur
Calcutta
BURMA
Dwarka
(VALLABHĀCHĀRYA, 1479-1532)
Narbada
Junāgadh
NARSIMHA MEHTĀ, 15th C.
INDIA
Mahanadi
G.D.&D.
MAHARASHTRA
ORISSA
Irrawaddy
D.&N.H.
EKNĀTH, 1548-1600
Paithan
CAITANYA, d. 1537
Puri
JÑĀNEŚWAR, 1275-96
TUKĀRĀM, 1598-1649
Godavari
Alandi
Dehu
NĀMDEV, 1270-1350
BASAVANNA, 1106-1167
Pandharpur
Bhima
Kalyāṇa
Bhadrācalam
RĀMDĀS, 17th C.
BAY OF BENGAL
ARABIAN SEA
ANDHRA PRADESH
Krishna
G.D.&D.
PURANDARADĀSA, 1480-1564
Tungabhadra
Vijayanagar
KARNATAKA (MYSORE)
MĀṆIKKAVĀSAGAR, 9th C.
Tiruvārur SUNDARAMŪRTI, 8th C.
Chidambaram
RĀMĀNUJA, 1050-1137
Kaveri
Tiruvāmur APPAR, 6th-7th C.
Śrīrangam
Tanjore
KERALA
TAMIL NADU (MADRAS)
TYĀGARĀJA, 1767-1847
ANDAMAN AND NICOBAR IS.
LAKSHADWEEP
NAMMĀLVĀR, 9th C.
Kurugur
Cape Comorin
SRI LANKA (CEYLON)
MALDIVES

# INTRODUCTION

Bardwell L. Smith

## I

Nearly a decade has passed since the publication of *Krishna: Myths, Rites, and Attitudes*, edited by Milton Singer.[1] This remarkable collection of eight essays has become a landmark both in terms of the topic examined and the variety of disciplinary approaches utilized. Though indebted to this publication, the present volume has taken on a different assignment. In the main, the essays contained here, at least in Part One, investigate forms of Vaiṣṇavism alongside other modes of the *bhakti* movement as a way of furthering understanding not of the Kṛṣṇa legend and cult but of the wider movement of which these are central ingredients. While the primary focus here also is on Vaiṣṇava bhakti and Vaiṣṇava mythology, both parts of this volume deal with certain features of Śaivism in order to place the former in somewhat broader perspective. Moreover, while Bengali forms of the Vaiṣṇava movement are the principal concern in Part One, two of the essays extend the picture, one looking at a pilgrimage to Rāmdevrā in Rajasthan, the other examining the basic literature in English on aspects of the wider bhakti movement throughout India.

Early in the process of soliciting essays it was decided to begin the collection with chapters on two important *bhaktas*, followed in each case by chapters in which the movements inspired by these persons would be analyzed.[2] Among the the many possibilities within Bengali Vaiṣṇavism no two figures stand out as more important than Caitanya (1486-1533) and Rāmakrishna (1836-86) and no two movements are more different than those which emerged through their influence.

---

[1] Milton Singer, ed., *Krishna: Myths, Rites, and Attitudes* (Honolulu: East-West Center Press, 1966).

[2] Originally, several of the essays for this volume were written for the 1971 meetings of the American Academy of Religion. Of those appearing here several have been rewritten since then and others solicited especially for this collection. Of the eight contributors six are historians of religion, one is a historian of modern India and one is principally trained in the social sciences. All specialize in Indian thought and culture.

The fifth essay is included for several reasons: first, it provides a contemporary example of bhaktas on pilgrimage, helping therefore to shed light on similar phenomena in the past; second, it is written from the standpoint of a participant-observer, unlike the others; and third, it deals with a figure generally unknown to Western scholars, namely, Rāmdev, the fifteenth century rājpūt martial hero-saint who was regarded by his devotees as an *avatāra* not of Viṣṇu but of Kṛṣṇa. The final chapter in this section is a bibliographical essay analyzing materials available in English for the study of bhakti from many perspectives. Part Two of the collection takes a different tack and attempts to reinterpret two important myths in epic and *purāṇic* literature which provide insight from the Sanskritic tradition upon Vaiṣṇava mythology, which in its variant forms had diverse influence upon and was doubtlessly influenced over the centuries by the more popular bhakti phenomenon.

As one considers the many themes which further relate these essays to each other and to Vaiṣṇavism more generally, a number of important ones appear. *First*, even within Bengal, not to mention the larger Vaiṣṇava scene, the significance of the historical, cultural and social contexts within which specific bhakti movements emerge and grow is central to understanding their inner ingredients as well as their impact upon the times.[3] The degree to which the Gauṛīya Vaiṣṇavas of the seventeenth century, for instance, who revered as their savior Kṛṣṇa-caitanya, were influenced by the situation of Muslim-dominated Bengal not only in their relationship to the social order but in their sense of what constituted devotion to Caitanya is matched by the impact late nineteenth and early twentieth century exposure to Western intellectual and social currents had upon the movement which succeeded Śrī Rāmakrishna. *Second*, within move-

[3] Another sort of influence upon Bengali Vaiṣṇavism is not traced in these essays, namely, its religious roots prior to Caitanya. This is an interesting and important subject and has recently been explored by Friedhelm Hardy in an excellent article entitled "Mādhavêndra Purī: A Link between Bengal Vaiṣṇavism and South Indian *Bhakti*," *Journal of the Royal Asiatic Society of Great Britain and Ireland*, No. 1, 1974, pp. 23-41. While carefully qualifying himself, the author's main thesis is: "Mādhavêndra Purī [15th century] appeared to be the figure of central importance for the *bhakti* of Caitanya, and on formal-poetic and historical grounds it seems likely that Mādhavêndra himself was under the influence of a particular South Indian *bhakti* milieu. One can therefore conclude that there is reason to believe that certain elements of Āḻvār *bhakti* entered Bengal Vaiṣṇavism." On the other hand, "the 700 years or so intervening between the Āḻvārs and Caitanya obviously caused considerable changes, modifications, extensions, and eliminations in the character of the *bhakti*."

ments which endure can be observed a continuing tension between patterns of institutionalization and patterns resisting routinization, those stressing the original vitality and ecstatic religious experience instead. This too is often a feature of the times, though it comes inevitably with the passing of the founder, if not before. To some degree this stems from different concerns shown by prominent figures within any movement. One case in point is the difference in emphasis within the Caitanya movement between what took place in Vṛndāban, as this was shaped by the six Gosvāmins, and what developed in both Bengal and Purī where intense devotion to Kṛṣṇa was preferred to the more scholarly concerns for doctrine and the shaping of ritual. This has been noted by Edward Dimock in the Singer volume and is explored further here by Joseph O'Connell in a somewhat different vein.[4] And *third*, within the continuing dilemma of institutionalization, one may observe the almost inevitable appropriation by the brahmanic tradition of bhakti movements, converting them into its own image and yet being modified itself in the process. The exceptions or at least the varieties found within this familiar process are as important, however, as the general rule. Indeed, it is more valid to portray the process as creating enduring tensions between the several ingredients than as one which results in popular forms of religious expression being appropriated by the so-called Great Tradition. Too often the relationship is seen in unilinear rather than dialectic terms, ignoring complex variables involving personalities, social structure, and a host of dynamic influences. In general, tensions existing between popular and more traditional forms of religion are themselves compounded by recurring organizational patterns of which various cycles of emergence, institutionalization, stagnation and renewal are common. Furthermore, it is only partially valid to term bhakti movements as popular, for their leadership often comes from those born to higher castes, even if their appeal is largely to lower caste groups because of the emphasis upon egalitarian ideals and the promise that birth presents no barrier in access to the Divine. This commonly experienced tension between leadership and other members, stemming in part from different social origins, provides some of the dialectic within these movements and further blurs the line between 'popular' and 'traditional'.

[4] Cf. Edward C. Dimock, Jr. "Doctrine and Practice among Vaiṣṇavas of Bengal," in Singer, *op. cit.*, pp. 44-46.

## II

Turning to more specific parallels between the practice of bhakti in the life and thought of figures such as Caitanya and Rāmakrishna, one enters the core of Vaiṣṇavism. In the essays by Norvin Hein, Joseph O'Connell and Walter Neevel there are several aspects of Vaiṣṇava devotion which merit highlighting at this point. Central to these movements is the conviction that in the Kali Age, the age of corruption and disorder within the four yugas, the only appropriate path or yoga is one of bhakti or devotion. The Kali Age is a reality on all levels—personal, historical, cosmological. The religious sensitivity of a Caitanya or a Rāmakrishna makes vivid in word and style of life the powerlessness of man to cope with the utterly fragmented nature of existence, his inability even to perceive the cosmic harmony except in relationship to divine love. The seriousness with which this is taken makes it impossible for them to accept as obligatory the traditional *varṇāśrama-dharma*, with its sacralizing of caste and ritual, of work and knowledge. While neither Caitanya nor Rāmakrishna felt it necessary to repudiate the various practices of sincere Hindus, it is clear that both saw loving devotion (*prema-bhakti*) alone as finally appropriate to the times, as well as to their own spiritual plight. And, among the Gauṛīya Vaiṣṇavas it was believed that devotion to Kṛṣṇa is the great secret which gives meaning to everything else. The response of devotion is therefore proportionate to the awareness of a pollution transcending caste and occurring at every stage of religious consciousness. Desire for liberation from this is what leads men to chant the Divine Name, evoking in them a sense of the divine presence and making vivid the conviction that this reality cleanses men from the deepest defilements which they experience. This is, of course, related to the *avatāra* concept of the Divine's descent into human affairs, which is basic in varying forms to all bhakti movements and which is superimposed upon the essentially pessimistic doctrine of the Kali Age, freeing the latter of mechanistic connotations. In fact, in the person of Rāmakrishna, a determinism of a positive sort enters in, whereby "only the Divine Mother is responsible for what happens in the world." Dependence upon this power, however, is naturally seen as the sole source of genuine freedom from the ravages of the Kali Age, a theme sounded originally perhaps in the *Bhāgavata Purāṇa*.

A second ingredient common to Vaiṣṇava bhakti in Bengal is the devotional response of *līlā*, or childlike playfulness, to the experience of being possessed by the Divine. Traditionally part of the broader Vaiṣṇavite heritage, particularly in the Rādhā-Kṛṣṇa stories, it takes the form of relief from anxious searching and becomes a kind of abandon enabling Rāmakrishna, for instance, to exclaim: "I don't want liberation; I want love of God." Or, in Caitanya, the chanting itself becomes a *līlākīrtan* telling of Kṛṣṇa's sportive deeds (*līlās*). The attitude of gay abandon may be seen as the ultimate in confident or trustful devotion (*śraddhā*), based as it is upon the realization that nothing finally exists apart from the Divine, that reality is therefore more "a mansion of mirth" to be enjoyed in loving play than "a framework of illusion" from which flight alone is appropriate. As Neevel's essay makes clear, this resembles a kind of divine determinism where human effort is of no avail (for salvation), yet in which the first fruit of genuine dependence (*prapatti*) is the freedom to enjoy the Divine in its infinite forms. One is presented with the reality of persons who have experienced release from the suffering of incompleteness and separation (*viraha*). The expression of trust and devotion, whether in ecstatic form or not, arises from the wonder of a divine love which heals and cleanses as men are drawn deeper into relationship to its power. This same sense of joy, stemming from belief in the compassion and miracles of Rāmdev, comes through in Mira Binford's depiction of the *bhajan* gatherings at Rāmdevrā. Though it is clear that the fervor of reunion (*milana*) with the Divine is never a constant experience, this is outweighed by the sensation that further search is needless. It was this realization that transformed Rāmakrishna "from the 'madman' of his early years into the saintly teacher" later on and that convinced Caitanya that "the sole purpose of life was the love and praise of Kṛṣṇa."

A third recurring element derives from the experience of union with the Divine, namely, man's awareness that "all the aspects of the natural world, including all the powers within himself, are manifestations of the divine *śakti*" or power. Walter Neevel's essay on Rāmakrishna's transformation through tantric *sādhana* argues convincingly for this as the key to understanding not only the life of Rāmakrishna but the true nature of *sādhana* (means, instrument, discipline) itself. The realization that the whole world was filled with the Divine alone both frees the devotee from frenzied questing and provides a vision of the world as inseparable from the Divine. The theme of union is both individual and universal, as oneness with the Divine experienced personally opens up awareness of the divine presence throughout the universe. This theme was expressed vividly in the twelfth century poem, *Gītagovinda*, by Jayadeva. In this, "the myth of Rādhā is the individualisation of all the love and delight and sweetness that was there in the Kṛṣṇa-legend. She is the quintessence of Vaiṣṇavism, especially in Bengal at the time of Jayadeva and later with Caitanya and his followers. The individualisation and the sublimation of the love-relation between the human soul and the Divine is to a great extent the work of Jayadeva." [5] In Vaiṣṇava consciousness there is finally no separation between the sensual and the spiritual, no ultimate dichotomy between the human and the Divine. As Edward Dimock has indicated, "the Vaiṣṇava devotee or poet often sees himself as a woman, a *gopī*, so complete is his transformation in *bhāva*." [6] And, one might add, so complete is his transformed awareness of the world's inseparability from the Divine that the assumption of female identity by the male seeker after God becomes a paradigm which provides the most intimate form of human longing with dimensions that are cosmic. The pilgrimage of Rāmakrishna, both in the beginning as he was drawn to Kālī as a *śākta* devotee and later as he found oneness with the Divine Mother through tantric *sādhana*, is an important instance of this. So too in a different sense was the ritualizing of perceived oneness by Caitanya in the *nagarkīrtan* which expressed his certitude in the omnipresence of divine grace and which symbolically portrayed this through weaving the entire community into the community of song.

A fourth factor emerging from these essays on Vaiṣṇava bhakti relates to the problems organizations and communities have in sustaining their membership, purpose, and vitality over time. The problem of continuity is examined especially in the chapters by O'Connell, Pangborn and Binford, each of which focuses on how the original experience and vision of the *āveśāvatāra* (the one possessed

---

[5] Ranajit Sarkar, *Gītagovinda: Towards a Total Understanding* (Groningen: Institute of Indian Studies, 1974), No. 2, p. 5. It is also important to say here, as Friedhelm Hardy does in his article referred to above, that there was only literary and no direct religious influence of Jayadeva's *Gītagovinda* upon Caitanya. Works of this kind "acquired a religious meaning only through the peculiar religious attitude of Caitanya and his followers, which could superimpose new interpretations on literary works by means of the *rasa*-theory. Thus although these earlier texts formed the *material* for the peculiar blend of religion and literature in Bengal Vaiṣṇavism, they do not offer an explanation of Caitanya's bhakti." Cf. Hardy. *op. cit.*, p. 24.

[6] Dimock, *op. cit.*, p. 221.

by God) can be sustained within the community of devotees and also extended to others. The patterns that are possible are extraordinarily diverse. The essays by O'Connell and Pangborn, for example, provide contrasting models: one which depicts the virtual desacralizing of the social order by the Gauṛīya Vaiṣṇavas of the seventeenth century, the other underscoring the considerable social involvement of the Rāmakrishna Order during this century. As is frequently true, later generations create patterns which the founding fathers would not recognize. It is nevertheless a truism that without organizational development movements do not survive. Hence, the dilemma of institutionalization, of how to maintain forms of continuity which are compatible in spirit with the founder's example if not his intent. The two examples mentioned above show the extremes of an overly literal concern for interior religious discipline at the cost of failing to develop a social ethic of use to Vaiṣṇava Hindus in Muslim-dominated Bengal *and* the relatively successful combining of spiritual discipline with intellectual pursuits and social service by the devotees of Rāmakrishna during the past several decades.

Again, the contexts within these movements existed are crucial, but factors of a more intentional sort were no less important. As Cyrus Pangborn indicates, it was the genius of Vivekānanda first to recognize that the tradition of "so many Sannyāsins wandering about [was] all madness," then to begin developing an organizational structure and style without which the movement might have disappeared, as has that of Caitanya. On the other hand, one can never be sure. How does one explain the continuing vitality of the Rāmdev movement? Here, while organizational elements are clearly visible, they are of a very different sort from those of the Rāmakrishna Order, which was highly influenced by Western organizational practices. Instead, they are more typical of the lineaments found in most bhakti pilgrimages to sacred places. To be sure, the shape and direction of this folk-cult have been modified over time and given organizational cohesiveness not only by the elements of Muslim-Hindu syncretism but also by the movement's recently developed appeal to urban-based non-untouchables as well as to the predominantly untouchable adherents. The inclusion of three essays depicting completely different approaches to the problem of continuity provides further evidence of Vaiṣṇavism's diversity in its structures, ideology and practices.

III

Part Two of this collection represents an effort to identify strata of Vaiṣṇava thought in mythic form which have influenced the legend and cult surrounding Kṛṣṇa. By coming to terms with dimensions of existence as portrayed in myth and symbol, which bewilder as much as they illuminate, one appreciates how seriously this tradition takes religious inquiry, not simply religious practice. The final two essays, therefore, illustrate in different ways how this process takes place within the Hindu framework. The first focuses more directly upon the concept of myth itself and examines a number of structural dimensions as seen through a particular archetypal myth; the second provides an alternative example of how Hindu mythology gives shape to religious consciousness. Both chapters follow naturally from the preceeding ones, exploring further how levels of meaning and ambiguity inhere within all authentic representational form and serve to suggest their actual presence throughout life.

Among several possible nodal points in these essays, at least three seem significant here in helping to clarify the role of Vaiṣṇava mythology in Hindu culture. The first is the manner in which divine reality is alternately disclosed and masked within mythology, the intention being as much to deceive as to reveal, lest men confuse representations with reality itself. The very employment of *māyā* not only to confound the forces of evil but to shake pious complacency takes dramatic and cognitive form, forcing one to move beyond appearances. While often conscious devices in the hands of artist or poet, they stand for deeper experiences of hiddenness and disclosure within history itself, which men can neither predict nor control. This is no less true of the hiddenness of reality within the human sphere than of the divine nature, in part because it is the nature of existence always to be changing, making each portrayal false by definition. Yet beyond this lies the fundamentally mysterious character of reality which resists being made captive to any form. Myth and symbol, therefore, create paradigms of disclosure and disguise which concomitantly assist *and* arrest one's compulsion to see. In an important sense, hiddenness itself *is* disclosure, for theophanies portraying the Divine in "dear, familiar form" may be less revelatory than those which blind one to easy access. The evidences of divine presence can no more be taken for granted than those of its apparent abcense.

In the churning of the ocean which issues forth in poison as well as in the elixir of immortality one has an image portraying not simply the cryptic nature of reality but its basic ambiguousness. "The sacred becomes profanized and the profane is sacralized." The essays by Bruce Long and Alf Hiltebeitel depict in various ways how the divine presence appears now as bestower of grace, now as destroyer. In Bengali Vaiṣṇavism, of course, one finds the classic mode of this in the image of Kālī. She is the terrifyingly wild aspect of the Divine and at the same time, at least within Bengali devotional tradition, "the benign, the loving, the comforting". The chapter by Hiltebeitel explicitly notes this dialectical portrayal of divine presence and mien: first, "Kṛṣṇa moves about like Time or Death, cutting up creatures with his *cakra*: indeed, 'the form of that soul of all creatures became very terrible' "; and then, "Kṛṣṇa, with Arjuna here, thus fulfills his role as *avatāra*: restoring *dharma* and renewing the world order." As Hiltebeitel continues, "We might say that Arjuna and Kṛṣṇa—Nara and Nārāyaṇa—are initiated here into their *capacity* to destroy and 'recreate,' but without symbolizing, in any direct way, an anticipation of the *fashion* in which they will do so in the great battle."

A second point of orientation within these essays is the accent upon the longing to return to perfect or divine origins that lies universally at the core of man's religious impulse. If awareness of divine grace and beauty arouses wonder and delight, the intense experience of its absence plunges man into despair. The longing of man to experience original and ultimate harmony is basic. The myth of the eternal return is based upon the belief, depicted through Long's interpretation, that "in precosmogonic times, before the cosmos had assumed its present forms, all things existed in a state of primordial unity and absolute stasis," and upon the conviction that phenomenal existence is pervaded by divine presence and power. Throughout Hindu tradition one finds a tension between eventual return and present possibility. In any case, the yearning is not something which has yet to occur, but for a reality once experienced and now lost. The burning of the forest, in fact, is to restore to the forces of dharma a territory which has become "an abode of enemies of the gods".

Part of the dilemma behind the apparently unmanifest nature of divine grace is that it is hidden from view by human blindness. *Māyā* is not simply a cosmic game played by Lord Viṣṇu for benign purposes; it is also the consequence of human pride and self-deception. As such, it is the obscuring of reality and tantamount to denying its fundamental unity. It is out of this disorder that divine grace erupts, in the *pralaya* (dissolution or destruction), or into which it descends. Within the tantric tradition, specifically among the followers of Kālī, it is through the discipline of devotion that all socially and personally relative distinctions between cleanness and uncleanness are overcome, for in the Age of Kali only the most intense longing (as in a Caitanya or Rāmakrishna) burns away all desires but one, thus freeing man's vision to perceive the Divine in all places and to experience the primordial unity.

Thirdly, constituent with most forms of Hindu mythology and symbolism ultimately is the dialectic operating throughout the universe, "the alteration of all cosmic elements between polar opposites of day and night, good and evil, life and death," "the complementary aspects of the unitary reality that is Being itself." The Churning of the Ocean myth, for example, serves to preserve this balance graphically: "This primordial and perpetual conflict between opposed but related cosmic forces at one and the same time establishes the world in existence and threatens it with extinction."[7] The repeated theophanies of Kṛṣṇa must be seen in this perspective, within the cyclical round of reversals and triumphs that constitutes the struggle between the Devas and the Asuras, for equally characteristic of Hindu mythology as the hidden or disclosed presence of the Divine is the active working of demonic forces. The disordering of cosmic harmony is constant; the balance between good and evil is precarious and ambiguous at best. However central are the themes of divine grace and of human devotion in response, these take on authentic power only by repeated focussing upon the interplay of forces within

[7] In this particular myth Viṣṇu is depicted by Long as the principle of mediation, identifying with all positions, simultaneously unifying the polarities and polarizing the unity. For another perceptive analysis of this theme see Wendy Doniger O'Flaherty, *Asceticism and Eroticism in the Mythology of Śiva* (London: Oxford University Press, 1973). On page 36 she writes: "The mediating principle that tends to resolve the oppositions is in most cases Śiva himself. Among ascetics he is a libertine and among libertines an ascetic; conflicts which they cannot resolve, or can attempt to resolve only by compromise, he simply absorbs into himself and expresses in terms of other conflicts. Where there is excess, he opposes and controls it; where there is no action, he himself becomes excessively active. He emphasizes that aspect of himself which is unexpected, inappropriate, shattering any attempt to achieve a superficial reconciliation of the conflict through mere logical compromise. Mediating characters of this type are essential to all mythologies which deal in contradictions".

the universe. The Churning of the Ocean motif is the note of realism, representing not the negation of cosmic harmony but the fact that significant human harmony and order are forged within the crucible of conflict. Both themes inject, therefore, a note of lucidity to all forms of bhakti, whether they be chanting of the Divine Name or pilgrimages to sacred places, which otherwise slip easily into sentimentality, if not perfunctory piety.

In conclusion, the attempt within Hindu tradition to understand, represent and experience reality through cultic and mythological forms is a history of profusion balanced by restraint. Belief and practice, myth and symbol weave themselves into religious consciousness, ritual, doctrine and teaching, as well as into every art form from poetry and drama to sculpture and dance. Forms capture movement in frieze-like fashion, pointing beyond stasis and outside themselves. Controlled creation seizes one's attention, only to thrust it away from portrayal and toward the portrayed. At their best, they seek more to understand than to depict, to involve one in the quest for meaning more than to delineate its shape. In this effort they are consistent with the experience even of the most saintly *sādhaka* whose recurring tastes of union (*milana*) with the Divine are all the more sweet because his sense of separation (*viraha*) is no less vivid.

RELIGIOUS EXPERIENCE
AND ITS INSTITUTIONALIZATION

# CAITANYA'S ECSTASIES AND THE THEOLOGY OF THE NAME

NORVIN J. HEIN*

The man on whom this study focuses is usually called Caitanya, but that name has been shortened for convenience. His full monastic designation, conferred upon him by the guru who initiated him into the ascetic life, is *Śrīkṛṣṇa-Caitanya*, "He Who Has Consciousness of Kṛṣṇa." The complete name is worthy of notice because it points toward the most memorable characteristic of the man. Caitanya has a place in history because he was a visionary and a stimulator in others of similar sensitivity.

Caitanya set in motion the first powerful wave of Hindu resurgence of the sixteenth century. His style of worship spread far beyond the circle of his acknowledged disciples and has its echoes throughout the whole of Hindu theism. His direct tradition lives on in a vigorous Caitanyite sect that is actively missionary. Its meetings for emotional singing are held regularly today in about fifty centers in North America.

In addition to its significance in Indian cultural history, the religion of Caitanya has a typological importance. As we describe Caitanya's attitudes and practices, readers may recognize the characteristics of religious movements originating far from the banks of the Ganges. In Caitanya there may be a more thorough development of techniques and a more thoughtful theological explication of the basic experience than can be observed in other manifestations of this type of religion. India is nothing if not systematic in the cultivation and analysis of the varieties of internal religious life.

We approach Caitanya as an exemplar of a type of religion, not as a problem in biography. We shall survey his life only selectively, for materials particularly relevant to the interpretation of his religious experience, limiting ourselves to non-controversial biographical data that need no documentation. We shall take the liberty, from time to time, of amplifying our picture with materials from the

* The author thanks the members of the American Academy of Religion who commented so helpfully on this paper, and is particularly grateful to Professor Joseph T. O'Connell of St. Michael's College, University of Toronto, whose careful scrutiny of the document has tempered the interpretations at many points.

lives and writings of Caitanya's predecessors and successors when we believe that their outlook was homogeneous with his own. We are not attempting to describe the peculiarly personal religious life of Caitanya, but to delineate his faith as it was shared with, and interpreted by, his tradition.

## I

Caitanya was born in 1486 in a brahman family in Bengal. For almost three hundred years Bengal had been under the firm control of Muslims. The aristocracy of the land were Muslims, and prestige and the power of decision lay with Muslims. To the lowest classes of old Bengal the coming of Islam may have been a liberation, but for those who were deeply committed to the Hindu tradition it was a disaster. The upper-class Hindu survived under Muslim rule by the Muslim's unsteady tolerance. So far as he was an idolator, the Hindu in Muslim eyes was a blasphemous person whose customs were rightly subject to stringent repression. The obvious way toward freedom and influence was through conversion to Islam or accommodation to Muslim ways. Those who remained Hindu suffered economic and political handicaps in obtaining the means of cultural self-expression. They were left with few of the freedoms that give meaning and satisfaction to life.

The Hindu establishment's first defense against Muslim pressure was a retreat into a tight orthodox pattern of living, under the direction of brahman priests and scholars. Rituals were elaborated to signalize Hindus' complete loyalty to their indigenous tradition. Less respectable social groups, under the unhappy restraints of the time, found an undeniable remnant of satisfaction in religious exaggeration of sexuality. Caitanya, too, bore the special burdens of his people and period in addition to those common to all humanity; but he was to deal with them in a religious reaction of yet another kind.

Caitanya's childhood home was the town of Navadvīp, a center of the brahmanism just mentioned. It was a university town if we use the phrase loosely: a complex of famous Sanskrit schools was located there. Students came from far and wide to study the scholastic traditions of Hinduism, and especially the relatively secular subjects of logic and grammar. Caitanya's mother was a daughter of a scholar of the place. Caitanya learned Sanskrit in childhood as a matter of course, and became accomplished in grammar especially. In his mid-teens he was already a bright young graduate of one of the Sanskrit schools. He founded a school of his own and joined the proud elite of the city.

As an established schoolmaster, Caitanya was pleased with himself and confident of his powers. He was a handsome fellow with an ideal complexion, shoulder-long hair, and a magnetic way. Ambitious and worldly, he had un unashamed interest in getting fees. Along with the rest of the learned community, he was contemptuous of the "vulgar" *bhakti* religion followed by certain of the people of the area. Caitanya belonged to a Vaiṣṇava family, but he brushed aside the efforts of relatives to interest him in serious worship of Viṣṇu in any form. When Īśvara Purī, a monk who was a friend of the family, tried to involve him in a study of Vaiṣṇava scriptures, all Caitanya would do was to pick the passages apart from a literary point of view and ridicule the standard of their grammar.

Yet there was cause for seriousness in the family history of this supercilious young man. He was the ninth or tenth child of his parents, in a house made emptier and emptier by tragedies. The oldest children died in childhood, leaving only Caitanya, his parents, and his older brother. When Caitanya was in his early teens this elder brother abandoned the world as a *sannyāsī* and left home never to be seen again. Then Caitanya's father died. Shortly thereafter his first wife died a sudden accidental death.

As the only surviving son of his father, it fell to Caitanya to perform a traditional ritual for the peace of his soul: in 1508 he was sent to Gayā in Bihar to offer there the *śrāddha* on behalf of his father's spirit. In pursuit of that duty, and with its many sombre associations on his mind, it was necessary for him to enter a shrine displaying footprints in stone that were said to have been left by Viṣṇu when once upon a time he descended to earth to insure the preservation of man. The feet of Viṣṇu are therefore a symbol of the divine presence and help. They have a power of suggestion that a non-Hindu can scarcely imagine. And at that shrine at Gayā Caitanya chanced also to meet again the ascetic Īśvara Purī, who had reminded him once before of the claims of his Vaiṣṇava faith.

Just what happened then in Caitanya's inner self, he was never able to narrate in words. In later life the very mention of the word "Gayā" made him break into tears and lose all power of speech. But it was some kind of mystical vision that burst in upon his consciousness there for the first time. The inenarrable event shaped the remainder of his years, and gave a distinctive character to the lives of millions not yet born.

Īśvara Purī communicated to Caitanya a mantra that initiated him into the worship of Kṛṣṇa. He returned to Navadvīp another man. He would talk of nothing but Kṛṣṇa. He paid no attention to his dress and appearance. For his classes in Sanskrit grammar he had no taste now, and no time. His school dissolved. He ignored his scholarly friends, slept on the bare earth, hardly ate, spent his time laughing and weeping and shouting Kṛṣṇa's name. He saw visions of Kṛṣṇa in the clouds and ran after them with his eyes full of tears, crying "O God, do not hide your face from me!" Even his mother thought that he had gone mad.

In the town of Navadvīp there was a circle of Viṣṇu-devotees that was able to appreciate and accept such behavior. Its members were accustomed to assemble nightly in the courtyard of the house of a certain Śrīvās to sing songs in praise of Kṛṣṇa. The orthodox of Navadvīp spoke contemptuously of this group because of the non-intellectual nature of its activities. Even the general public looked down on its members because of the indiscriminate welcome that they gave to persons of mean social status. Caitanya joined them. His capacity for visions, his absolute conviction, his contagious enthusiasm and his talent in speech and song made Caitanya their leader at once. While people outside were still questioning his sanity, the devotees of this circle were beginning to say that he might be Kṛṣṇa himself returning to earth in a new body.

Here in these evening meetings Caitanya developed the methods of chanting and singing that have survived to this day, and cultivated publicly for the first time the possessed states that occur still among his followers and others whom he has influenced. The group's sessions of ecstatic singing—their only form of organized worship—followed the pattern of no established ritual and required the offices of no priest. The formalities of brahmanism were ignored. The requirements of cultivating their distinctive kind of religious feeling shaped the pattern of their religious activities.

The kind of hymn that filled their evenings goes by the general name of *kīrtan*. A *kīrtan* is a congregational song that magnifies a deity by mentioning his honorific names or praiseworthy deeds. Caitanya took the leadership in such singing in the Navadvīp meetings. He is believed by his followers to have been the creator of the several types of kīrtan that have come down to us from his time and circle. The singing of this group certainly attracted hearers through a fascinating novelty of some kind, but it appears that most of their characteristic types of song had an earlier history. The fresh element seems to have been the use of a special kind of melody, new or revived, that had an unusual appeal. Caitanya's personal contributions included a clear expressive voice of great charm, and, above all, a passionate acceptance of the message of the songs.

The biographers of Caitanya love to dwell on—even to exaggerate—the wild extravagance of Caitanya's behavior as the leading participant in these religious gatherings. The sessions always began with instrumental music of a distinctive character. Then Caitanya would lead off vocally, singing the names of Kṛṣṇa in a fine penetrating voice, uttering each name clearly and with an intensity of feeling that stirred an immediate response in the hearts of the devotees assembled around him. When the emotion in the crowd and in himself reached a certain tension, he would spring up from his seat, raise his arms high and wide and move about amidst the crowd, dancing and singing, shouting the words in ecstasy until perspiration ran down his face and the veins stood out on his brow. Cold thrills surged through his body, the hairs of his head bristled, he trembled and wept. Fits often came on him in which he would stiffen and fall. Then he would sometimes jump up and bound out of the throng and climb a nearby tree—or he would lie for a long time on the ground in a frothing fit, or in exhausted stupefaction, or in a trance. He came out of these lapses of consciousness reluctantly, as if torn away from happy visions.

Soon the fervor that was generated in Caitanya's circle flowed over. Forgetting their former taste for privacy, the devotees took their singing into the streets. A kind of singing procession now developed that is known as *nagarkīrtan*. For the rest of Caitanya's life the world was to know him as a center of commotion in public places, a leader of singing roaring crowds that were set afire by his love of Kṛṣṇa and by his sense of Kṛṣṇa's presence.

The religious tumults that Caitanya now stirred up in Navadvīp did not win immediate admiration from the brahman scholars of the city. They complained to the Muslim governor of the place about the noise in the streets. The governor declared nagarkīrtan a public nuisance and issued an ordinance forbidding any further processions of the kind. According to some of Caitanya's biographers, he responded with a modern tactic: he sent more than a dozen nagarkīrtan processions simultaneously through the streets to converge on the governor's palace, and besieged him with such powerful song that even his stout Muslim heart was overcome and he gave Caitanya's people liberty to sing in the streets at will. And that is what Caitanya did, essentially, all the rest of his life.

After a year or so as a lay devotee, Caitanya underwent the rite of *sannyāsa*, gave up his childhood name of Viśvambhara Miśra, and assumed the monastic name by which he is now known. His formal renunciation of the world brought little change in his style of life; it merely symbolized his resolve to dedicate the whole of his time to the worship of Kṛṣṇa. Soon he settled permanently at the great Vaiṣṇava pilgrimage center at Purī on the seacoast of Orissa. Before the millions of pilgrims who came to Purī annually for the Jagannāth car festival, he cut a great figure as leader of the singers and dancers that performed in the processions of the chariots of the gods. He sent certain learned disciples to restore the holy settlements of Mathurā and Vṛndāban and to begin writing the manuals and theological works needed by his movement. His death, which occurred in 1533 at Purī, is the subject of conflicting stories: that he drowned by rushing into the sea in one of his ecstatic visions, or that he died of an infection in a foot that he had injured while dancing in a frenzy. In either case it was his capacity for boundless emotion that brought him death, as it had brought him life.

## II

With this simple sketch as biographical background, we can now center in upon our major interest: Caitanya's worship and its special theological supports.

Caitanya held back nothing from the fulfilment of the end of his existence as he understood it, and for him the sole purpose of life was the love and praise of Kṛṣṇa. In the little poem of eight Sanskrit verses called *Śikṣāṣṭakam* that is his only known writing, he expressed his characteristic dedication and his total longing for God:

> When shall my eyes be filled with flooding tears,
> My mouth be choked with stammering praise,
> The hairs of my body thrill with rapture
> At the uttering of Thy Name?

Let Him crush me in embrace as his beloved
Or by His absence strike me to the quick!
Let the Libertine deal out whate'er He may,
Still He only, no other, is Lord of My Life! [1]

Caitanya never actually repudiated the pious duties that occupy the time of many earnest Hindus. After his death, his learned disciples listed in their scholastic manuals as many as sixty-four devout practices as suitable for observance by members of the sect.[2] Caitanya himself participated only fitfully or casually in such rituals. He threw himself continually into only one defined practice—the worship described in the first verse above—the chanting of the Divine Name.

The early writers on Caitanya's life commonly use the word *saṃkīrtan* in referring to his activities in song. *Saṃkīrtan* or *kīrtan* is a general term for any singing of a god's praises that employs a certain old style of instrumental music and antiphonal exchanges between a chief singer and a chorus. Within this broad heading various sub-classes can be distinguished by names that refer to their content or setting. We have already noticed the word *nagarkīrtan* referring to processional singing in a city (*nagar*). *Līlākīrtan* describes performances that praise Kṛṣṇa by telling of his sportive deeds (*līlās*) in the words of old Vaiṣṇava narrative and lyric poems. *Namkīrtan* is the chanting of stanzas made up largely or entirely of divine names reiterated. *Nāmkīrtan* was Caitanya's characteristic religious practice.

The content and feeling of Caitanya's nāmkīrtan can be illustrated by quoting an example preserved by his earliest biographer.[3] We are

---

[1] Nayanaṃ galadambudhārayā
Vadanaṃ gadgadaruddhayā girā
Pulakair nicitam vapuḥ kadā
Tava nāmagrahane bhaviṣyati?
Āśliṣya vā pādaratāṃ pinaṣṭu mām
Adarśanān marmahatāṃ karotu vā.
Yathātathā vā vidadhātu lampaṭo
Matprāṇanāthas tu sa eva nā 'paraḥ!

—Rupa Gosvāmin, ed. Sushil Kumar De, *The Padyāvalī* (University of Dacca, 1934), No. 93 p. 39, and No. 337 p. 152.

[2] Sixty-four types of *vaidhi bhakti* are mentioned in Rūpagosvāmin's *Bhaktirasāmṛtasindhu* and are described in great detail in Gopala Bhaṭṭa's *Haribhaktivilāsa*. See S. K. De, *Vaiṣṇava Faith and Movement in Bengal* (Calcutta, General Printers and Publishers Limited, 1942), pp. 129, 340-395.

[3] Murāri Gupta, *Śrīkṛṣṇacaitanyacaritāmṛta* 2.2.26 as quoted by Raghava Chaitanya Das, *The Divine Name* (Bombay, the author, 1954), p. 380n., and often by others.

told that Caitanya, from the time of his conversion onward, frequently sang the following and used it as a basis for sermonic exhortations:

> Harer nāma, Harer nāma, Harer nāmaiva kevalam!
> Kalau nāstyeva, nāstyeva, nāstyeva gatir anyathā!
>
> Hari's name! Hari's name! Just Hari's name alone!
> In the Kali Age there just is not, is not, is not any
> other way!

In nāmkīrtan such lines are repeated over and over, rhythmically, with intense feeling that begins with deep awareness of the meaning of the divine names that they contain. Another old nāmkīrtan, whose author is said to have been Caitanya himself, has the form of a Sanskrit prayer, as follows:

> Rāma Rāghava rakṣa mām
> Kṛṣṇa Keśava trāhi mām!
>
> O Rāma the Rāghava protect me,
> O Kṛṣṇa of the long locks, take me across!

The lines above are full sentences; but it is not necessary for nāmkīrtan to be grammatically complete or to have a rational meaning. The fact that the names refer to the Deity gives them significance enough. The texts of many kīrtans are no more than a series of names of Viṣṇu, repeated over and over in various orders. A very common nāmkīrtan contains no declarative statement whatever, but only names in the vocative case:

> Hare Kṛṣṇa, Hare Kṛṣṇa,
> Kṛṣṇa Kṛṣṇa, Hare Hare,
> Hare Rāma, Hare Rāma,
> Rāma Rāma, Hare Hare!

In the singing of verses like these, each line, separately, is incanted by the leader first, and the whole assembly repeats each line after him, one by one. As the verse is gone through again and again, the leader steps up the tempo. When the speed of utterance approaches the utmost possible, the whole group, in unison, begins to shout the lines, at the same time beating out the rhythm with sharply-timed clapping of hands. The singers begin to sway and to let themselves go in ungoverned gestures. Faces flush. From the line of instrumental accompanists the bell-like peal of small brass cymbals swells up with the rising shouting and pierces through it. The whole process approaches a crashing, breath-taking crescendo. The point of explosion is reached: eyes flash, mouths drop open, a tremor runs through the entire assembly. The Power, the Presence, has been felt!

At such times, they say, Caitanya used to dance in ecstasy with all consciousness of his body gone.[4] His principal Bengali biography reports how he used to behave in Purī at the height of his participation in nagarkīrtan around the car of Jagannāth:

> In the midst of the wild dance a strange delirium came upon the master. At the same moment all eight kinds of *sāttvik* emotion were stirred up within him. His hair stood on end, with flesh and skin all bristly like a *śimul* tree full of thorns . . . From his whole body ran sweat mixed with blood, while with choked voice he stammered incoherently. His tears fell like water from a fountain . . . At one moment he seemed stupefied, the next he rolled on the ground; now his hands and feet were motionless like dried sticks, again he lay prone on the ground almost bereft of breath . . . At times water fell from his eyes and nose, and froth from his mouth.[5]

We have in literature an illuminating account of similar emotional phenomena that occurred at a kīrtan festival held under the patronage of the Rājā of Kheturi in the first decade of the 17th century. Of one of the participants named Narottama, we read that "mystic visions came to Narottama often during this concert of music, and he was so overpowered by them that at one time he swooned away. For some time the songs had to be stopped and all were busy trying to restore him to his senses, and when this was done, he looked divinely inspired as though just returned from the presence of God." [6] To express their appreciation of the meaning of such experiences some of the

---

[4] A. A. Bake, "Çri Chaitanya Mahaprabhu," Koninklijke Nederlandsche Akademie van Wetenschappen, Afd. Letterkunde, *Mededelingen*, Nieuwe Reeks, Deel 11, No. 8, pp. 279-305, reprinted by Noord-Hollandsche Uitgevers Maatschappij, Amsterdam, 1948, p. 9/287. Though the Caitanya sect worships Kṛṣṇa as God in his highest nature, notice that the names of Rāma are acceptable divine names, as referring to an incarnation of Kṛṣṇa and thus to the same godhead. To magnify Rāma is not to lessen Kṛṣṇa but to recall the breadth of his protective operations. It is noteworthy that *mukti*, the most persistent longing of the Hindu soul, is also in evidence here. Though Caitanyite writers often belittle *mukti* as an object of aspiration, the singers here cry out, "Trāhi mām, take me over (this stream *saṃsāra*, the world)." In Bengal, land of rivers, God is a ferryman and worshippers pray, "Take me to the Other Shore."

[5] Kṛṣṇadāsa Kavirāja, *Caitanyacaritāmṛta* II.13, translated by Melville T. Kennedy in his *The Chaitanya Movement* (Calcutta, Association Press, 1925), p. 44.

[6] D. C. Sen, *The Vaishnava Literature of Medieval Bengal* (University of Calcutta, 1917), p. 130.

participants used the language of erotic love. A singer named Gokul Dās sang this verse:

> O Lucky night that I spent,
> I beheld the moonlike face of my love!
> My youth, my life became blessed
> And everything around assumed an air of joy.
> My home has become a true home today,
> And my body a worthy one indeed.
> Providence has favored me tonight
> And all my doubts are removed.[7]

Providence has favored me, I beheld the face of my Love, my doubts are removed—these words bespeak a decisive divine self-disclosure. The poet means to say: God was present, I have met Him. My life has come to fruition; before I wondered, now I know.

Kīrtan is able to bring to many people an effective certitude regarding God's existence and power. Their faith arises with, and out of, certain extraordinary internal sensations and bodily phenomena. The tingling of the flesh that arises in the singer is understood to be no mere physical titilation but a response to a genuine dynamic Presence. He is sure that he is indwelt by, and communes with, God himself. Caitanya believed that he had been blest by such realization, and his contemporaries affirmed his belief in the very name that they gave him.

Writers belonging to this bhakti tradition support their belief in the supernatural nature of kīrtan by asserting that miraculous benefits come from the practice. Unlike ordinary Hindu rites, the chanting of the Name does not depend for its effectiveness upon performance in any particular time or place or state of purity.[8] It causes power to flow in from an omnipotent source and sweep away forever old weaknesses, blemishes and oppressions. The Name confers unflinching love of Kṛṣṇa and turns one's entire life to devotion.[9] Writers cite the *Bhāgavata Purāṇa* to affirm the superiority of the cleansing power of the Name in comparison with the entire register of Hindu rituals of purification, which can indeed remove the consequence of individual offenses, but leave the root of sin untouched, whereas the Name removes the very source of pollution

---

[7] *Ibid.*

[8] Raghava Chaitanya Das, *op. cit.*, p. 370, quoting Gopāla Bhaṭṭa, *Haribhaktivilāsa* 2.11.411, *na deśakālaniyamo na śaucāśaucanirṇayah. . .*

[9] Das, *op. cit.*, p. 225.

by regenerating the mind.[10] Hanumanprasad Poddar, modern writer and devotee, says that the temptations to evil living that once were all but irresistible become through this practice easy to withstand, and that the Name burns up old sins as fire consumes piled hay. The roaring sound of the Name goes out and purges away the sins of all who hear—even those of the birds and beasts. People who have transgressed all the laws of morality and religion can nevertheless obtain salvation through the uttering of Hari's Name.[11] It would seem that the Name can do whatever God himself can do! Advocates say that the religion of chanting the Name is now the world's only effective religion. In proof of their claim they quote *Bhāgavata purāṇa* 12.3.52:

> What was obtained in the Kṛta Age by meditation on Viṣṇu,
> In the Tretā Age by sacrificing with oblations,
> In the Dvāpara Age by image worship,
> In the Kali Age comes by *kīrtan* of Hari.[12]

The position of the faith as the one universal religion for today is supported further by pointing out its universal accessibility, in that "everyone irrespective of caste, colour, creed, community, sex, age, space or time is allowed to enter or join." [13]

The followers of Caitanya are not awed even by the prestige of Śaṅkara's *advaita*. Quoting the *Caitanyacaritāmṛta* they say that the bliss that comes of chanting the name of Kṛṣṇa makes insignificant in comparison the bliss that the *jñānī* feels in experiencing the Undifferentiated *Brahman* and merging into it: the Name is a surging ocean of joy that makes the monists' *samādhi* look like the puddle of water that gathers in the hoofprint of a cow.[14] In India, that is strong language. It cannot means less than this: that many who have followed this pathway of religion have undergone an experience in which their gravest anxieties dissolve. They attain a sense of puri-

[10] *Bhāgavata Purāṇa* 6.2.7-12, vol. I p. 716 in edition of V. Ramaswamy Sastrulu and Sons, Madras, 1937. On the power of the Name in the *Bhāgavata Purāṇa* and other writings, see also Adalbert Gail, *Bhakti im Bhāgavatapurāṇa* (Wiesbaden, Otto Harrassowitz, Münchener Indologische Studien, Band 6, 1969), pp. 77f., 95f.

[11] Hanumanprasad Poddar, *The Divine Name and Its Practice* (Gorakhpur, Gita Press, n.d.), pp. 7, 14, 84.

[12] Kṛte yad dhyāyato Viṣṇum, tretāyām yajato makhaiḥ,
Dvāpare paricaryāyām, kalau taddharikīrtanāt.

[13] Bhakti Pradip Tirtha, *Sayings of Vaishnava Saints* (Puri, A. R. Patnaik, 1949), p. 11.

[14] Raghava Chaitanya Das, *op. cit.*, p. 218, quoting Kṛṣṇadāsa Kavirāja, *Caitanyacaritāmṛta*, 7.96-98.

fication, relief, victory and release. They have utmost confidence in the reality of the transformation they have undergone. For them, further search is needless—is out of the question!

The outsider's problem of understanding is not a difficulty in believing that the experiences described by the devotees actually occur. The accounts of the Hindu writers are consistent. The emotional phenomena described have been experienced in some degree by many non-Hindus, and many who have not known them personally, accept their actuality on the testimony of acquaintances whose veracity they trust. The uncanny moving power within is a ubiquitous factor in religious psychology. We have no reason to suppose that these particular reports are fictions. The difficulty lies, rather, in appreciating the expansive construction that is placed on these internal experiences. How is the *bhakta* able to be confident that these events are revelatory, ultimate in knowledge, saving, the very action of God?

The ability of a religious tradition to convince and reassure depends not only on its success in producing its characteristic experience, but also on its ability to surround the experience with effective theological explication. Ecstatic religious movements like that of Caitanya are often disappointingly inarticulate in their theology. But Hindus in general attach great importance to subjective states and give thoughtful attention to their analysis and interpretation. From ecstatics who are Hindu we dare therefore to expect explanatory ideas of some kind. In particular, a tradition as lasting as Caitanya's is likely to have had something beyond dogmatic identifications to offer the minds of its adherents. I am not aware that anyone has searched seriously, however, for Caitanyite theological teachings on kīrtan. The special undertaking of this study was to gather together any easily-available Vaiṣṇava doctrines that may have been intended to explain the experiences of these kīrtan-singers. The materials found are enough to justify a rudimentary account of Bengal Vaiṣṇavism's thinking about the Names of God. The Caitanyite theology of the Name is not elaborate. But well-developed theories about this deep-felt matter of the names of God are not easy to find anywhere. In comparison with the reflections of other groups, the Caitanyites' theological effort in this connection may even be sophisticated. It is not the whole of Caitanyite theology, of course, anymore than kīrtan is the whole of Caitanyite religious practice. The ecstatic trances of Caitanya himself were often precipitated by other means, especially by his contemplation of the forms of Rādhā and Kṛṣṇa as physical idols or as merely mental images. For the later Caitanyite movement also, the contemplation of the erotic sports of this Divine Pair has remained a vital second focus of meditation, vision, and theological interpretation. The singing of kīrtan is the more easily available and popular practice, however, and its conceptual framework is important.

The fundamental Vaiṣṇava idea about the Name is suggested in an often-quoted Sanskrit verse in which Kṛṣṇa promises that he will himself be present in the singing of kīrtan.

Nāham vasāmi Vaikuṇṭhe
  na yogihṛdaye ravau.
Madbhaktā yatra gāyanti
  tatra tiṣṭhāmi Nārada.[15]

I dwell not in Vaikuṇṭha
  nor in the hearts of yogis, nor in the sun;
Where my devotees are singing,
  there, O Nārada, stand I!

Now, "in the hearts of yogis" is exactly the place where many Hindus would deem God most likely to be present. Not so these bhaktas. Their method is not isolation, introspection, and arduous self-effort. Their trust is in the grace of God.[16] The background of their trust is two thousand years of Vaiṣṇava teaching about the willingness of God to intervene and assist man in the realization of his highest end. This confidence appears as early as the *Bhagavadgītā*, in which Kṛṣṇa says (4.7) that he descends to earth in age after age to destroy evil and establish true religion. In *Bhagavadgītā* 18:66 Kṛṣṇa promises salvation even to great sinners if they come to him in complete trust. The Vaiṣṇava God is a God who can be expected to be available to his worshippers' need.

How is God's presence in the circle of the singers actualized and

---

[15] Bake, *op. cit.*, p. 7/285.

[16] Another striking expression of this Caitanyite depreciation of yoga is found in Priyā Dās' commentary on Nābhādās' *Bhaktamāl* (Bombay, Śrīveṅkateśvara Steam Press, *saṃvat* 1888), p. 238:

Prem bhakti ekau palak, koṭi varaṣko yog,
Prem bhakti sab yog hai, yog prem bina rog!
Loving devotion for one moment
  equals yoga for ten million years
Loving devotion's the whole of yoga,
  yoga without love's a disease!

certified? In the line of those Vaiṣṇavas who use the *Bhāgavata Purāṇa*, there is a special understanding that the instrument through which the Divine Presence is mediated is the sung Name itself. The chanting of the names of God is a human activity, admittedly; but it is an occasion for a superhuman activity—the descent of God into the presence of His devotees. The voicing of a divine name brings realization of God's presence because a name of God is not just a sound, referring to a reality that is something other than itself. In the common fund of Hindu thought, a metaphysical status and function pertains to a thing's name. A name, in comparison with a thing's phenomenal aspect, is the principle of its individuality real or imagined—a subtler level of its reality and an approach to the essence of the thing named. In an advaita system that finally denies the truth of all individualizations, a divine name cannot express highest Divinity, or offer an approach to the Divine Being that is more than preliminary in function.[17] But for bhaktas like the Caitanyites and perhaps others,[18] who accept individualizations as real and acknowledge real personality in men and in God, a true name of God is a genuine modality of God's being or is God himself. That is why, in the reciting of sacred names, the mysterious Presence is often felt: God is there.

Even within the Caitanyite tradition, there is divergence in the way in which the relation between God and the Name is understood. Sometimes the divine names are described as outflows of the power of God. This seems to have been the view of Caitanya himself, as we see it in the second verse of his *Śikṣāṣṭakam*:

> Thou possessest name upon name, in multitude.
> In each of them is fixed Thy power entire,
> Bound by no rule of time of recitation.[19]

By the end of the sixteenth century the theologians of Caitanya's movement developed a stronger claim than this. They dared to say, not merely that the *Power* of God is present in such recitation, but that, when the Name is uttered in faith, God *Himself* is present. The

[17] For *advaita* views of *nāma* see *Chāndogya Upaniṣad* 6:1.4-6, 6:4.1-4, and S. Radhakrishnan, *Indian Philosophy* I (London, George Allen and Unwin Ltd.), 1923ff, p. 188n.

[18] See W. H. McLeod, *Gurū Nānak and the Sikh Religion* (Oxford, Clarendon Press, 1968), pp. 189-196.

[19] Nāmnāmakāri bahudhā nijasarvaśaktis
Tatrārpitā niyamitaḥ smaraṇe na kālaḥ.
—Rupa Gosvāmin, ed. Sushil Kumar De, *op. cit.*, No. 31, p. 13.

Vṛndāban Gosvāmins call this belief the doctrine of *Nāmanāminoradvaita* or *Nāmanāminorabheda*, "the non-difference between the Named One and the Name." [20] Jīva Gosvāmin in his *Bhagavat-Saṃdarbha* states the main point bluntly: *bhagavat-svarūpam eva nāma*, "The Name is the very essence of the Lord." [21]

The doctors of the sect warn, however, that one must not expect the Divine Presence to be realized through uttering any and every name of God that human fancy can concoct. Names that are products of the imagination of man are insubstantial and of no effect. Jīva Gosvāmin says again in the book just mentioned, ". . . it is by the use of names that are celebrated in *scripture* that the Lord himself is instantly known . . . The inherent effectiveness of these must be recognized, and the fictitious nature of the others." [22] Modern Caitanyites stress the fact that kīrtan, as they practice it, uses no names save those that occur in sacred texts. As words of revelation, such names are transcendental (*aprākṛita*) in nature, and utterly different from the merely aural names that are constantly being created by speculative minds. Scriptural names, when sung with faith, bring the full being and power of God into immediate presence.[23] They are the end, as well as the means, of the religious life.

This conception of the Name as a descending and saving agency is similar in some ways to the ancient Vaiṣṇava idea of an *avatāra*. The kinship of conceptions was recognized by the Caitanyite theologians. At several points in the evolution of the sectarian thought they considered including the Name under this old and honored heading. It was possible, first, to see the Name—a heavenly reality that has "descended" and assumed a form available to the senses—as itself a type of avatāra. Jīva Gosvāmin in one passage actualizes this possibility by remarking about the Name, "Speaking of *avatāras*, this is an *avatāra* of the Lord in the form of syllables: "*varṇarūpenāvatāro 'yam*." [24]

[20] S. K. De, "Philosophy of Bengal Vaiṣṇavism" in his *Bengal's Contribution to Sanskrit Literature and Studies in Bengal Vaisnavism* (Calcutta, Firma K. L. Mukhopadhyaya, 1960), p. 120.

[21] Quoted by De, *Vaiṣṇava Faith and Movement in Bengal* (Calcutta, General Printers and Publishers, 1942), p. 219 n. 9.

[22] Ato yaiḥ śāstre'ti-prasiddhair nāmabhiḥ śrī-bhagavān eva jaṭiti pratīto bhavati. . . teṣām svataḥ-siddhatvam anyeṣam kalpanāmayatvaṃ jñeyam. (Quoted in De, *Vaiṣṇava Faith*, p. 220).

[23] Nisikanta Sannyal, *Sree Krishna Chaitanya* (Madras, Gaudiya Math, 1933), pp. 576, 601f.

[24] *Avatārāntaravat parameśvarasya varṇarūpeṇāvatāro'yam*, quoted by De, *Vaiṣṇava Faith*, p. 220.

A second adaptation to incarnational thinking lay in the possibility of seeing the Name as the means whereby possessed individuals become avatāras "by adoption," so to speak. This type of reasoning took the form of an early effort to connect the Name with the sect's well-established *āveśa* class of avatāra. An *āveśāvatāra* is a Divine Incarnation who is made such by the fact that the Lord enters into that individual and possesses him. The category covered a class of saints who were preeminent by reason of extraordinary charisma. The supernormal qualities of ecstatic devotees could easily be said to come about through the agency of the Name, and the view that Caitanya became an *āveśa* or "possessed" avatāra through his singing of kīrtan was plausible and had some explanatory value. We are not surprised, therefore to find that Caitanya was called an *āveśāvatāra* at a very early time by his biographer Murāri Gupta.[25]

But in the end the concept of avatāra did not satisfy. An avatāra of any kind is not quite the full cosmic Being of God. An *āveśāvatāra* in particular is not the infinite Lord. Rūpa Gosvāmin says that *āveśāvatāras* arise when the Lord enters into and exalts particular souls, but they are avatāras by analogy only, not equatable with real avatāras because they are limited in duration and limited in degree of immanence of the divine power.[26] Jīva Gosvāmin says in similar vein that *āveśāvatāras* possess a great portion of the divine energy but are never representative of the fullness of the Deity.[27]

The Bengal Vaiṣṇavas quickly dropped these early attempts to understand the Name as a *varṇāvatāra*, or as the source of *āveśāvatāras*. Apparently they could risk no impairment of their trust that the Name on the lips of devotees brings contact with Highest Godhead.[28] If an *āveśāvatāra* is not an eternal and full manifestation of the Deity, then the completeness and finality of any process that brings such avatāras into being is lost also. Perhaps it was for this reason that the Bengal Vaiṣṇavas rejected for their founder the label of *āveśāvatāra*, with its flaw of incompleteness, and identified Caitanya, as a matter of fact, with Kṛṣṇa Himself. With regard to the nature of the Name, no doctrine would do that claimed less than *bhagavat-svarūpam eva nāma*, "The Name is the very essence of the Lord." Once that truth

---

[25] De, *Vaiṣṇava Faith*, pp. 338, 175.

[26] De, *op. cit.*, p. 221.

[27] De, *op. cit.*, p. 240.

[28] For an emphatic modern defense of the unqualified divinity of the Name see Raghava Chaitanya Das, *op. cit.*, pp. 582-592; also Sannyal, *op. cit.*, pp. 638-40.

is established beyond doubt, any believer who "knows the Name"—who hears and sings and feels it—is assured that he has arrived at Truth, the ultimate solution, the chief end of man. In singing the Name in the company of the saints, his doubts flee away, divine power rises up within him, the impossible becomes possible, the burden of the past is lifted from him, he has accomplished the purpose of his life, and he can look with composure upon death itself.

Because it is the Name that is to be known, the Bengal Vaiṣṇava's call to the religious life is not a call to the lonely hermitage, but an invitation to a community of song. The significance of such singing for believers oppressed by the frustrations of mortality is apparent in a kīrtan collected by Professor Bake, that was written as recently as 1943:

Dance, O Mind
and spread your arms
and sing the name of God;
sing Hari once.

The birds and beasts wake up and sing
once ev'ry watch;
how then should you, created human,
yet still remain unconscious? . . .

If you neglect the Name
stark danger looms
when the great Crossing comes
and you stand all alone.

Remember well the Name
and dance and spread your arms!
Sing Hari,
Oh, sing Hari! [29]

## BIBLIOGRAPHY

Bake, Arnold A., "Kirtan in Bengal," *Indian Art and Letters*, n.s. XXI (1947), pp. 34-40.

——, "Çri Chaitanya Mahaprabhu," *Mededeelingen der Koninklijke Nederlandsche Akademie van Wetenschappen*, Afd. Letterkunde, Nieuwe Reeks, Deel 11, No. 8, pp. 279-305. Reprinted by Noord-Hollandsche Uitgevers Maatschappij, Amsterdam, 1948.

Chakravarti, Sudhindra Chandra, *Philosophical Foundations of Bengal Vaisnavism* (Calcutta, Academic Publishers, 1969).

[29] Bake, *op. cit.*, pp. 7f.

Chakravartī, Sukumāra, *Caitanya et sa théorie de l'amour divin—prema* (Paris, Les Presses Universitaires de France, 1933).

Datta, Phulrenu, *La Société Bengalie au XVIe siècle* (Paris, Editions Litteraires de France, 1938).

De, Sushil Kumar, *Bengal's Contribution to Sanskrit Literature and Studies in Bengal Vaisnavism* (Calcutta, Firma K. L. Mukhopadhyaya, 1960).

——, *Early History of the Vaiṣṇava Faith and Movement in Bengal* (Calcutta, General Printers and Publishers Limited, 1942).

Dimock, Edward C., Jr., "Doctrine and Practice among the Vaiṣṇavas of Bengal," *History of Religions* III (Summer 1963), pp. 106-127.

——' "The Place of Gauracandrikā in Bengali Vaiṣṇava Lyrics," *Journal of the American Oriental Society* LXXVIII (July-Sept. 1958), pp. 153-169.

Eidlitz, Walther, "*Kṛṣṇa-Caitanya, sein Leben und seine Lehre* (Stockholm, Almquist & Wiksell, 1968, Stockholm Studies in Comparative Religion No. 7).

Gonda, Jan, *Notes on Names and the Name of God in Ancient India*. Amsterdam, North-Holland Publishers (Verhandelingen der Koninklijke Nederlandse Akademie van Wetenschappen, Afd. Letterkunde, Nieuwe Reeks, Deel 75, No. 4), 1970.

Judah, J. Stillson, *Hare Krishna and the Counterculture* (New York, John Wiley and Sons, 1974).

Kennedy, Melville T., *The Chaitanya Movement* (Calcutta, Association Press, 1925).

Kṛṣṇadāsa Kavirāja, Eng. tr. Nagendra Kumar Ray, *Sri Sri Chaitanya Charitamrita*, 3 vols. in 6 (Calcutta, Nagendra Kumar Ray, 1954ff.).

Law, Narendra Nath, *Śrī Kṛṣṇa and Śrī Caitanya* (London, Luzac & Co., 1949). Reprinted from *Indian Historical Quarterly* XXIII (Dec. 1947) pp. 261-299, and XXIV (March 1948), pp. 19-66.

Poddar, Hanumanprasad, *The Divine Name and Its Practice* (Gorakhpur, Gita Press, n.d.).

Raghav Chaitanya Das, *The Divine Name* (Bombay, the author, 1954).

Rupa Gosvāmin, ed. Sushil Kumar De, *The Padyāvalī* (U. of Dacca, 1934).

Sen, Dineschandra, *The Vaisnava Literature of Mediaeval Bengal* (University of Calcutta, 1917).

# CAITANYA'S FOLLOWERS AND THE *BHAGAVAD-GĪTĀ*:

## *A Case Study in Bhakti and the Secular*

JOSEPH T. O'CONNELL

The *Bhagavad-gītā* is a Vaiṣṇava text that has enjoyed the widest currency in India for the last two millenia. It is thus reasonable to ask how the Gauṛīya Vaiṣṇavas (i.e., those revering as their savior Kṛṣṇa-caitanya of Bengal) understood the *Bhagavad-gītā*. It is a bit surprising to find that not until the end of the seventeenth century, more than a century and a half after the death of Caitanya, did any Gauṛīya Vaiṣṇava produce a commentary upon the *Gītā* that is extant today.

There was available to the Gauṛīya Vaiṣṇavas the commentary on the *Gītā* by Śrīdhara Svāmin (fl. 1400), whose commentary on the *Bhāgavata Purāṇa* they so much admired. But while the latter commentary receives praise and copious citation by Gauṛīyas, the former goes more or less unmentioned. Nor did the existence of Śrīdhara's respected commentary on the *Bhāgavata* dissuade several Gauṛīyas from trying their hand at comments of their own. It is said that Advaita Ācārya, a senior contemporary and highly regarded associate of Caitanya, commented upon the *Gītā*, but had he produced a formal written document of this sort it is most unlikely that his descendants and spiritual successors, otherwise jealous of their heritage from Advaita, would have let it slip into oblivion.[1]

Advaita had learned the devotional interpretation of the *Bhagavad-gītā*, it is reported, from his preceptor, Mādhavēndra Purī (the guru's guru of Caitanya). But apart from the small circle of Mādhavēndra's disciples there were few students of Sanskrit texts at Navadvīpa, the town in Bengal where Caitanya was born, who did not subordinate the teachings on devotion (*bhakti*) to the teachings on knowledge (of a gnostic and impersonal sort, *jñāna*) or on work

[1] Krishna-dāsa Kavirāja, *Caitanya-caritāmṛta*, ed. Bhakti Vilās Tīrtha, 5th ed. (Māyāpur, India: Caitanya Maṭha, G.A. 470 or A.D. 1956), 1:13:64. Hereafter cited as CC. Nāgendra Nāth Basu, ed., *Viśvakoṣa* (Calcutta, B.A. 1318 or A.D. 1911), II, 138, mentions one Sūrya-dāsa Paṇḍita as author of a commentary on the *Gītā*, but does not indicate if he was a Gauṛīya Vaiṣṇava; standard Gauṛīya Vaiṣṇava reference books mention no such text.

(in the sense of traditional social and ritual performance, *karma*), or so one of the best of Caitanya's biographers, Vṛndāvanadāsa, laments.[2] The lament of the biographer points directly at the problem which the *Gītā* posed for the Gauṛīya Vaiṣṇavas: it does not give unambiguous enough pre-eminence to devotion over the other spiritual disciplines of knowledge and work. In particular, the *Gītā* is silent on the winsome sports of Kṛṣṇa as a child and on his amorous sports (*līlās*) as an adolescent young man, sports which the Gauṛīya Vaiṣṇavas confidently believe to reveal the essence of divine life and the perfection of religious life, loving devotion (*prema-bhakti*).[3]

Several of the biographers of Caitanya evidently were well-versed in the *Gītā*, since they quote it with some frequency. The famous six Gosvāmins of Vṛndāban, most of whom made substantial contributions to the Sanskrit literature of the Gauṛīya Vaiṣṇava movement, were aware of the *Bhagavad-gītā*, but generally were most sparing in their citation of it, according to the tables prepared by S. K. De. Only the second generation Gosvāmin, Jīva, quotes the *Gītā* with any profusion. None of the six is known to have authored a commentary upon the famous text. Of much more importance to them and to the Gauṛīya Vaiṣṇavas generally were the *Bhāgavata Purāṇa* and other Vaiṣṇava texts telling of the amorous pastimes of Kṛṣṇa.[4]

The first extant Gauṛīya Vaiṣṇava commentary upon the *Bhagavad-gītā* is the *Sārārtha-varṣiṇī* (also mentioned as *Sārārtha-darśinī*) of Viśvanātha Cakravartin, a brahman born in northern Bengal in the second half of the seventeenth century. Most of his copious writing in Sanskrit was done as a recluse at or near Vṛndāban. He was steeped in the distinctive Gauṛīya Vaiṣṇava literature, especially that of Rūpa Gosvāmin dealing with the mood of loving devotion (*prema-bhakti-rasa*). Even though his work appears too late to have had an impact upon the Gauṛīya Vaiṣṇavas' view of the polity and the societal community of Bengal prior to British rule, he is sufficiently typical of Gauṛīya Vaiṣṇava piety that it is worthwhile to consider briefly his treatment of the *Bhagavad-gītā*. There is another commentary on the *Gītā* by a Vaiṣṇava from Orissa said to have been a

[2] Vṛndāvana-dāsa, *Caitanya-bhāgavata*, ed. Bhakti Kevala Auḍulomi, 3rd ed. (Calcutta: Gauṛīya Mission, 1961), 1:2:72-73.

[3] Sushil Kumar De, *Early History of the Vaiṣṇava Faith and Movement in Bengal*, 2nd ed. (Calcutta: F. K. L. Mukhopadhyay, 1961); Edward C. Dimock, Jr., *The Place of the Hidden Moon* (Chicago: University of Chicago Press, 1966). Both are valuable accounts of the Gauṛīya Vaiṣṇava movement.

[4] De, *Early History*, pp. 201, 220, 253, 414-15.

disciple of Viśvanātha, namely Baladeva Vidyābhūṣaṇa. I have not considered his eighteenth century document because Baladeva represents the impingement of a more philosophical attitude toward devotion, perhaps influenced by the tradition of Madhva, upon the traditionally aesthetic attitude of the Gauṛīya Vaiṣṇavas. Likewise, I have not considered the ideas of the Gauṛīya Mission and its several related revival movements in the last century, since it is the Vaiṣṇavas' stance toward public affairs from the sixteenth to the early eighteenth century, a period of Muslim domination, with which this paper is concerned.[5]

The one document after the *Bhāgavata Purāṇa* that is the most influential among the Gauṛīya Vaiṣṇavas is the *Caitanya-caritāmṛta*, a Bengali biography and theological compendium completed by Kṛṣṇa-dāsa Kavirāja, the heir to the intellectual and spiritual legacy of the Gosvāmins of Vṛndāban, in the second decade of the seventeenth century. What I propose to do in this paper is to examine the ways Kṛṣṇa-dāsa and Viśvanātha respectively exegete passages from the *Bhagavad-gītā* and to relate this doctrinal information to a set of biographical data showing a high degree of involvement by Gauṛīya Vaiṣṇavas in the Muslim-dominated political and administrative regime ruling Bengal in the early sixteenth century. In the examination of Kṛṣṇa-dāsa's and Viśvanātha's interpretations of the *Gītā* I shall focus upon their treatment of *karma*, traditional socio-ritual work. This is because it is in work (*karma*) that sacredness and particular forms of socio-political organization are fused. In the epic context which the *Bhagavad-gītā* portrays, the sacred normative order (*dharma*) is that characterized by the brahmanical system of castes (*varṇa*) and states in life (*āśrama*). A good king is one who enforces *varṇāśrama-dharma*; a good warrior one who risks his life in defense of it. The *Bhagavad-gītā* explicitly affirms and legitimates on sacred grounds the system of *varṇāśramadharma*, even though it has much else to say about the religious life. The Gauṛiya Vaiṣṇavas, on the contrary, tend to withdraw both legitimation and censure from the social and political spheres by confining the area of genuinely sacred activity to the interior devotional life of the individual.[6]

[5] Viśvanātha Cakravartin, *Sārārtha-varṣiṇī Ṭīkā* in Adhara Candra Cakravartin, ed., *Śrīmad-bhagavad-gītā* (Calcutta: Tārā Library, B.A. 1361 or A.D. 1954). Hereafter, the *Bhagavad-gītā* will be cited as *Gītā* and the *Sārārtha-varṣiṇī* as Comment on *Gītā*.

[6] For extended discussion of these issues see Joseph T. O'Connell, "Social Implications of the Gauṛīya Vaiṣṇava Movement," Ph.D. dissertation, Harvard 1970.

## I. *Kṛṣṇa-dāsa's Interpretation of the Gītā*

The chart appended to this article lists those verses of the *Bhagavad-gītā* which Kṛṣṇa-dāsa quotes in the *Caitanya-caritāmṛta* and indicates where these occur in the editions of the Caitanya Maṭha and of Rādhā Govinda Nāth.[7] Since our present concern is the attitude Vaiṣṇavas take toward traditional patterns of action which may simultaneously have ritual and social, and often economic, political and military significances, i.e., their attitude toward performance of work (*karma*), I have simply noted the several passages which have little or no relevance to the question of work, but which speak to some other theological question. The next group includes passages which appear to be more or less favorable to the performance of work. Kṛṣṇa-dāsa's exegesis of such passages is extremely interesting and rather daring, I think. Finally, there are those passages, slightly more numerous, which seem to be unfavorable to the performance of work, passages which Kṛṣṇa-dāsa, like the Gauṛīya Vaiṣṇavas generally, interprets in a way favorable to devotion, but not favorable to work or knowledge (*jñāna*).

### Verses indifferent to work (*karma*)

The passages from the *Bhagavad-gītā* having no direct bearing upon the issue of karma treat of the following points: God pervades and upholds the universe (*Gītā* 10:41-42); God has a spiritual nature beyond matter (*Gītā* 7:4-5); display of Kṛṣṇa's majesty (*aiśvarya*) diminishes the spontaneity of love (*Gītā* 11:41-42); fools despise Kṛṣṇa in His human form (*Gītā* 9:11); and, those who deny the supremacy of Kṛṣṇa go to perdition (*Gītā* 16:19).

### Verses favorable to performance of work

Kṛṣṇa-dāsa quotes four verses from the *Gītā* early in the first book of the *Caitanya-caritāmṛta* to support one basic point: "If (the Lord) Himself does not perform it, *dharma*, normative order, fails to be propagated." (CC 1:3:21) The verses appealed to are: *Gītā* 4:7-8, which state that whenever dharma is in decline and its opposite in the ascendancy, the Lord incarnates Himself, in age after age for the rescue of the good, the destruction of the wicked, and the establishment of dharma; *Gītā* 3:24, which states that if He did

---

[7] Krishna-dāsa Kavirāja, *Caitanya-caritāmṛta*, ed. Rādhā Govinda Nāth, 4th ed., 6 vols. (Calcutta: Sādhanā Prakāśanī, n.d.).

not perform His work these worlds would perish, He would be the agent of mixing (of castes), and He would thus destroy these creatures; and, *Gītā* 3:21, which says that whatever the best do, lesser men imitate, whatever standard such a one sets, the world follows. Kṛṣṇa-dāsa goes on to say that while a mere portion of the deity, a partial *avatāra*, is capable of establishing the normative order appropriate for any particular age (*yuga-dharma*) only the Lord in person is able to distribute the love appropriate to Kṛṣṇa's pastoral village (*vraja-prema*) (CC 1:3:26). Caitanya is Kṛṣṇa in person descended for two purposes: the propagation of the dharma of the current *kali* age, propagation of the divine name (*nāmer pracāra*) (CC 1:3:40); and, the more transcending work of loving devotion (*prema-bhakti*). Kṛṣṇa-dāsa thus, like other Gauṛīya Vaiṣṇavas, maintains the traditional idea of a divine descent to propagate a system of normative order (*dharma*) but, by having recourse to the notion of several ages (*yuga*), radically alters the kind of dharma now valid. In place of the just war to maintain the brahmanic system of socially and ritually exclusive castes, the work required to support dharma is a combination of singing the names of God and fostering amorous devotion to Kṛṣṇa and his beloved Rādhā. Kṛṣṇa-dāsa, interestingly enough, says nothing at all about the word *saṅkarasya*, "of mixing" (castes), a problem that looms large in Kṛṣṇa's charge to Arjuna in the *Bhagavad-gītā*.

One of the verses just mentioned, *Gītā* 3:21, stating that lesser men follow the example of the best, appears again in the *Caitanya-caritāmṛta* (2:17:178) not as a sanction for rigor in upholding the order of castes and states in life, as the context in the *Gītā* seems to require, but as a justification for laxity. Kṛṣṇa-dāsa appeals to this verse to explain why Caitanya, contrary to the usual practice of a brahman ascetic (*sannyāsin*), took food at the house of a brahman of questionable ritual purity. The explanation is that Caitanya simply followed the precedent of that excellent person, Mādhavēndra Purī, the guru of Caitanya's own guru, who had eaten at the same house years before.

Another passage in the *Bhagavad-gītā* (4:11) enunciates the principle that the Lord favors His devotees in ways proportionate to how they worship Him, for persons ply the road to Him in all sorts of ways. This principle can be construed broadly enough to include performance of social and ritual duties, as the *Gītā* does. However, as Kṛṣṇa-dāsa applies the verse the first time, it seems restricted to the interpersonal, devotional relationships of child to father, friend to friend, and lover to beloved. The second citing of the verse is in a special context which has little bearing on the argument of this paper. Kṛṣṇa-dāsa explains that the promise of Kṛṣṇa to respond in the proportionate or reciprocal fashion to His devotee appears to be violated in the incident in the *Bhāgavata Purāṇa* where married girls long to meet Kṛṣṇa but are locked in their houses. In this case, Kṛṣṇa allows them to meet Him in their meditation. Neither of these applications of *Gītā* 4:11 explicitly rules out the performance of social and ritual duties as worthwhile expressions of devotion, but neither do they give any support to such an interpretation.

A related idea appears in *Gītā* 7:16, where Kṛṣṇa states that four types of well-behaved persons worship Him: the suffering, those desiring knowledge, those seeking rewards, and those possessing knowledge. Well-behaved (*sukṛtino*) may, as Gauṛīya editors and commentators take it, refer to fidelity to the dharma of castes and states in life. Hence the mere citation of the verse constitutes a mild endorsement of the performance of karma in line with *varṇāśrama-dharma*. Kṛṣṇa-dāsa even says that the four types of well-behaved persons are most fortunate (*mahābhāgyavān*) (CC 2:14:91), but quickly adds that they should abandon the corporal and spiritual desires which motivate them and become exclusively motivated by devotion (*śuddha-bhaktimān*). He has nothing more to say in this section about being well-behaved: precisely what it involves, whether it is a *sine qua non* of further development, or a coincidental, but not essential, circumstance.

One of the foremost principles in the *Bhagavad-gītā*, especially in the early chapters in which the issue of righteous warfare in behalf of *varṇāśrama-dharma* is in focus, is that one may and should perform works which bring rewards and repercussions in this life and beyond but should dedicate all the rewards and repercussions to Kṛṣṇa. On this principle public and domestic activities can be of major religious importance. This pivotal idea is practically ignored in the more than ten thousand couplets of the *Caitanya-caritāmṛta*. The idea is suggested in *Gītā* 9:27, which appears once (CC 2:8:60). An intimate associate of Caitanya, Rāmānanda Rāya, is presented as reciting to Caitanya a series of scriptural statements on the goal of religious discipline. The first suggestion is that devotion comes from exercise of the dharma proper to oneself. Caitanya says that this is superficial (*bāhya*) and asks for something more. Then Rāmānanda says, "Dedication of one's works to Krishna, this is the essence of all piety," and recites *Gītā* 9:27 in support. Again, Caitanya puts the suggestion aside as superficial and the two move on toward ever more intimate modalities of loving devotion.

There is explicit mention of work in *Gītā* 6:3 (*karma*) and *Gītā* 6:4 (*karmasu*) both of which are cited by Kṛṣṇa-dāsa (CC 2:24:153-54). The first states that for one desirous of attaining *yoga*, the instrumental cause is karma; the second says that when a person no longer has attachment to the objects of sense nor to works (*karmasu*) and has abandoned all schemes he is said to have reached *yoga*. The context in the *Caitanya-caritāmṛta* is a laborious exposition of the sixty-four ways Caitanya was able to construe a verse from the *Bhāgavata Purāṇa* (1:7:10; i.e., *ātmārāmāś ca . . .*) to show that various types of holy men authentically worship Kṛṣṇa not because of the varieties of knowledge (*jñāna*) or release (*mokṣa*) to which they are aspiring or which they have attained, but because they have grown attracted toward Kṛṣṇa by His grace, directly or by associating with devotees of Kṛṣṇa (CC 2:24:155). There is no discussion of the significance of karma in this case; it is referred to only as part of the scriptural passage cited to fill out the sixty-four-fold interpretation.

Moderation in spiritual discipline is the theme of *Gītā* 6:16-17, moderation in eating, sleeping, rest and works. Kṛṣṇa-dāsa relays these verses as part of an advice by an older ascetic, Rāmacandra Purī, to Caitanya, who had grown thin from excessive fasting. There is no consideration of moderation in domestic or public affairs on the part of householders (CC 3:8:61-67).

The eleven verses from the *Bhagavad-gītā* cited in the *Caitanya-caritāmṛta* which more or less explicitly seem to endorse performance of traditional social and ritual works do not receive any comment or application by Kṛṣṇa-dāsa which would constitute an appeal for efforts to maintain or re-establish *varṇāśrama-dharma*, despite the very didactic character of the book. At most, it is admitted that exercise of one's proper dharma and dedication of one's work to Kṛṣṇa are valid but superficial types of devotion. Accidental mention of work or dharma in a few verses cited as scriptural implies that some validity attaches to such work in keeping with normative order of castes and states in life, but whether such validity is still operative, whether it is important enough to encourage are other matters. The overwhelming concern of Kṛṣṇa-dāsa is exposition of devotion to Kṛṣṇa as revealed through Caitanya. Other matters are ignored or subordinated to this one. The dharma appropriate to the present age is recitation of the names of Kṛṣṇa. The ultimate dharma surpassing all others is loving devotion to Kṛṣṇa as epitomized in His beloved Rādhā. To establish firmly both these dharmas is the purpose of Kṛṣṇa's descent as Caitanya. To save the world from the mixing of castes is the least of Caitanya's objectives, or so it would seem from a reading of the *Caitanya-caritāmṛta* of Kṛṣṇa-dāsa.

Verses not favorable to work

Several verses from the *Bhagavad-gītā* which state or imply that performance of work is unnecessary or baneful in the quest for devotion find their way into the *Caitanya-caritāmṛta* and a few of these are cited three times, presumably reflecting the author's high regard for them as scriptural proof texts. One such text is *Gītā* 10 : 10, which states that the Lord gives to those who constantly and attentively worship Him with love a mental control (*buddhi-yogam*) by which they may attain to Him. This is offered as proof of a statement (CC 1 : 1 : 47) that Kṛṣṇa, by dwelling within one's soul (*antar-yāmī*) reveals Himself as a teacher. It appears again (CC 2 : 24 : 167)— in that sixty-four-fold interpretation of how saints are saved— to support the contention that devotion does not grow into love without a person's being attentive or disciplined. Later in the same exegesis (CC 2:24 : 186) the verse re-appears after a paraphrase of it in the Bengali text. There is no extended discussion of the verse in any of the contexts in which it is cited. While there is no overt disparagement of work in the service of dharma, there seems to be more than a hint that it is by the more direct intervention of Kṛṣṇa Himself that devotion, at least the higher loving devotion, comes to a person, rather than by work. *Gītā* 10 : 8, cited as CC 2 : 24 : 183, has similar import.

Another of the verses from the *Gītā* that Kṛṣṇa-dāsa cites three times is *Gītā* 7 : 14, which states that by resort to Kṛṣṇa one passes beyond the snares of material illusion (*māyā*), which is an aspect of Kṛṣṇa Himself. Kṛṣṇa-dāsa uses this text to support these assertions: by the mercy of Kṛṣṇa extended through holy men and scriptures souls long caught in māyā pass beyond it (CC 2 : 20 : 121); release comes not from knowledge which is without devotion, but from devotion to Kṛṣṇa (CC 2 : 22 : 23); and release from māyā is dependent upon that release which is focussed upon Kṛṣṇa (CC 2 : 24 : 131). Like the previous example this contains no explicit denigration of the performance of works, but rather directs human attention toward awareness of Kṛṣṇa as the effective element in the process of salvation. The only extended passage from the *Gītā*, i.e., 12:13-20, carried into the *Caitanya-caritāmṛta* (2:23:100-107) has much the same force. The virtues of the person who is dear to Kṛṣṇa are listed at length. They emphasize tranquilitity, indifference to changes in the external environment, and trusting devotion to Kṛṣṇa.

The next example is much the same, although the verse in the *Gītā* itself (18:54), stating that the soul which is at peace and has realized Brahman attains to the highest devotion to the Lord, seems to attribute slightly less instrumental significance to devotion than do the assertions it is called upon to support. In CC 2:8:65 it illustrates yet another of the relatively superficial types of piety, knowledge mixed with devotion (*jñāna-miśrā bhakti*), that is set aside by Caitanya in favor of unadulterated devotion. In CC 2:24:127 it supports the principle that one whose release is through devotion worships Kṛṣṇa, while one whose (alleged) release is through dry knowledge (*śuṣka-jñāne*) falls into sin (*aparādhe*). It appears a third time (CC 2:25:148) to prove that one should continuously sing the praises of Kṛṣṇa's name in order to receive release through love. In these passages there is evidence of a consistent Gauṛīya Vaiṣṇava polemic against the claims of knowledge (*jñāna*) as a means of genuine release. The parallel polemic against work (*karma*) would depict a discipline of pure work as folly, work mixed with devotion as effective but not optimally so, with pure devotion as the active ingredient in the mix. It appears in Gauṛīya Vaiṣṇava literature, but not with the frequency and urgency of the polemic against knowledge, which presumably was the greater challenge at the time.

A forceful statement of the polemic against work is CC 2:9:263:

> All scriptures advise disparagement of work (*karma-nindā*) and the abandonment of work (*karma-tyāga*). Loving devotion for Krishna never comes from work.

In support of this Kṛṣṇa-dāsa appeals to *Gītā* 18:66 wherein Krishna recommends that one forsake all dharmas and promises that He will save from all sins. The context of this is a discussion in which Caitanya is presented as criticizing the view of one Raghuvarya Tīrtha that the best religious practice is dedicating to Kṛṣṇa one's dharma of caste and state in life and that the best religious attainment is enjoyment of five-fold release. *Gītā* 18:66 reappears (CC 2:22:91) to substantiate the statement:

> Forsaking all the foregoing and also the *dharma* of caste and state in life, becoming humble, one attains the sole refuge of Krishna. (CC 2:22:90)

The third occurrence of *Gītā* 18:66 is in CC 2:8:63, where it supports Rāmānanda Rāya's advocacy of abandonment of one's personal dharma as the essence of beatitude, one of the views that Caitanya sets aside as superficial.

*Gītā* 18:64-65 has Kṛṣṇa reveal the highest secret to Arjuna, i.e., that He is going to save Arjuna, if Arjuna remains devoted to Him, because Arjuna is dear to Him. Kṛṣṇa-dāsa writes that Kṛṣṇa gave this message through Arjuna to the whole world. Kṛṣṇa-dāsa goes on to declare:

> The former directives—for Vedic *dharma*, work, yoga, knowledge—all are terminated and the final directive is in force. If there is trust (*śraddhā*) in this directive, then one abandons all work and worships Krishna. (CC 2:22:60)

The crucial point then becomes trust in Kṛṣṇa. So long as this is wanting, there is some scope for other religious practices; when it is effectively present, only devotion to Kṛṣṇa is appropriate.

Kṛṣṇa-dāsa draws upon two verses from the *Gītā* to explain Caitanya's willingness to embrace two allegedly defiling persons, Haridāsa, the Vaiṣṇava saint of Muslim background, and Sanātana, the brahman Vaiṣṇava who was disgraced in some circles for close association with Muslims and who was diseased. *Gītā* 6:8 says that a yogi sees no difference between a clod of earth and a piece of gold; *Gītā* 5:18 says that the wise look upon cow and dog, brahman and eater of dogs as equivalent. Caitanya's behavior does not seem to have been part of an effort to do away with caste and ritual pollution altogether, as some modern enthusiasts have contended, but it was sufficiently liberal in these regards to gain for him a contemporary reputation for universal love of persons whom others would dare not touch.

The basic policy of Kṛṣṇa-dāsa in appealing to passages from the *Bhagavad-gītā* which do not favor performance of traditional social and ritual work is to argue from them to the fundamental superiority and uniqueness of devotion. Since devotion is the active ingredient in the mixtures of devotion and work and knowledge and since Kṛṣṇa by his grace bestows devotion upon whom he will, there is no basic need for work or knowledge in the ultimate religious quest.

## II. *Viśvanātha Cakravartin's Commentary upon the Bhagavad-gītā*

Viśvānatha Cakravartin composed the *Sārārtha-varṣiṇī*, a commentary upon the *Bhagavad-gītā*, toward the end of the seventeenth century. His views are close to those of Kṛṣṇa-dāsa in most respects. Viśvanātha says that the first six chapters of the *Gītā* treat of the discipline of work free of desire (*niṣkāma-karma-yoga*), the middle six treat of devotion (*bhakti-yoga*), and the final six treat of knowledge (*jñāna-yoga*). Like Kṛṣṇa-dāsa, Viśvanātha considers work and knowledge to be effective at all only when mixed with some devotion. Devotion receives the central position in the *Gītā* because it is the most secret, the most respected (since it gives vitality to the other two disciplines), and because it is the most rare.[8] If we take the rareness (difficulty of attainment, *durlabhatvāt*) in a quantitative sense, there would be a difference of mood from Kṛṣṇa-dāsa's enthusiasm over the current ease of access to devotion, but the word may simply indicate excellence. There is a major difference between the two Vaiṣṇavas in their treatment of Caitanya and a wide divergence in concern for contemporary history. While the biographer subordinates the *Gītā* to the demands of explaining Caitanya's life and teachings in concrete historical scenes, the commentator salutes Caitanya in a couplet at the outset and thereafter ignores him and anything having to do with contemporary history.

There are a great many passages in the *Sārārtha-varṣiṇī* wherein Viśvanātha shows how one can subordinate work, and also knowledge, to devotion. I would like to focus attention upon those relatively few passages in which his comments on work give some inkling of his view of the importance of domestic and public affairs to a committed Vaiṣṇava. Two passages in the *Gītā* make explicit reference to the social implications of fighting an (apparently) unjust war (1:26-46) or failing to fight a just one (3:21-25). Viśvanātha says next to nothing in comment upon these verses, apart from grammatical or lexical notes, a fact in itself indicative of his priorities. It is interior religious discipline and not social ethics with which he is concerned. He does mention, in commenting upon *Gītā* 3:16-17, that a person who is incapable of working without desire should continue the traditional Vedic practices which nourish the gods, the ancestors and the living in the great wheel of sacred ecology.

[8] Comment on *Gītā* 1:1.

He also devotes seven lines of explanation to *Gītā* 3:35, which states that one should perform one's proper dharma even if badly in preference to executing another's dharma well. Viśvanātha restates Arjuna's appeal that he would rather do something less violent than the dharma of a warrior and then paraphrases the requirement stated by Kṛṣṇa. This is an explicit admission that violence in some cases is or at some time has been obligatory, but it is a perfunctory one, presumably reflecting the general Gauṛīya Vaiṣṇava preference for a non-violent way of life and the practical fact that there was almost a total absence of kshatriyas among the Hindus of Bengal upon whom such an injunction could be binding. Like Kṛṣṇa-dāsa, Viśvanātha shared the conviction that the higher dharma of the current age is devoted singing of the names of God.

Viśvanātha has little else to say explicitly about domestic and public responsibilities, but his brief references to the notion of "holding the world(s)/people(s) together" or "the general welfare" (*loka-saṃgraham*) are worth looking at. The expression occurs in *Gītā* 3:20, where Viśvanātha briefly glosses it as, "You should do work to uphold teaching, (i.e., good example) in the world" (*loke śikṣā-grahaṇārtham*). In his one line of comment upon *Gītā* 3:25, where the expression appears again, he fails to mention it. In another document of his, a commentary upon the *Bhakti-rasāmṛta-sindhuḥ* of Rūpa, Viśvanātha quotes *Gītā* 3:20 precisely because of the idea of "holding the world together." In that context Rūpa quotes the *Bhāgavata Purāṇa* 3:33:6 (*yannāmadheya-* . . .) to sustain his contention that devotion is able to efface the effects of sins that have already begun to bear fruit (*prārabdha*), i.e., have caused a person's current birth in a defiled tribe or caste. The verse says that even an eater of dogs, i.e., a Caṇḍāla, is fit for the oblations of Vedic sacrifice (*savanāya*) if he has taken the name of God. Viśvanātha and the other commentators, Jīva and Mukunda, agree that in practice Vaiṣṇava Caṇḍālas do not participate in Vedic sacrifices, but they differ in explaining the discrepancy between bold principle and cautious practice.[8]

Viśvanātha answers the objector's query of why the Caṇḍāla fails to sacrifice if he is qualified by asserting that since he is a pure devotee such a person has no trust (*śraddhā*) in work. Hence he does not perform it. On the other hand, he points out, it is true that

[9] Rūpa Gosvāmin, *Bhakti-rasāmṛta-sindhuḥ*, ed. Haridās Dās, 2nd ed. (Navadvīpa: Haribol Kuṭī, G.A. 475 or A.D. 1961), 1:1:21-22.

householders of good families (who also are pure Vaiṣṇavas) perform such work for the sake of holding the world together though they too lack trust in it. Here he quotes *Gītā* 3:20. He then adds that the Caṇḍāla Vaiṣṇava is further deterred from performing work for which he is qualified by fear of censure from persons not acquainted with devotional scriptures. Unfortunately for our purposes, but quite understandable in view of the context into which the proof texts from the *Bhāgavata* and the *Gītā* have been drawn, there is no precise delineation of what Viśvanātha means by "holding the world together" (*loka-saṃgraham*). Could it embrace a sense of public responsibility in a world not governed on the pattern of *varṇāśrama-dharma*? Do actions other than Vedic rituals contribute to holding the world together? Were there no scoffers to censure them, would Vaiṣṇava Caṇḍālas perform and Vaiṣṇava brahmans discard Vedic rites? Does *loka-saṃgraham* suggest merely negative avoidance of discord or a more positive commitment to physical and social well-being? Viśvanātha does not say.

What he does say about work seems to exclude two extreme positions: that *varṇāśrama-dharma* is wrong in itself and must be opposed; and, that *varṇāśrama-dharma* is in any way necessary to the ultimate religious quest, devotion to Kṛṣṇa. Between these extremes there seems to be an open field for personally idiosyncratic resolutions of the tension between devotion to Kṛṣṇa and everything else in the world. The crucial factor, according to Viśvanātha, is trust (*śraddhā*). If a person is performing work with his trust anywhere but exclusively in devotion to Kṛṣṇa, then, according to *Gītā* 3:26, one should not create conflict in conscience for him, should not try to undermine his confidence in what he is doing (so long as there is a vein of trust in devotion running through his trust in knowledge, work, etc.). But once he trusts devotion alone, it is a different matter:

> Knowledge depends upon purity of the mind and this purity depends upon performing work without desire. Devotion, however, depends upon its own efficacy and is not dependent upon anything, not even upon purity of mind. If one should be able to arouse trust (*śraddhā*) in devotion, then (one should create) conflicts in conscience (*buddhi-bhedam*) on the part of those who perform work, because there is no eligibility for work on the part of those who trust in devotion. (Comment on *Gītā* 3:26)

Performance of work even without desire may serve some extrinsic purpose, but neither it nor knowledge is integral to the fundamental religious goal, devotion to Kṛṣṇa.

Like most Sanskrit texts composed by Gauṛīya Vaiṣṇavas, the *Sārārtha-varṣiṇī* practically ignores contemporary history and the relationship between devotion and worldly responsibility. It would be unwarranted, however, to assume from this silence a fundamental Gauṛīya Vaiṣṇava denial of value to living in history, although the prior renunciation of family and world by most of the authors of these Sanskrit texts indicates that those individuals were inclined personally in such a direction. Viśvanātha's commentary leaves open a wide range of ways of coping with the tensions between the historical and the eternal, the world and Kṛṣṇa. I am inclined to view this reticent stance of Viśvanātha and other Gauṛīya Vaiṣṇavas as symptomatic of an implicit policy of flexibility and freedom for the individual Vaiṣṇava and for local groups of Vaiṣṇavas in fostering devotion while participating in domestic and public affairs. The Gauṛīya Vaiṣṇava interpretation of the *Bhagavad-gītā*, especially as represented in the most influential Bengali document of the movement, the *Caitanya-caritāmṛta* of Kṛṣṇa-dāsa, seems to be open to a fairly modern and secular orientation to the facts of religious plurality and social and technological change. Secular in this context, of course, does not mean anti-clerical or anti-spiritual, but rather viewing a wide range of activity as religiously neutral, free of ascribed ritual forms, fit for being performed alongside persons of different communal background and different piety. To gain a more concrete picture of Gauṛīya Vaiṣṇava participation in public affairs under a Muslim-dominated regime we may turn to the biographies of Caitanya, most of which are written in Bengali.

## III. *Gauṛīya Vaiṣṇava Participation in the Secular Affairs of Muslim-dominated Bengal*

This section contains an enumeration of Gauṛīya Vaiṣṇavas contemporary with Caitanya who were involved in the commerce, collection of revenue, administration and personal service of Husain Shāh, his successor and immediate predecessors from the end of the fifteenth century to the middle of the sixteenth. There is some evidence, though less plentiful, of similar involvement of important Gauṛīya Vaiṣṇavas in the subsequent Mughal administrations of Bengal.

Two brothers of Kāyastha (clerk) caste, Hiraṇya and Govardhana, were in charge of revenue collection at Saptagrām, the leading port on the Hugli River, located a few miles above what is now Calcutta. They had incurred the wrath of a Muslim whom they had supplanted in this lucrative position, but managed to survive his harassment. Both brothers are regarded by Vaiṣṇavas as great devotees and patrons of Vaiṣṇavas and brahmans. Among the persons they patronized were Caitanya himself, his father, Jagannātha Miśra, and his maternal grandfather, Nilāmbara Cakravartin, who is said to have regarded the two Kāyasthas as brothers (he himself being a brahman). The venerable Advaita Ācārya, whose prayers are said to have prompted Kṛṣṇa to descend as Caitanya, was a special object of their patronage, in recognition of which he introduced Raghunātha-dāsa, Govardhana's son, to Caitanya. The son, unwilling to submit to the worldly demands of householder and revenue collector subsequently ran away to Caitanya, and became an ascetic and poet, one of the noted six Gosvāmins of Vṛndāban. Govardhana sought to win back his son through the good offices of another rich Vaiṣṇava, a Baidya (medical caste) named Śivānanda Sena. Śivānanda was the devotee who organized and financed the annual pilgrimage of Gauṛīya Vaiṣṇavas from Bengal to Purī in Orissa to see Caitanya and the Jagannātha deity. I have not discovered the source of Śivānanda's wealth, but in view of his origins in Kulīnagrām, a town from which a number of Hindus used to go to Gauṛa to serve at the royal court, it is not improbable that he held some royal commission, perhaps as collector of revenue at Kāñcaṛāpāṛa, the village to which he had moved. Śivānanda was a devotional poet in his own right and his son, Paramānanda Sena, alias Kavikarṇapūra, wrote extensively in Sanskrit on poetics and Vaiṣṇava devotion. His works include a formal poem (*kāvya*) and a drama (*nāṭaka*) on the life of Caitanya.[10]

Nīlāmbara Cakravartin, Caitanya's grandfather, had other good connections. The Muslim inspector (*qāẓī*) whom Caitanya challenged over the right of Vaiṣṇavas to undertake loud devotional processions in Navadvīpa is reported to have claimed the relationship of "village brother" with Nīlāmbara, in view of which he sought to treat Caitanya, then in his early twenties, as his nephew. Nīlāmbara was known also to the royal pundit at Purī, Sarvabhauma Bhaṭṭācārya, as the fellow student of the latter's father. This network of quasi-brotherly ties is one of several indications that Gauṛīya Vaiṣṇavas exercised an

[10] CC 2:15:93-97; 2:16: 217-226; 3:6:180ff.; Haridās Dās, *Gauṛīya-vaiṣṇava-jīvana* (Navadvīpa: Haribol Kuṭī, G.A. 465 or A.D. 1951), I, 199; idem, *Gauṛīya-vaiṣṇava-tīrtha* (Navadvīpa: Haribol Kuṭī, G.A. 465 or A.D. 1951), p. 10.

informal diplomatic function of mediating between the Hindu kingdom of Orissa and the Muslim dominated kingdom of Bengal, or Gauṛa.[11]

Returning to Caitanya we find that his second marriage was to the daughter of a brahman, Sanātana Miśra, a royal pandit (*rāja-paṇḍita*), apparently in the employ of Husain Shāh. Buddhimanta Khān, a landholder or collector of revenue in the vicinity of Navadvīpa, financed the wedding as he had financed devotional festivals for the Vaiṣṇavas in Navadvīpa. This is the Buddhimanta Khān who pattronized Ānanda Bhaṭṭa, author of the *Ballāla Carita* (A.D. 1510), a book on social issues stressing the position of Kāyasthas as second to brahmans in a world that is devoid of kshatriyas. The editor of the *Ballāla-carita*, Haraprasād Śāstrī, considers the little book to be part of an agitation arising from Nityānanda's (Caitanya's energetic and unconventional disciple) efforts at "encorporating the wealthy but presecuted Suvarṇavaniks (goldsmiths) into the new and rising Vaiṣṇava community." [12] Many of the leading Vaiṣṇava brahmans in and near Navadvīpa at the time of Caitanya were newcomers who seem to have made common cause with members of other castes seeking greater prestige and influence. In the process they ran afoul of older inhabitants of the area, especially Śākta brahmans accustomed to offering bloody sacrifices. Those depicted in the biographies of Caitanya as most hostile to the Vaiṣṇavas usually are not Muslims, but Śākta brahmans.

Nityānanda's marriage late in life suggests the influence of certain lay Vaiṣṇavas. That Nityānanda, who had been a celibate mendicant should have married two girls in his old age is surprising, and a scandal in some quarters. His father-in-law, Sūrya-dāsa, who is widely hailed as a devotee and who may have authored some devotional lyrics, was mortally afraid over his failure to marry off his daughters. The reasons for his failure are not given. Possibly his contacts with the Muslims had incurred for him some ritual pollution. Here again there was a wealthy zamindar in the background ready to finance the celebration, one Kṛṣṇa-dāsa, son of Hari Hoṛa, a zamindar of Baṛagāchi, north of Navadvīpa. Both are remembered as devotees. Another zamindar associated with Nityānanda's family is the pious Kamalākānta Piplāi, paternal grandfather of Nityānanda's daughter-in-

[11] CC 1:17:148-149; 2:6:52-53.

[12] Vṛndāvana-dāsa, *Caitanya-bhāgavata*, 1:15:40-72; *Ballāla-carita* (Calcutta: Hare Press, S.A. 1823 or A.D. 1901), p. vii.

law. Hari-dās Dās reports that the grandson of Kamalākānta, one Rājīvalocana, received a grant of land from the Mughal governor at Dacca. Such a seventeenth century transaction seems to be anachronistic, but is barely possible. A greater strain on the historian's credulity is placed by the story that Nityānanda's son, Vīrabhadra, received from the Muslim ruler a black stone that wept miraculously, from which stone were made several images of Kṛṣṇa. Less fanciful evidence of the good favor of the Nityānanda family with the Muslim rulers is an extant document guaranteeing the family's possession of lands north of Calcutta.[13]

A disciple of Caitanya especially noted for combining loving devotion with the external trappings of wealth and pomp is Puṇḍarīka Vidyānidhi, a brahman with residences in Navadvīpa and near Chittagong. Caitanya assigned to him for training in loving devotion Gadādhara, a young man who became so sensitive to the moods of Rādhā that some Gauṛīya Vaiṣṇavas believe him to be an incarnation of Rādhā herself.[14] Two brothers who, like Vidyānidhi, combined loving devotion and wealth, Sanātana and Rūpa, came from a family of South Indian brahmans who had migrated to Bengal in the latter part of the fifteenth century. The family had a seat at Rāmakeli, near the capital of Gauṛa, and extensive holdings of land in East Bengal. Sanātana and Rūpa were for a time chief minister (or departmental head) (*sarakāra mallika*) and private secretary for Husain Shāh. They and their nephew, Jīva, are among the most prolific of the six Gosvāmins of Vṛndāban. The brothers resigned from Husain's service on the occasion of a campaign against Orissa, in protest against attacking brahmans, devotees and deities in that Hindu kingdom.[15]

Other Gauṛīya Vaiṣṇavas employed at the court in Gauṛa include: Mukundadāsa, a Baidya from Śrīkhaṇḍa, friend of Caitanya, and

---

[13] Comment of the editor upon CC 1:11:25; Kṣīrod-bihārī Gosvāmin, *Śrīman-nityānanda vaṃsāvallī* (Calcutta: Kṣīrod-bihārī Gosvāmin, B.A. 1337 or 1930), pp. 158-60, 163; Nityānanda-dāsa, *Prema-vilāsa*, ed. Yaśodā Lāl Tālukdār (Calcutta: Patrika Press, B.A.1320 or A.D. 1913), pp. 250-51; Haridās Dās, *Gauṛīya-vaiṣṇava-jīvana*, I, 15-17, 228. The Bhāgavatācārya Pāṭha-bāṛi north of Calcutta holds the document guaranteeing lands to the family of Nityānanda.

[14] Vṛndāvana-dāsa, *Caitanya-bhāgavata* 2:7 passim; Nityānanda-dāsa, *Prema-vilāsa*, pp. 216-17; Kavikarṇapūra, *Gauragaṇoddeśa-dīpikā*, 4th Murshidabad ed. (Berhampur: Rādhā-ramaṇa Press, B.A. 1329 or A.D. 1922), v. 147.

[15] Narahari Cakravartin, *Bhakti-ratnākara*, ed. Nanda Lāl Vidyā-sāgar (Calcutta: Gauṛīya Mission, 1960), I, 526-851; CC 2:19 passim.

private physician to Husain Shāh;[16] Dāmodara Sena, alias Yaśorāja Khān, author of *Krishna-maṅgala*, "an officer of the sultan Husain Shāh";[17] Keśava Khān, alias Keśava-chatrī, a Kāyastha, writer of devotional lyrics, bodyguard of the king (as were his father and grandfather before him);[18] Gopinātha Vasu, a minister (*wazīr*) at court, son of another official, Subuddhi Khān;[19] Subuddhi Rāya, onetime superior of Husain Shāh who rose in power upon Husain's ascension to the throne, only to be chastised reluctantly by the king (at the urging of his queen), after which chastisement he retired to Mathurā to pray and assist Bengali pilgrims;[20] and Mālādhara Vasu, alias Guṇarāja Khān, author of *Śrī-krishna-vijaya*, a Kāyastha of Kulīnagrām, "probably a revenue officer of the sultan Rukn-ud-dīn Barbak Shah."[21] Caitanya appreciated Mālādhara's poem and showered his affection upon Mālādhara's kin, Satyarāja Khān (title received from Rukn-ud-dīn Barbak Shāh) and Rāmānanda Vasu, both noted devotees.[22] The younger brother of the royal physician mentioned above (Mukunda-dāsa) was Narahari Sarakāra, one of the most influential poets and spiritual directors of Caitanya's generation. Though a Baidya from Śrīkhaṇḍa, he had a number of brahmans among his disciples, an indication perhaps of his political as well as spiritual prestige.[23]

In Navadvīpa one Subhānanda Rāya, a pious Vaiṣṇava and a man of influence, is said to have been on friendly terms with the king, a predecessor of Husain. His son also was pious and influential, we are told, but his grandsons, Jagannātha and Mādhava, despite their good Vaiṣṇava names, were lecherous drinkers who abused their powers and molested simple people. The conversion of the pair to a pious life of devotion is a famous event in the annals of the Gauṛīya Vaiṣṇavas.[24] South of Navadvīpa, guarding the border with Orissa, was a Kāyastha named Rāmacandra Khān, remembered as the devotee

[16] Haridās Dās, *Gauṛīya-vaiṣṇava-jīvana*, I, 99-100, 158. Mukunda-dāsa is reported to have fainted once from seeing in Husain a physical resemblance to Kṛṣṇa.

[17] Sukumar Sen, *History of Bengali Literature*, pp. 70, 115.

[18] CC 2:1:171ff.; Vṛndāvana-dāsa, *Caitanya-bhāgavata*, 3:4:48ff.; M. A. Rahim, *Social and Cultural History of Bengal* (Karachi: Pakistan Historical Society, 1963), I, 249.

[19] Haridās Dās, *Gauṛīya-vaiṣṇava-jīvana*, I, 112.

[20] CC 2:25:179ff.

[21] Sukumar Sen, *History of Bengali Literature*, p. 69.

[22] Jadunath Sarkar, *History of Bengal*, Vol. 2, *Muslim Period, 1200-1757* (Dacca: University of Dacca, 1948), p. 136.

[23] Haridās Dās, *Gauṛīya-vaiṣṇava-jīvana*, I, 99.

[24] Nityānanda-dāsa, *Prema-vilāsa*, p. 214.

responsible for securing a safe-conduct for Caitanya en route to Purī during a period of hostility between Gauṛa and Orissa.[25] Gauṛīya Vaiṣṇavas in general had ample reasons for wanting to see the peace maintained: access to Caitanya and the Jagannātha deity at Purī; economic interests centered upon trade and gathering of revenue; the fundamentally non-violent character of Vaiṣṇava ethics; and, conviction that Caitanya was Kṛṣṇa descended to earth to establish a new age in which loving devotion would prevail over the violence that had marred the past.

In addition to Rāmacandra's mini-truce, the resignation of Rūpa and Sanātana and the quasi-fraternal links between Vaiṣṇavas, other Hindus and certain Muslims, the evidence that Gauḍīya Vaiṣṇavas pursued a policy of reconciliation between Orissa and Bengal includes Caitanya's own behavior, though such evidence is quite scanty. It would distort the evidence, I think, to claim that diplomacy was a major concern for Caitanya, however large such a consideration may have played in the minds of some of his lay followers. His decision to settle at Purī, rather than at the more distant Vṛndāban, is said to have been a concession to his mother and devotees, but an indirect result was to expand cultural and commercial ties between Bengal and Orissa. Caitanya avoided contact with the Hindu king of Orissa, Pratāpa Rudra, as he had refused to meet with Husain Shāh near Gauṛa.[26] One alleged meeting with Pratāpa Rudra provides a remarkable glimpse of Caitanya's view of power politics, if indeed the account is genuine. For Bimanbehari Majumdar, editor of the critical edition of the only text containing this episode, the *Caitanya-maṅgala* of Jayānanda, after weighing the evidence for Jayānanda's reliability, concludes simply that it is "extremely difficult" to decide. According to Jayānanda, Caitanya had just arrived in Orissa (A.D. 1510) when Pratāpa Rudra informed him of an anticipated invasion of Bengal:

> The king begged of the divine Caitanya his blessing.
> The Lord heartily ridiculed Pratāpa Rudra:
> "The king of the five Gauṛas is Kāla-yavana.
> See how many lions and tigers there are inside him.
> The Yavana (foreigner, Muslim) will tear up Orissa.
> Jagannātha will depart from Nīlācala (Purī) for some time.
> . . . . . . . . . . . . . . . . . . . . . . . . . .
> You acquire kingdoms by conquering the Kāñcī region;

---

[25] Vṛndāvana-dāsa, *Caitanya-bhāgavata*, 3:2:82ff.; Haridās Dās, *Gauṛīya-vaiṣṇava-jīvana*, I, 178-79.

[26] CC 2:2:47ff.; 2:1:221ff.

I see no way of overcoming Gaura."

. . . . . . . . . . . . . . . . . . . . . . . . . . .

Hearing the Lord oppose it (Bengali campaign),
Pratāpa went off to make war upon Vijayānagara.[27]

Even if the account is not a faithful one—and the pragmatism of Caitanya in suggesting conquest of weaker Hindu kingdoms to the south runs against the grain of loving passivism in the image of Caitanya that we usually get—still the survival of the episode in a fairly popular biography of Caitanya suggests that the scene was considered plausible and proper by Gauṛīya Vaiṣṇavas of the time. It is a far cry from Kṛṣṇa's command that Arjuna destroy even his own relatives to preserve *varṇāśrama-dharma* way back in the waning of the Dvāpara Age.

*Table I*

*Verses of the Bhagavad-gītā cited in the Caitanya-bhāgavata*

| *Gītā* | *Gauṛīya Maṭha* | *Nāth* | *Gītā* | *Gauṛīya Maṭha* | *Nāth* |
|---|---|---|---|---|---|
| 3:21 | 1:3:25 | 4 | 7:16 | 2:24:89 | 29 |
| | 2:17:178 | 10 | | | |
| | | | 9:11 | 2:25:38 | 7 |
| 3:24 | 1:3:24 | 3 | | | |
| | | | 9:27 | 2:8:60 | 5 |
| 4:7 | 1:3:22 | — | | | |
| | | | 10:8 | 2:24:183 | 68 |
| 4:8 | 1:3:23 | 2 | | | |
| | | | 10:10 | 1:1:49 | 20 |
| 4:11 | 1:4:20 | 2 | | 2:24:167 | 59 |
| | 1:4:178 | 28 | | 2:24:186 | 70 |
| 5:18 | 3:4:177 | 7 | 10:41-42 | 2:20:373-74 | 61-62 |
| 6:3-4 | 2:24:153-54 | 53-54 | 11:41 | 2:19:199 | 28 |
| 6:8 | 3:4:178 | 8 | 11:42 | 2:19:— | 29 |
| 6:16-17 | 3:8:65-66 | 4-5 | 12:13-20 | 2:23:100-07 | 50-57 |
| 7:4 | 2:6:164 | — | 16:19 | 2:25:39 | 8 |
| 7:5 | 1:7:118 | 6 | 18:54 | 2:8:65 | 8 |
| | 2:6:165 | 12 | | 2:24:127 | 41 |
| | 2:20:116 | 10 | | 2:25:148 | 43 |
| 7:14 | 2:20:121 | 12 | 18:64-65 | 2:22:57-58 | 23-24 |
| | 2:22:23 | 7 | | | |
| | 2:24:133 | 45 | 18:66 | 2:9:265 | 22 |
| | | | | 2:22:91 | — |
| | | | | 2:8:63 | 7 |

Book, chapter, and verse numbers are given in full for the Gauṛīya Maṭha edition of the *Caitanya-caritāmṛta*. Rādhā Govinda Nāth numbers Sanskrit verses independently within each chapter; his chapter and book numbering coincides with that of the Gauṛīya Maṭha.

[27] Jayānanda, *Caitanya-maṅgala*, ed. Bimanbehari Majumdar and Sukhamay Mukhopadhyay (Calcutta: The Asiatic Society, 1971), pp. xxxiii, 218.

# THE TRANSFORMATION OF ŚRĪ RĀMAKRISHNA*

Walter G. Neevel, Jr

Śrī Rāmakrishna (1836-86) was a multifaceted and mystifying figure. To some he remains a madman; to many others, a saint. In my opinion he was both. Indeed, the most intriguing question about his life and spiritual pilgrimage was how he was transformed from the one into the other, from the "madman" of his early years into the saintly teacher of the later years. He struggled through loss, despair and self-destructive frenzy to emerge as a sensitive and wise man, and as an incarnation of all that is held sacred by millions of persons within India and elsewhere.

The primary purpose of this essay is to seek an understanding of this transformation, for far beyond its healing and renewing effects upon one individual it has had wide-spread and enduring influence upon the religious life of India. The integrity and authenticity of what he came to personify became a central factor in the modern renewal of the Hindu religious tradition, inspiring in his followers both a conviction as to the vitality of their tradition and a capacity to nurture and develop that vitality.

However, the very dynamism of the renewed tradition that sprang from Śrī Rāmakrishna, while making dramatically clear his greatness and significance, at the same time poses obstacles to any attempt to understand the precise nature of his spiritual development. All living traditions naturally and inevitably reinterpret the sources of their inspiration as their contexts and concerns change. In these reinterpretations, certain aspects are highlighted while others are de-emphasized, leading to an obscuration of the particular nature of the original inspiration. The intent in a healthy tradition, of course, is not to obscure or distort the original, but rather to continue and extend its beneficial influence in the new circumstances.

The effects of this inevitable reinterpretation were especially dramatic in the case of Śrī Rāmakrishna because his greatest disciple, Swami Vivekānanda, almost immediately projected on a world-wide

---

* This essay was written in 1964 at Yale Divinity School under the guidance of Professor Norvin J. Hein. The writer owes a debt of gratitude to Professor Hein for his encouragement and his assistance in the final editing.

scale the message of his Master, the *paramahaṃsa* of Dakshineśwar who had never been out of India and only rarely out of his native Bengal. To his world-wide audience, Swami Vivekānanda quite naturally emphasized his Master's teaching of the "truth" within all religions; and it is with this "universalism" that Śrī Rāmakrishna and the Rāmakrishna Mission, which Swami Vivekānanda founded, are most commonly associated. While this universal aspect is certainly there in his teachings, it is not to my mind the most appropriate focal point for an understanding of Śrī Rāmakrishna himself. Indeed, his most striking characteristic was his "particularity." He was consumately Hindu—in Romain Rolland's phrasing, "... the consumation of two thousand years of the spiritual life of three hundred million people." [1] Śrī Rāmakrishna had only the most cursory acquaintance with anything outside of Hindu religion and culture; and his universality developed out of the widely inclusive nature of his particularity. If we are to understand him adequately, our focus must be on the latter rather than the former.

A second shift of focus that poses an obstacle to our task was caused by the fact that Swami Vivekānanda and the later Rāmakrishna Mission have presented their Master's life and teachings in terms of a systematic philosophy generally called "Neo-Vedānta" or "Neo-Advaita," indicating that it is a reinterpretation of the classical *Advaita Vedānta* of the great philosopher Śaṅkarācārya. However, when one turns from the later systematic and biographical writings to the well-attested sayings of Śrī Rāmakrishna himself, one finds oneself in a confusion of unsystematic and seemingly conflicting materials, a confusion that is at first only heightened, and not resolved, by the contrasting clarity of the later presentations. While Śrī Rāmakrishna was an intelligent person capable of subtle speculation, his dialogues clearly reveal him to have been a mystic and *bhakta* who disparaged the power of the intellect, denied the possibility and necessity of rational understanding of the Divine, and held in small honor those who were preoccupied with philosophical and theological considerations. He often broke into song with words such as these:

> Who is there that can understand what Mother Kālī is?
> Even the six darśanas are powerless to reveal her . . .[2]

---

[1] Romain Rolland, *Prophets of the New India* (N. Y., Albert and Charles Boni, 1930), p. xxvi.

[2] Swami Nikhilananda, trans., *The Gospel of Sri Ramakrishna* (N. Y., Ramakrishna-Vivekananda Center, 1952), p. 618.

O Mother, make me mad with Thy love!
What need have I of knowledge or reason?
Make me drunk with love's Wine . . .[3]

In striking contrast, later representatives of the Rāmakrishna Mission maintain that "Philosophy was the substantial core, the central theme, the very soul of every religion." [4]

While this latter shift of emphasis may have been influenced by the strongly intellectual and philosophical bent of the *jñānī*, Swami Vivekānanda, the determinative factor once again may have been the wider, largely American and European audience to which this missionary movement has by and large directed its English writings. Without doubt the Rāmakrishna Mission has had as its major goal the revitalization of the Hindu tradition within India. However, as a mission it was also concerned with making an impact abroad, especially within those lands that had sent Christian missionaries to India. This particular concern or bias is felt most strongly, of course, in those presentations composed in English. In these works and lectures, Swami Vivekānanda and the succeeding Rāmakrishna missionaries were concerned to present the Hindu tradition and Śrī Rāmakrishna's message in the manner most comprehensible and appealing to Americans and Europeans. The Upaniṣads and the Vedānta school of religious thought (*darśana*) based upon them had already found ready acceptance and praise, especially within certain non-traditional and non-Christian circles. Moreover, the currency of transcendental idealism and vitalistic monism within Western philosophy provided a ready basis for an acceptance of the profundity of Śaṅkarācārya's idealistic non-dualism (*a-dvaita*). Since Śrī Rāmakrishna held such a widely inclusive Hindu position, it was not at all difficult to emphasize or highlight the more appealing and acceptable Vedāntic and *advaitic* aspects of his teachings. However, this tendency—together with the corresponding tendency to de-emphasize certain other more popular, emotional and exotic aspects that might be offensive to Western sensibilities—is a major obstacle in the way of a reader who is dependent upon English sources coming to an understanding of Śrī Rāmakrishna himself. My hope is that with the current shift in the cultural winds and with the presence of saffron-robed ecstatics dancing and chanting the names of Krishna on American street corners, it is

[3] *Ibid.*, p. 399.
[4] Haridas Bhattacharyya, ed., *The Cultural Heritage of India*, IV (Calcutta, The Ramakrishna Mission, 1956), p. 714.

now possible to present Śrī Rāmakrishna in his own Hindu garb.

There is a third shift of focus within the Rāmakrishna Mission as organized by Swami Vivekānanda that has caused a great deal of confusion regarding the relationship between this movement on the one hand and both Śrī Rāmakrishna and the entire previous Hindu tradition on the other. Śrī Rāmakrishna is quite commonly viewed as an "other-worldly" mystic concerned only with God and not with the service of man within the world.[5] On the other hand, Swami Vivekānanda proclaimed a life-affirming philosophy, and the Rāmakrishna Mission has organized a dynamic social service program operating hospitals, clinics, colleges, libraries, etc., throughout India. Since neither Śrī Rāmakrishna's teachings as commonly understood nor Śaṅkara's acosmic non-dualism with its rejection of the ultimate reality of the world would seem to support the dynamic social concern generated by Swami Vivekānanda, it is not unusual to find it asserted that his Neo-Vedānta is "Hinduism reborn—a new creation, not merely revived and reconstructed."[6] In such a view, the source of this "new creation" is usually traced to the dynamic nature of Swami Vivekānanda's personality and/or the impact of Western and Christian realism and ethical concern. While these factors were certainly major ones in the continued development and reinterpretation of this tradition, I believe that if we can view Śrī Rāmakrishna in his own terms rather than those of Śaṅkara's *advaita*, we can accept at face value Swami Vivekānanda's claim that his social concern was inspired directly by his Master. For, although Śrī Rāmakrishna did not engage directly in social service, his teachings did provide a traditional Hindu basis for a dynamic and life-affirming world-view that Swami Vivekānanda in turn developed into an ethical philosophy more adequate for Hindus living in a modern context.

This essay, then, represents an attempt to understand the original inspiration of Swami Vivekānanda and the Rāmakrishna Mission, i.e., the religious experience and teachings of Śrī Rāmakrishna. It is written by one of the many who have been impressed by the contributions of this movement to the revitalization of the Hindu

[5] Leo Schneiderman, "Ramakrishna: Personality and Social Factors in the Growth of a Religious Movement," *J. for the Scientific Study of Religion*, VIII (1969), pp. 60-71.

[6] Paul D. Devanandan, *The Concept of Maya* (London, Lutterworth Press, 1950), p. 227.

tradition, but who have also been confused by the relation between the later systematization of Rāmakrishna's experience and teachings and the image presented in the most authentic expressions of his own mind, the transcriptions of his public discussions during the last four years of his life. The conclusions presented herein are my effort to resolve this confusion; they derive whatever value they possess from my detailed comparative analysis of all available English translations of the above transcriptions. In light of the many obstacles confronting this task, not the least being my lack of a command of the Bengali originals of the major sources, the tentative nature of my conclusions should be clear to all. However, my hope is that I have been successful in presenting some sense of Śrī Rāmakrishna's surprisingly coherent if unsystematic synthesis of many diverse Hindu traditions, of the spiritual experience and transformation upon which his synthesis was based, and of his impact upon the continuing development of the Hindu tradition.

## Methodology

In attempting to make a fresh analysis of the religious experience and teachings of Śrī Rāmakrishna there are great methodological problems. Rāmakrishna, while literate in Bengali, had no interest in writing and left no published or manuscript works of his own. All of the information that we have about him has been mediated through his disciples or, in a few cases, through other persons who had contact with him. While his disciples have been and are sincerely concerned to advance Rāmakrishna's genuine message, their conception of that message was crystalized during a period after the death of the Master when the powerful personality of Swami Vivekānanda was dominant in their circle.

As has been noted in the introduction, Vivekānanda's development of his Master's teachings was carried out under the pressures of concerns and circumstances that were of relatively little importance in Rāmakrishna's own context. Therefore, the central critical problem we face is that of distinguishing the role played by these later changes of emphasis and focus in shaping our sources of information on his life and teachings.

A major aspect of this critical problem is the fact that the disciples who are our channels of information believed Śrī Rāmakrishna to have been from birth an *avatāra*, an incarnation of the Divine, and consequently expected in him the manifestation of extraordinary powers. On the negative side, this belief may have encouraged the development of legends that are now mingled with the facts about Rāmakrishna. On the positive side, however, the great reverence arising from such faith was also, in general, a factor making for careful preservation of his teachings. His disciples have preserved his sayings in exceptional fullness. In the case of sayings that were initially preserved as oral tradition and only written down much later, this reverence is not enough to justify trust in the text of the documents.

With regard to the main body of the recorded teachings of Śrī Rāmakrishna, however, we may have much greater confidence in their authenticity. During the last four years of his life (1882-1886), a large number of his public and private utterances were recorded in a diary, shortly after they were heard, by Mahendranāth Gupta, a devoted disciple. Mahendranāth met Rāmakrishna shortly after being graduated from college. He was a teacher at a school in Calcutta during their association. He was, therefore, a well-educated scribe. Apparently he possessed a fine memory, for his notes are widely praised as having "the value of almost stenographic records." [7] Both Rāmakrishna's wife and Swami Vivekānanda have testified that Mahendranāth did not interject his own personality into his materials but presented the teachings of Rāmakrishna faithfully.[8] Without a doubt, then, we come the closest to Rāmakrishna in Mahendranāth's recordings, where the overlay of traditions is least significant. These recordings, then, will be our major source and the authority against which all other sources must be judged.

It was in the Bengali language, of course, that Śrī Rāmakrishna spoke and Mahendranāth wrote in his diary. Mahendranāth's work was first published in Bengali, under the pseudonym "M," as *Śrī Śrī Rāmakrishna Kathāmṛita* ("The Nectar of the Story of Śrī Rāmakrishna") in five volumes, the first appearing in 1897 and the last in 1932.[9] To estimate the quality of the several English translations of these sayings is important in the work of this essay. My lack of competence in Bengali makes this problem of testing the translations as difficult as it is necessary. However, an examination and compari-

[7] Swami Nikhilananda, trans., *The Gospel of Sri Ramakrishna*, p. vii.

[8] Nikhilananda, *Gospel of Sri Ramakrishna*, abridged edition (N. Y., Ramakrishna-Vivekananda Center, 1958), pp. vii-viii.

[9] Nikhilananda, *The Gospel of Sri Ramakrishna*, p. vii.

son of the various English publications themselves has been found to provide a realistic basis for an impression of the quality of the translations and well-based preferences in use of editions.

The first English edition of a portion of Mahendranāth's recordings, translated by the scribe himself, was published also in 1897 as *Gospel of Sri Ramakrishna* (*According to M., a son of the Lord and disciple*) or *The Ideal Man for India and for the World*, Part I (The Brahmavadin Office, Madras). I am in possession of a 1907 reprint of this edition (hereafter referred to as *Madras I*). A second edition of this Part I was published in 1911 by the Srī Rāmakrishna Math, Mylapore, Madras. According to the editor, this second edition was "completely revised by the author," Mahendranāth.[10] I do not have this second edition but do have a copy of the fifth edition (hereafter *Madras 5th*) published under the same auspices in 1930. The editor of *Madras 5th* mentions no revisions done for his publication and a comparison between the first and fifth editions shows that Mahendranāth's revisions for the second edition consisted mainly of a modernization of the English style. Although the pagination differs, there seems to be little substantive difference between the 1907 reprint of the first edition and the fifth edition of 1930.

A further portion of the sayings of Rāmakrishna was first translated and published in 1922 by the Śrī Rāmakrishna Math, Mylapore, Madras, as *Gospel of Sri Ramakrishna* (*According to M., a son of the Lord and disciple*), Vol. II. This publication was apparently projected when the first English volume was being prepared. I have the second, 1928 edition of this book (hereafter referred to as *Madras II*). The prefaces to the first and second editions, which appear in my copy, do not identify the translator of this second volume into English. Since Mahendranāth's name is not mentioned, it is safest to assume that the volume was translated from the Bengali edition by someone else. Moreover, for the second edition "the language has been edited and improved by a Western friend."[11] Because these two critical persons are unknown, the trustworthiness of their work is a matter of question, but comparisons with parallel sections in Swami Nikhilānanda's translation (to be described later) show general agreement. Each of these two volumes published in Madras spans the four year period of Mahendranāth's association with Rāmakrishna, the

[10] *Madras 5th*, p. iii.
[11] *Madras II*, p. vi.

second volume being composed of episodes not included in the first. The two volumes together leave a large proportion of the Bengali edition still untranslated.

Another relatively early English edition is *The Gospel of Ramakrishna* revised in 1907 by Swami Abhedānanda from Mahendranāth's original English text. I possess a 1947 edition of this work (referred to hereafter as *S. Abhed.*). From all indications this 1947 edition reproduced unchanged the text published by Swami Abhedānanda forty years before. This book calls itself "the authorized English edition of the 'Gospel of Ramakrishna.'" [12] Abhedānanda, at the time in charge of the original Vedanta Society headquarters in New York City, says in the introduction: "At the request of 'M' I have edited and remodelled the large portion of His English manuscript; while the remaining portions I have translated directly from the Bengali edition of his notes." [13] A comparison with the general layout and content of *Madras I* indicates that the manuscript Mahendranāth sent to Abhedānanda must have been substantially the same as that published in Madras in 1897. But the comparison also illustrates that Abhedānanda was extremely free in his use of Mahendranāth's text, altering radically the chronological order of the episodes and also the order of the dialogue within the episodes. For his own reasons he often interpolated his text with materials taken out of context from other parts of the English text or translated from the Bengali text. At at least one point he distorted the meaning of a passage radically by omitting certain sections and interpolating other sections.[14] In general, Abhedānanda's edition can be said to obscure the order and the direct and fresh character of Mahendranāth's original diary and is not a reliable source. The fact that Swami Nikhilānanda (see below) does not mention this edition while he does cite the Madras editions may indicate that he shares this evaluation.[15] We shall not make any primary use of it. But for certain critical purposes, such as determining the true text when the Madras transla-

[12] *The Gospel of Ramakrishna*, revised by Swami Abhedananda from M.'s Original English Text (Boston, Beacon Press, 1947), p. vii.

[13] *Ibid.*, p. viii-ix.

[14] Cf. *S. Abhed.*, Ch. IX, pp. 261ff, with conversation of June 25, 1884, *Madras I*, pp. 220ff, and *S. Nikhil.*, pp. 462-72. *S. Abhed.* makes several insertions (on pp. 271, 273, 274-83) and omissions (on pp. 269, 272, 273) which greatly heighten the emphasis on *jñāna yoga* and *advaita* and obscure the original emphasis on *bhakti yoga* (cf. especially *Madras I*, pp. 231ff and *S. Nikhil.*, pp. 468f.).

[15] *S. Nikhil.*, p. vii.

tions and that of Swami Nikhilānanda disagree, Abhedānanda's edition has some utility.

A third and relatively independent translation of Mahendranāth's Bengali work is Swami Nikhilānanda's *The Gospel of Sri Ramakrishna* published by the Rāmakrishna-Vivekānanda Center in New York in 1942. I have a copy of its second printing in 1952 (hereafter called *S. Nikhil.*). Nikhilānanda has published in this work a virtually complete translation of the Bengali edition, "omitting only a few pages of no particular interest to English-speaking readers." [16] The Swami says that he has made a literal translation and that "often literary grace has been sacrificed for the sake of literal translation." [17] A comparison of selections of his work with parallel passages in the Madras editions gives apparent confirmation to the claim to literalness. Whereas *S. Abhed.* omitted all dates (again obscuring the original nature of the diary), both *S. Nikhil.* and the Madras editions date their materials. *S. Nikhil.* includes more episodes and is thus more complete, but the Madras editions reproduce completely all that Mahendranāth recorded for any day that they reproduce at all. Therefore, there are large blocks of material that are complete and dated in both editions and thus easily open to comparison. For the most part, the wording or at least the meaning of texts in *S. Nikhil.* and in *Madras I* and *Madras 5th* corresponds closely. For the one and only date on which I have found sequential and substantive disagreement between them, *S. Nikhil.* and *S. Abhed.* agree—suggesting that the Madras edition might have altered the original at this point.[18] My general conclusion is that Swami Nikhilānanda has produced a faithful translation and has preserved the order and character of the original carefully.

Swami Nikhilānanda has not, however, allowed his hands to be completely tied by his literalistic tendencies. Relative to the Madras texts, his translation shows minor omissions, additions or rewordings that alter the emphasis to some degree, and occasionally there are disagreements on the translation of specific religious terms. These variations occur with differing frequencies and degrees of significance. We shall consider some of the more important and consistent variations as they become relevant to our discussion.

My final opinion is that both the Madras and the Nikhilānanda

---

[16] *Ibid.*

[17] *Ibid.*

[18] On August 5, 1882, cf. *Madras I*, pp. 67ff; *S. Nikhil.*, pp. 99ff; and *S. Abhed.*, pp. 99ff.

translation are basically accurate and reliable efforts. Therefore, by a critical comparison of them, it should be possible to get as close to Śrī Rāmakrishna's original teachings as is possible without a knowledge of Bengali and to have an adequate degree of certainty about their meaning.

The remaining major sources upon which this essay is based are the various biographies and biographical sketches of Śrī Rāmakrishna, especially those standard works produced by his direct disciples. These sources are essential for any full understanding of his earlier life and spiritual development. As has been noted, his recorded teachings all come from his last four years, although they do contain a considerable number of scattered references to his earlier experiences.[19] However, as will be established later, these biographies have been heavily influenced by the later systematic reinterpretation of the tradition. Therefore, they must be utilized with critical caution and checked against the recorded sayings whenever possible. Essentially, this essay will be such a critical comparison between the image of Rāmakrishna presented in the standard biographies and that which emerges from a detailed study of his recorded teachings.

The basic biography in Bengali is the five-volume *Śrī Śrī Rāmakrishna Līlā-prasanga* by Swami Saradānanda, a direct disciple. It was begun in 1909 and left partially incomplete at the author's death in 1927. I have used the English translation of this work by Swami Jagadānanda that was published in 1952 under the title *Sri Ramakrishna The Great Master* (Madras, Sri Ramakrishna Math), hereafter referred to as *The Great Master*.[20] The other major traditional biographical source in English appeared in 1925 as the *Life of Sri Ramakrishna Compiled from Various Authentic Sources* (Mayavati, Almora, Himalayas; Advaita Ashrama), hereafter called *Life of Sri Ramakrishna*.[21] The publishers of this compilation state in the preface that it draws upon the major Bengali biographies, Mahendranāth's diary and recollections of other direct disciples and that it was prepared specifically for the "English-reading public." They also reveal

---

[19] E.g., *S. Nikhil.*, pp. 185, 187, 239-40, 297, 305, 407, 619, 779, 813-14, 830-33. etc.

[20] In the later, more readily available editions there have been some slight changes of wording and of pagination. The page references for the 3rd edition, 1963, will be given in brackets.

[21] This work was thoroughly revised in 1928. Wherever possible the corresponding references for the 2nd revised edition, 1964 reprinting, will be given in brackets.

their sensitivity to the problems caused by "the free introduction of the 'supernatural' element in the book." [22] This sensitivity has not led them to omit miraculous happenings from their account, but it may have caused them to eliminate some legends which had no basis in fact.

Of the many other biographical accounts, only one necessitates special mention here. It is the brief sketch in F. Max Müller's *Ramakrishna: His Life and Sayings* which represents an early and relatively independent source of biographical data. Müller had been dismayed at the "strangely exaggerated" and contradictory accounts of Rāmakrishna's life that were then (1898) in circulation. He states:

> I applied therefore to one of his most eminent pupils, Vivekananda, asking him to write down for me what he could tell of his own knowledge of his venerable teacher, and I received from him a full description of his Master's life. . . . I give it as much as possible unaltered. . . . . I had made it as clear as possible to Vivekananda that the accounts hitherto published of his Master, however edifying they might be to his followers, would sound perfectly absurd to European students . . . Vivekananda himself is a man who knows England and America well, and perfectly understood what I meant.[23]

Although Müller claims still to see "the irrepressible miraculising tendencies of devoted disciples," [24] we can assume that Vivekānanda, under these admonitions from the leading Indologist of the day, made every effort to make his account as factual and accurate as possible.

Having examined the major sources to be used, let us make explicit some of the principles of interpretation to be used in this study of Śrī Rāmakrishna's life and teachings. Our primary objective is, of course, to represent the character of his spiritual experience and teachings faithfully and accurately and in its own terms. However, in our systematic attempt to arrive at a clear and rational understanding, we must be careful not to impose these academic qualities arbitrarily upon Śrī Rāmakrishna himself. While he was quite intelligent and capable of understanding the nuances of philosophical and theological speculation, he refused to allow his teachings to be restricted by the requirements of rational systematic discourse. There is evidence that

[22] *Life of Sri Ramakrishna*, pp. i-iii.

[23] F. Max Müller, *Ramakrishna, His Life and Sayings* (London, Longmans, Green & Co., 1898) [reprinted Mayavati, Almora, Himalayas, Advaita Ashrama, 1951], pp. 24, 29-30.

[24] *Ibid.*, p. 30.

the character of his utterances could vary considerably with his spiritual state at the particular time [25] and that the particular aspect of his teachings that he would emphasize on a particular occasion was often accommodated to the particular viewpoint, needs and qualifications of the person with whom he was conversing.[26] To appreciate the meaning of Śrī Ramakrishna's utterances, we must not treat them as atomic units each one of which, in isolation, represents a system and can be made the source of logical deductions about the whole of his outlook. Rather, to grasp his meaning, we must view his statements in relation to the factors involved in the situation in which they were given, in relation to other statements made in other situations, and, most importantly, in relation to his spiritual and religious experience.

On the problem of the interpretation of Rāmakrishna's total message, J. N. Farquhar has made an insightful statement: "The character of Ramakrishna was singularly simple. He seemed to be capable of only a single motive, namely, a passion for God. That ruled and filled him. . . . when we follow that clue, every detail of his character and life falls into place." [27] Such is indeed the case, although the many diverse directions in which this single motive led Śrī Rāmakrishna often obscure the basic simplicity. The point to be made is that we are dealing with a man who claimed to know nothing but God. While his quick mind enabled him to acquire a wide and detailed knowledge of the Hindu religious tradition, he taught only that which he believed he had actually experienced as real and true. And herein lay his greatness and his ability to move the spirits of men. He spoke as one having authority. If we would understand what he said, we must comprehend the spiritual travail and inspiration which lay behind his words.

## Life and Teachings of Śrī Rāmakrishna According to the Rāmakrishna Mission

As has been said, central to our task is the problem of discerning the relationship between the spiritual experiences and teachings of Śrī Rāmakrishna and the Rāmakrishna Mission's systematic inter-

---

[26] *Ibid.*, p. 58.

[26] *Life of Sri Ramakrishna*, p. 373.

[27] John N. Farquhar, *Modern Religious Movements in India* (New York, The Macmillan Co., 1919), p. 195.

pretation of these experiences and teachings. This problem can be dealt with most effectively by comparing the picture presented in the major biographies mentioned above with the image that emerges from Mahendranāth's diary. In the two major biographies composed or compiled 23 to 39 years after Rāmakrishna's death, the interpretive role of the Rāmakrishna Mission was of primary importance since the disciples had to separate the facts from the overgrowth of legends and to establish the chronology and sequence of events with few definite guidelines. As Swami Saradānanda himself reveals,

> We entertained great doubts at the time of writing the present Part of the book, whether we should be able to ascertain the dates of all the important events of the Master's life. Although he told many of us the facts of his life as a spiritual aspirant, he never narrated them chronologically to anyone. Consequently the events of this period of his life have remained confused and complicated in the minds of his devotees. But as the result of investigation, we have now been able to ascertain, by his grace, the dates of many of those events.[28]

This statement raises the question of the precise nature of the historical principles employed by Saradānanda to determine the sequential structure of Rāmakrishna's experience. This question is especially important because most of the other biographical material produced subsequently by the Rāmakrishna Mission "closely follows the chronology and treatment of the great Bengali work . . . by Swami Saradananda." [29]

In light of this question, it is useful to examine the manner in which Saradānanda resolves the complex controversy over the date of Śrī Rāmakrishna's birth. From Mahendranāth's diary, we learn that he was born on "the second day of the bright fortnight of the moon" under the zodiacal sign *Kumbha* (Aquarius.)[30] We also learn that his birthday (the day of his natal star, *Pūrvabhadrapada* or Pegasi) was celebrated on March 11th in 1883, February 16th in 1885 and March 7th in 1886.[31] Swami Vivekānanda first gave the date of his birth as February 20, 1833.[32] In 1907 the official version was changed to "Wednesday, the 20th of February 1834, or the 10th of Falgun

[28] *The Great Master*, p. 75 [3rd ed., p. 73].
[29] *Life of Sri Ramakrishna*, p. ii.
[30] *S. Nikhil.*, pp. 813-14.
[31] *Ibid.*, pp. 186, 691, 940-41.
[32] Müller, *Ramakrishna, His Life and Sayings*, 1898, p. 30; Swami Vivekananda, *My Master* (N. Y., Baker and Taylor, 1901), p. 70.

1756 Saka, the second lunar day of the light fortnight." [33] Saradānanda acknowledges this disagreement and claims to have resolved it:

> There has continued till now a controversy about the year of the Master's birth. For he himself told us that his original horoscope was lost and that the one cast afterwards was full of errors. We have been able to solve that dispute by consulting a number of almanacs more than a hundred years old. To ascertain the dates, therefore, of the events of the Master's life has become easy for us.[34]

Saradānanda's research revealed

> that the boy had come into the world at an especially auspicious moment.
>
> It was the sixth day of Phalgun in . . . 1757 of the Saka year, or Wednesday, February 17, A.D. 1836. . . . The auspicious second lunar day of the bright fortnight and the twenty-fifth of the lunar constellations (Pūrvabhadrapada) had combined to bring about the happy astrological conjunction called the Siddhiyoga.[35]

Furthermore,

> The result of this natal arrangement of the planets is, according to the *Bhrigu Samhita*, that the man becomes the head of a religious movement, virtuous, highly honoured, always engaged in doing virtuous deeds; he lives in a temple, and gets a large following of disciples; he is called a great man by all, and is born of the spirit of Lord Narayana; he is worshipped by all.[36]

Several points should be noted with regard to Swami Saradānanda's method of resolving this dispute. Firstly, it is clear that his solution was not finally conclusive since the official decision on the date was subsequently revised to February 18, 1836.[37] Secondly, simply determining the date of Śrī Rāmakrishna's birth does not, as Saradānanda claims, make it "easy for us" to ascertain the dates of the many events that previously had "remained confused and complicated in the minds of his devotees." While there are a few fixed dates and Rāmakrishna does give some evidence as to the sequence of certain events, a great deal of guesswork remains; and it is misleading to obscure the tentative nature of any historical reconstruction of the events of his life. Thirdly, one's doubts are raised when the lost and erroneously recast horoscope is eventually reconstructed to produce such fore-

---

[33] *Madras I*, p. 1.
[34] *The Great Master*, p. 75 [3rd ed., p. 73].
[35] *Ibid.*, p. 42 [3rd ed., p. 40].
[36] *Ibid.*, Appendix, p. ii [3rd ed., p. 960].
[37] *Life of Sri Ramakrishna*, pp. 15, 767 [2nd ed., pp. 13, 607].

casts as "the man becomes the head of a religious movement" and "he lives in a temple, and gets a large following of disciples." While the asterism under which a person was born is certainly useful for determining which years and dates are eligible for consideration, in light of the incomplete data and the continuing uncertainty, one must raise the question of whether or not the "especially auspicious" conditions of February 17, 1836, were not selected by Swami Saradānanda because they were the ones most conducive to producing the sort of person Śrī Rāmakrishna had become in the minds of his disciples.

The second and third points above in turn raise the question of how the many other uncertainties concerning the events of Śrī Rāmakrishna's life were resolved by Swami Saradānanda. *The Great Master* and subsequently *Life of Sri Ramakrishna* fit the Master's religious practices or disciplines (*sādhana*) into a very neat sequence, progressing through certain preliminary and lower forms of discipline and realization and culminating in his experiencing *nirvikalpa samādhi*, the formless mystical ideal of *Advaita Vedānta*. This essay argues that this reconstruction derived more from the views of Swami Vivekānanda and the later Rāmakrishna Mission than from the teaching of Śrī Rāmakrishna himself. I propose that Saradānanda and the other official biographers were moved to establish this particular order by their conviction that *Advaita Vedānta* is the ultimate expression of religious truth and therefore the ultimate and finally satisfying phase of Rāmakrishna's sādhana. To demonstrate the validity of this analysis I will first present a sketch of his life and sādhana in accordance with the standard biographies, criticizing them when there is sufficient evidence, and then contrast this orthodox view with the perspective found in earlier and more reliable historical materials.

Śrī Rāmakrishna was born into a Chattopādhyāya (or Chatterjee) family living in the Bengal village of Kamarpukur.[38] He was officially named Śambhu Chandra but was called Gadādhar, one of the names of Viṣṇu, because of a vision which his father was reported to have had shortly before the child's birth.[39] His was a pious and orthodox Vaiṣṇava brahman family having Rāmachandra as its tutelary deity.

[38] *Life of Sri Ramakrishna*, p. 1. Non-controversial biographical information which can be found easily either in this biography or in *The Great Master* will not be footnoted hereafter.

[39] *Ibid.*, pp. 16, 22.

This Vaiṣṇava background and the fact that names with Rāma in them were traditional in his family probably are the most important factors to be considered in tracing the unknown origin of the name Rāmakrishna which he later bore.[40] Rāmakrishna apparently acquired many of the characteristics of his own religious life from an ecstatic spirituality that was traditional in his family. Not only are visions attributed to his father and mother, Khudiram and Chandra Devī, but

> almost all the members of the Chatterjee family were open to psychic influences . . . Ramsila, the sister of Khudiram, had the goddess Sitala as her Chosen Ideal and while meditating on her she often lost her own consciousness and acted so much like that goddess that people often thought her to be possessed by her . . . Once when Ramsila was in such a mood, the boy Gadadhar was standing near. Instead of being afraid of what he saw, he said afterwards with a smile, "It would be a great fun if she who possessed my aunt got hold of me!" [41]

An event which would seem to have been determinative for the course of Rāmakrishna's religious experience was the death of his father at the age of 68 in 1843. Gadādhar was still a young boy and greatly missed his elderly father who had been quite indulgent with him. This loss quite naturally drew him closer to his mother. From this time forward, he spent a good deal of his time helping his mother with household duties, including daily worship of the household deities. Such activities also brought him into close enduring relationships with the other women of the village. It is probable that these contacts made it natural for the young boy, who always found it quite easy to identify with and imitate others, to develop both the feminine characteristics and behavior and the attraction to feminine aspects of the Divine, which manifested themselves so strongly as his religious life progressed. As he entered his teen-age years, he associated with and imitated women even more. He would go out dressed as a girl and especially loved to play the part of a *gopī* or cowherd girl longing for Śrī Kṛṣṇa.

Gadādhar's loss of his pious father led him also, his biographers suggest, to associate with wandering pilgrims and *sādhus* who would stay for some time at the rest-house in Kamarpukur. While Gadādhar's eldest brother probably assumed the formal role of father-substitute,

---

[40] Swami Apurvananda, *Sri Ramakrishna and Sarada Devi* (Mylapore, Madras, Sri Ramakrishna Math, 1961), p. 11.

[41] *Life of Sri Ramakrishna*, pp. 28-29 [2nd ed., pp. 18-19].

it may be that the boy transferred some degree of filial affection to these sādhus. Again it is clear that he identified with them, singing and praying with them, dressing like them, smearing his body with ashes. At any rate, as Gadādhar got older he became increasingly drawn to religious activities.

The most outstanding characteristic of Gadādhar was his artistic capability and sensitivity which, as is usual in India, came to be expressed in religious activities. He "could paint very well and could also model small images of the deities." [42] He would fascinate the villagers, especially the women, with his singing or chanting of religious songs and verses. Most outstanding of all was his dramatic ability. He liked to observe and identify with diverse types of people and could easily imitate their actions and voices. His memory was also excellent so he soon became one of the leading actors in the dramatic presentations with which the Hindus celebrate many of their religious festivals. A great deal of Rāmakrishna's knowledge of Hindu religion can be attributed to his memorizing portions of the *Mahābhārata*, the *Rāmāyaṇa* and other religious texts while participating in these dramas.

Gadādhar's artistic sensitivity made him quite open to the ecstatic type of spiritual experience which was common not only among his own family but in Bengal generally. His biographers place his first ecstatic trance in his sixth or seventh year shortly before the death of his father. Their doing so, however, conflicts with Rāmakrishna's quite explicit statement: "When I was ten or eleven years old and lived at Kamarpukur, I first experienced samadhi. As I was passing through a paddy-field, I saw something and was overwhelmed." [43] In a quote not found in Mahendranāth's diary, Rāmakrishna's give his description of what he saw:

> There appeared in one part of the sky a beautiful black cloud charged with rain ... Very soon the cloud covered almost the whole sky, when a flock of milk-white cranes flew against that black cloud. It looked so beautiful that I became very soon absorbed in an extraordinary mood. Such a state came upon me that my external consciousness was lost. I fell down ... People saw it and carried me home. This was the first time that I lost external consciousness in Bhavasamadhi.[44]

[42] *S. Nikhil.*, p. 240.

[43] *Ibid.*, p. 161; cf. *Ibid.*, p. 933; *Madras II*, p. 355; *Madras I*, p. 3. If If Rāmakrishna's birth were placed in 1833 rather than 1836, then this experience could have come shortly before his father's death.

[44] *The Great Master*, p. 103 [3rd ed., p. 101].

The second time came shortly after the first as he was singing to a group of women while going with them to worship at a temple of the goddess Visalakshī, and the third came a little later as he was portraying Śiva in a drama celebrating the *Śivarātri* festival.[45] From his tenth or eleventh year on, such trances became common. At first his family feared that he was an epileptic; but, as his health did not seem to suffer, they came to accept his experiences as true possessions by the Divine. It is clear that his ability to enter into trances so easily derived largely from his esthetic and emotional sensitivity—his capacity to so appreciate and identify with the beauty and harmony in what he saw and did that he would become totally overcome by ecstacy.

Before leaving his childhood we should consider the extent of his education. The followers of Rāmakrishna have sometimes magnified the importance of Rāmakrishna's intuitive insight by underemphasizing the amount of education which he had.[46] The fact is that he attended the village school, with differing degrees of regularity and intensity, for twelve years between the ages of five and seventeen.[47] The depth of his education must be estimated in light of the fact that he was an extremely creative and intelligent person but had a very strong will of his own. What interested him, he would easily master; what he did not like, he gave very little attention. As he progressed he became increasingly less interested in formal attendance at school, but it is quite clear that "he became proficient in reading books written in his mother tongue and in writing that language."[48] He read in the epics as well as in many other religious texts in Bengali, and he would even make manuscript copies of some of the works. Also, while he could not speak Sanskrit, he could understand it.[49] The point to be made is that we are not dealing with an uneducated or ignorant ecstatic. Rather, because of his intelligence, his interest, his own study and his subsequent contact with Hindus of all schools of thought, we should realize that we are dealing with a well versed Hindu thinker who, because of the ecstatic nature of his religious experience, refused to be bound in and restricted by what he viewed as dry, rationalistic requirements of systematic discourse.

---

[45] *S. Nikhil.*, p. 933; *Madras II*, p. 355; *Life of Sri Ramakrishna*, pp. 43ff.
[46] Cf. *The Great Master*, p. 370 [3rd ed., p. 366].
[47] *The Great Master*, p. 46; *Life of Sri Ramakrishna*, p. 64.
[48] *The Great Master*, p. 59 [3rd ed., p. 57].
[49] *S. Nikhil.*, p. 407.

Rāmakrishna's life adheres to the adage, "The child is the father of the man." All of the characteristics which we have mentioned continued to be expressed in his adult life. However, his fully developed teachings were produced only after many years of involved and arduous spiritual travail. The beginning of his adult life can be marked by his departure for Calcutta during his sixteenth or seventeenth year (1852) when he began to assist his oldest brother, Rāmkumār, with his duties as household priest to a number of Calcutta brahman families. Three years later (1855) he accompanied his brother to a large new temple on the banks of the Ganges at Dakshineśwar (near Calcutta) where Rāmkumār had been appointed chief priest. Built by a wealthy but low class (*śūdra*) woman who was a *śākta* (a devotee of *śakti*, the female and dynamic aspect of the Divine), the temple was primarily dedicated to the goddess Kālī but included a string of twelve smaller shrines dedicated to various manifestations of her consort Śiva. However, since this temple was meant to be a gathering place for devotees of all kinds, images of the divine pair Rādhā-Govinda were installed in a large and prominent temple in the complex in order to provide a place of worship for the many Vaiṣṇavas in the area. The Vaiṣṇava Rāmkumār "had long ago become initiated in the mantra of Śakti of his own accord" [50] and thus was qualified to be the priest of the Mother Kālī. There is little doubt that Rāmkumār assumed the office of śākta priest for a *śūdra* proprietor—a low position that many other brahmans had declined—in order to bolster his family's financial situation, and did so with no little pangs of both his and his brother's consciences.[51] This action, however, was of great consequence to Rāmakrishna's life in that it established as the setting for his sādhana a śākta temple mingling many strands of the Hindu tradition in its facilities and in the varied outlooks of its constant flow of pilgrims.

The Rāmakrishna Mission biographers relate Rāmakrishna's statement that his period of sādhana lasted for twelve years beginning with his coming to Dakshineśwar in 1855, although they also acknowledge that all of his spiritual practices cannot be fitted into this period.[52] Rāmakrishna soon attracted the attention of those responsible for the administration of the temple and within a few months was put in charge of the worship of Rādhā-Govinda. As Rāmkumār's

---

[50] *The Great Master*, p. 121 [3rd ed., p. 119].

[51] *Ibid.*, pp. 124-25 [3rd ed., pp. 122-23].

[52] *Ibid.*, p. 156 [3rd ed., p. 153].

health began to deteriorate, Rāmakrishna took over many of the duties associated with Kālī and began to feel drawn to her. After studying the rituals involved in the worship of Kālī, he was initiated into the *śakti mantra*; and, shortly before Rāmkumār's death, he assumed complete charge of the Kālī temple. In my opinion it is most probable that the beginning of his sādhana was marked by his śākta initiation in the year of his brother's death, 1856.

The first stage of Rāmakrishna's spiritual "discipline" as a śākta devotee of the Divine Mother was quite undisciplined. He became seized by a desire to have a vision of the Mother, a direct realization of Her reality. It is permissible to speculate that, as his biographers seem to suggest,[53] this youth, having again lost the one serving as his father, once more turned as a forsaken child to a mother-figure in the form of the goddess. In his quest for a vision of the Mother, he did not follow the traditional way of adhering to the teachings of one *guru* or of one particular school. Rather, independent and willful as always and driven by a frenzied devotion, he would try first one thing and then another as he learned of different practices from wandering sādhus. As he is reported to have said later in life, "I became positively insane for some time. The sādhus who frequented this temple told me to practice many things. I tried to follow them and the consequence was my austerities drove me to insanity." [54] He did indeed gain the reputation of a madman among many people, but those in charge of the temple were convinced that he was a saint. Soon he was spending all his time worshipping and serving the image of the goddess and importuning her to reveal herself to him—doing all this without regard for normal ritual and in ways quite shocking to normal sensibilities. Finally, an "intolerable anguish" drove him to seize Kālī's sword to end his life, and then—

> suddenly I had the wonderful vision of the Mother and fell down unconscious . . . in my heart of hearts, there was flowing a current of intense bliss, never experienced before, and I had the immediate knowledge of the light that was Mother . . . a boundless infinite conscious sea of light . . . a continuous succession of effulgent waves . . .[55]

While this classical mystical experience had been the object of his quest, it did not satisfy his desire. The pain of separation which

[53] *Ibid.*, p. 138 [3rd ed., p. 135].
[54] *Life of Sri Ramakrishna*, p. 375 [2nd ed., p. 282].
[55] *The Great Master*, p. 143 [3rd ed., pp. 140-41].

followed increased his longing all the more. Later Rāmakrishna was to say that "one must have the yearning for God of a child . . . when his mother is away." [56] It was during this period that he felt such yearning most acutely and most uncontrollably. He felt that after a true realization of God one should feel Her presence at all times; and, therefore, the recurrence of a sense of separation led him to question the validity of his visions, to wonder if they were not simply the illusions of his deranged mind. Therefore, he asked both for a more constant vision of the Mother and for signs of its validity—signs which, according to the biographers, were always given.

In this first period of questing experimentation, Śrī Rāmakrishna's Vaiṣṇava bhakti background also found expression. A *bhakta*'s love of the Lord can be expressed in a number of *bhāvas* or worshipful attitudes, all of which Rāmakrishna attempted to adopt. Toward Kālī he cultivated the *śānta-bhāva* or the passive "peaceful" attitude. He next assumed *dāsya-bhāva* or the attitude of a servant toward his master. In doing so, he completely identified himself with Hanumān, the monkey-god, who set the model of ideal servitude in his devotion to Rāma. Rāmakrishna ate and walked like a monkey, spent much of his time in trees and even fixed a tail to the end of his spine.

The vision which climaxed his *dāsya* experiment was interesting and significant. It was of Sītā rather than Rāma and when he recognized her he called her "Mother"—showing his attachment to the śakti or feminine aspect of the Divine. Moreover, it was a vision that occurred while he was fully conscious with his eyes open—the first which, rather than blotting out the natural world, revealed the Divine to him in natural and human form. This experience set the pattern for many of his later visions.[57] While he was simply sitting among some trees—not meditating—Sītā appeared as a luminous woman, approached him and merged into him, whereupon he was overcome with emotion and lapsed into the oblivion of *samādhi*.[58] This sequence reminds us of Śrī Rāmakrishna's entering into a trance while assuming the role of Śiva as a boy, and of his ease, as a child, in identifying with and adopting the character of others. We must keep this vision in mind because these tendencies—to identify himself with God, to identify God with the natural world

---

[56] *S. Nikhil.*, p. 673.

[57] Müller, *Ramakrishna, His Life and Sayings*, p. 51; Rolland, *Prophets of the New India*, p. 19.

[58] *The Great Master*, p. 161 [3rd ed., p. 158].

and to identify all of this with the śakti or feminine aspect of the Divine—became increasingly evident as his teachings developed.

Rāmakrishna's having these seemingly hallucinatory visions further convinced people that he was a madman. His behavior was bizarre. He now saw the image of Kālī as a living person, who could talk and play with him, who actually ate offerings of food and walked with him outside the temple. To the normal person he did indeed appear insane. Many were concerned about his physical health as well, because his austerities and his thoughtless disregard for himself were putting a tremendous strain upon his body. Therefore, in 1859 his friends decided that he should return to Kamarpukur for a vacation in hope that in the familiar surroundings he would return to normal.

His mother and family were of course concerned about his seeming madness. Under their watchful eyes, he did attain a somewhat more even keel and regained his health. His mother and brothers decided marriage would be a good steadying influence upon him by forcing him to accept responsibility and to keep his attention on normal affairs rather than on the dizzying heights of spiritual experiences. To please his family, Śrī Rāmakrishna agreed to marry, but, craftily, he selected a five-year-old bride who would continue to live with her family for a number of years and be of little bother to him. He and Śāradāmaṇi Devī were married in May, 1859.

Rāmakrishna returned to Dakshineśwar in 1860, and the outcome of his vacation was a renewed energy in his bhakti toward the Divine Mother. His spiritual madness and austerities again exacted a tremendous toll upon his physical health. His biographers call this a state of "divine inebriation." Visions of the type of the appearance of Sītā came to him constantly, at the slightest stimulation. Rāmakrishna claimed that his mind was so involved with these visions that he was not able either to shut his eyes or to sleep for six years. So great was the wear upon his body that he would at times pray the Mother to relieve the intensity of his devotion, only to be swept away by Her again. Soon, however, the unbridled greatness of this man's spiritual devotion was recognized by experienced persons, and his frenzied activity was channeled into more disciplined and constructive expressions.

Help came to Śrī Rāmakrishna in 1861 in the form of a middle-aged female ascetic who is usually called the *Bhairavī Brāhmaṇī* and who was a master of a śākta [59] form of tantric sādhana. Rāmakrishna and the *Bhairavī* were immediately drawn to each other—she recognizing in him the signs of an *avatāra* or incarnation of the Divine and he in his need being attracted to her as a motherly figure. Swami Saradānanda describes Rāmakrishna's reaction to this woman as follows:

> The Master then sat beside the Bhairavi and, like a child . . . to his mother, he went on narrating his extraordinary visions, the loss of external consciousness during talks on God, the burning sensation in his body, his sleeplessness and other peculiar bodily changes for which he was taken to be mad, and repeatedly asked her, "Mother, what are these things that happen to me? Have I actually become mad? Have I been seized with a fell disease for calling on Mother whole-heartedly?" [60]

The *Bhairavī* assured him that he was not mad but was experiencing phenomena that accompany *mahābhāva*, the supreme attitude of loving devotion toward the Divine (*prema-bhakti*). She said that the *bhakti śāstras* show that such symptoms occurred regularly in the lives of avatāras, especially in that of Śrī Caitanya (1486-1533). On the basis of these signs plus her own impressions of Rāmakrishna, she declared that he was an avatāra, an opinion which, though not universally agreed to, was accepted by at least two other prominent Vaiṣṇava scholars and tantric masters.[61] In this way and by helping to alleviate some of his physical sufferings, the *Bhairavī* won his confidence, became his first guru and remained one of his closest companions for nearly six years. She provided something which Rāmakrishna greatly lacked—discipline. Rāmakrishna had always been strong-willed and independent; his family, unable to control him, had been indulgent in allowing him his own way. In the *Bhairavī*, he found a mother-figure as strong-willed as himself, and he bowed before her at least for a time. Under her guidance he went through a full course of tantric sādhana over a period of three or four years.[62]

Rāmakrishna's followers tend to be apologetic about his taking

---

[59] Involving the *śakti* or female aspect of Śiva's "terrible" *Bhairava* forms of which there are eight. In these forms, Śiva rides on a dog and frequents the crematoria on which he repeats the destructive *Tāṇḍava* dance. See J. Dowson, *A Classical Dictionary of Hindu Mythology and Religion* (London, Routledge and Kegan Paul, 1961), p. 45; Jan Gonda, *Viṣṇuism and Śivaism* (London, Athlone Press, 1970), p. 132.

[60] *The Great Master*, p. 189 [3rd ed., p. 186].

[61] *Ibid.*, pp. 193, 499-525 [3rd ed., pp. 190, 495-521].

[62] *Ibid.*, p. 203 [3rd ed., p. 200].

up tantric practices because of the eroticism that has discredited tantric schools in general and those of Bengal in particular. Their anxiety about misunderstandings leads them, in my opinion, to underestimate and obscure the importance of tantric influences on his spiritual development. A casual perusal of their biographies suggests that Rāmakrishna's participation in tantric disciplines was simply one among many experiments which dot his path along the way to the final culmination and integration of all his experiences in the eventual advaitic realization.

We will suggest that his tantric sādhana was much more than casual or formal, and that in interpreting his teachings we can understand them more adequately in the categories of tantric thought and practice than in the concepts of Śaṅkara's *advaita* which the biographers primarily employ. Our defense of this suggestion will appear in our consideration below of his teachings as they appear in Mahendranāth's diary, their most authentic form. However, even from our present position it must be acknowledged that his tantric sādhana was of more than passing significance. As we have seen, at or near the beginning of his twelve years of intensive sādhana, he was initiated as a śākta temple priest, and his first period of undisciplined sādhana was dominated by his intense bhakti toward the śakti, Kālī. Adding to this first period the time spent under the *Bhairavī*, we see that at least two-thirds of this twelve years was devoted to a śākta variety of tantric sādhana.

The aim of tantric sādhana is to make the aspirant or *sādhaka* realize that all the aspects of the natural world, including all the powers within himself, are manifestations of the divine śakti.[63] Toward this end, the sādhana focuses attention upon the whole of life and the natural world, including aspects which are generally considered reprehensible or repulsive, and leads the sādhaka to see each and every one as the divine śakti. The biographers claim that Rāmakrishna was led through all the practices recommended in the sixty-four major Tantras. He began with the *mantra* rituals such as *japa* and *puraścaraṇa* (experiencing the divine in the sound of the names of God and of holy verses) and with many other preliminary rituals designed to purify the mind and establish self-control. He then proceeded to practices that broke down the barrier between the holy and the unholy by overcoming his aversion to such activities

[63] Sir John Woodroffe, *Shakti and Shakta* (London, Luzac and Co., 1929), p. 520. Cf. the vision of Sītā, p. 73 above.

as eating the leavings of dogs and jackals and touching his tongue to rotten flesh. He also became an adept at *Kuṇḍalinī yoga* whereby one becomes aware of and awakens the śakti as she exists within one's self and eventually achieves internally a union of the śakti with Śiva, the passive Absolute, which also exists within. Another course of tantric sādhana which he engaged in at least partially was the *Vāmācāra* or "left-hand" path which utilizes as means of liberation five activities which most Hindus abhor as sinful and binding, namely the eating of parched grain, meat and fish along with the drinking of wine and sexual intercourse. It must be remembered that this "left-hand" path is often followed only symbolically. Both Rāmakrishna and his biographers are adamant in insisting that he did not actually participate in the last two of these activities, that all he needed was a suggestion of them to produce the desired result. There is no reason to doubt their word although in the latter case the "suggestion" involved viewing "the supreme pleasure of a pair of lovers." [64]

Many—both Hindus and others—find it easy to condemn out-of-hand the type of activities in which he engaged. Rāmakrishna himself knew that this sādhana was a dangerous one and advised people to stay away from many aspects of it—especially actual participation in the *Vāmācāra* rites. Yet the beautiful lotus growing out of the mud and slime is the proper image for the ideal results of tantric sādhana. The Tantras intend not to promote licentiousness and degradation but rather to instill the strictest restraint, leading to the control, redirection and ultimate transformation of all aspects of life, especially those which are normally most destructive and enslaving. Throughout all the erotic temptations involved in this path, Rāmakrishna is reported to have maintained such restraint, retaining the attitude of an innocent child toward his mother, and to have emerged as a greatly changed person.

As Swami Saradānanda himself attests, "A root-and-branch change, the Master said, came over his previous nature at the time of the Tantric Sadhana." [65] In Rāmakrishna's own words we find the following testimony:

> I practiced the discipline of the Tantra under the bel-tree. At that time I could see no distinction between the sacred tulsi and any other plant . . . . Sometimes I rode on a dog and fed him with luchi, also

---

[64] *The Great Master*, p. 199 [3rd ed., p. 196].
[65] *Ibid.*, p. 203 [3rd ed., p. 200].

> eating part of the bread myself. I realized that the whole world was filled with God alone. [66]

In my opinion, this realization was the major determinant of all the rest of Rāmakrishna's life and of his teachings as we see them in his later years. We noted the beginnings of such a realization in his vision of Sītā, and we will see that the importance of this insight continues to develop throughout the rest of his life.

Perhaps the major question with regard to the life of Śrī Rāmakrishna is how he was transformed from the uncontrollable and self-destructive madman of the early years into the saintly and relatively self-controlled—if eccentric and ecstatic—teacher of the later years. My contention is that the healing and transforming factor was this tantric realization that "the whole world is filled with God alone." His early frenzy occurred because of his feelings of separation from the Divine Mother. He drove himself into supersensuous and abnormal states in attempts to realize Her. However, through his tantric sādhana he was able to harness his psychic energies and achieve an ability to adjust to—and even to enjoy—the normal conscious state of man. For he came to see the Mother not only in the ecstatic trance but all around him in the affairs of man and nature. The frenzy of separation abated and we find a man at ease with the world.

Not only did this tantric realization affect the state of his mental and physical well-being, but, in my opinion, it also determined the basic framework in which he viewed the significance of all his experiences and in which he set all of his teachings as they appear in Mahendranāth's diary. This is not to say that the totality of Rāmakrishna's message was formulated during his tantric sādhana, but rather that his experiences and insights, as they developed, were always thereafter incorporated into a basically tantric framework of concepts and values. This point will be elaborated more fully later.

As we have indicated, Rāmakrishna's biographers view his tantric

---

[66] *S. Nikhil.*, p. 544. We must not make any Western presuppositions about the gender of the word "God" in this statement. Unfortunately, Swami Nikhilānanda tends to use the words "God" and "Him" where the Madras translations more accurately use "Mother" and "Her." Cf. *S. Nikhil.*, p. 87 ("pray to God") with *Madras 5th*, p. 64 ("pray earnestly to the Divine Mother"); p. 116 ("It is His will") with *Madras II*, p. 10 ("It is Her wish"); p. 116 ("God Himself is Mahāmāyā") with *Madras II*, p. 11 ("She is Mahamaya Herself"); p. 197 ("sometimes God effaces") with *Madras II*, p. 124 ("She sometimes"); etc. Unfortunately, the statement quoted here is not reproduced in the Madras editions.

sādhana as simply one of the lower rungs on a ladder rising to his eventual advaitic samādhi.[67] They present him as proceeding upward then, as he experiments with more of the Vaiṣṇava *bhāvas*. We have seen that he had practiced at an early stage the *bhāvas* of *śānta* and *dāsya*. In 1864 he cultivated *vātsalya bhāva*, the attitude of a parent towards a child. As a doting mother, he cared for and played with a small metal image of Rāmalālā (Rāma as a sportive child), the image often coming to life before his eyes. Next he returned to a *bhāva* which had been his favorite as an adolescent—*mādhurya bhāva*, the attitude of the gopīs and Rādhā toward their lover, Kṛṣṇa. At the end of this sādhana, he is represented as reaching the next to the last rung, the highest realization of dualistic forms of sādhana—*savikalpa samādhi*, blissful union with the personal and attribute-possessing Kṛṣṇa. "He had tapped the fountain of Eternal Bliss and was immersed in it till the opportunity arrived for a grander realization—that of Advaita." [68]

To digress a bit, someone hearing of Rāmakrishna's antics during this Vaiṣṇava stage of sādhana might question my analysis that his tantric sādhana had overcome his madness, since he continued to behave eccentrically and to have many abnormal visions. But it is clear that the former frenzied, self-destructive character of these experiences had now vanished. Now Rāmakrishna went about his sādhana with the joy and openness of a child at play—with the same attitude that he had displayed as a child. His biographers affirm that it was during the tantric sādhana that this change took place.[69] Rāmakrishna himself tells us that he became as a child at play because he saw that the śakti was like a child at play (*līlā*) in all the world.[70] This process of identifying with and becoming like the creative source of the cosmos—a process which we have long noted in Rāmakrishna—is a central aspect of tantric sādhana.[71]

Returning to his biographers' interpretation of his sādhana, we finally come to the climax and the pinnacle as they present it—the realization of the truth of *advaita* in *nirvikalpa samādhi*, a union of complete identity with the undifferentiated *Brahman*. Later in 1864 a

---

[67] *The Great Master*, pp. 250, 409-91, 688, 768 [3rd ed., pp. 246, 486-87, 684, 765]; *S. Nikhil.*, pp. 20-31, gives a condensed rendering of this progression.

[68] *Life of Sri Ramakrishna*, p. 250 [2nd ed., p. 180].

[69] *The Great Master*, p. 205 [3rd ed., p. 202].

[70] *S. Nikhil.*, pp. 176, 490-91, 688, 769.

[71] Heinrich Zimmer, *Philosophies of India* (New York, Meridian Books, 1957), pp. 586-87.

*jñānī* called Totāpurī arrived at Dakshineśwar and immediately recognized Rāmakrishna's fitness for the path of *advaita*. He asked Rāmakrishna to receive instruction from him, and Rāmakrishna, having asked permission of Kālī, agreed. Selecting an auspicious day for beginning, Totāpurī first guided Rāmakrishna through the rites of *sannyāsa*, or renunciation of all ties to the world; and then he instructed him in the teaching of *advaita*—that "Brahman alone is real, and the world is illusory; I have no separate existence; I am that Brahman alone." [72] He then told Rāmakrishna to discriminate between the real and the unreal, to withdraw his mind from all that has name and form and to plunge within himself to experience the *ātman* which is *Brahman*. At first Rāmakrishna had difficulty doing as asked because his mind always fixed upon the "intimately familiar form of the universal Mother." [73] Finally, late on the first day and at a special urging from his guru, Rāmakrishna cut through even this name and form with the sword of discrimination and plunged into *nirvikalpa samādhi* in which he stayed for three days before Totāpurī could bring him back to the normal plane of consciousness. Totāpurī was so amazed at the speed with which Rāmakrishna achieved this realization that he broke one of the rules of sannyāsa and stayed with Rāmakrishna for eleven months to instruct him further in the teachings of *advaita* and to be instructed by Rāmakrishna in the importance and reality of the Divine Mother on the level of normal consciousness. Then we are told that for six months after Totāpurī left, Rāmakrishna remained almost constantly on the level of *nirvikalpa samādhi*—staying alive only because a sādhu adopted the task of forcing him periodically to return to consciousness and eat. Since it is believed a person usually does not return from this deepest samādhi and never does so after spending more than twenty-one days in that state, his disciples take his return as a certain sign that he was preserved by God for a special mission. As the six months drew to a close, he received a command from the Mother, "Remain in Bhavamukha; for the enlightenment of the people, remain in Bhavamukha" [74]—*bhāvamukha* being a state of existence intermediate between samādhi and normal consciousness in which one is always aware of both the world and its source and of their unity.[75] This

[72] *S. Nikhil.*, p. 593. Cf. *ibid.*, p. 859; *Madras I*, p. 225.
[73] *The Great Master*, p. 255 [3rd ed., p. 251].
[74] *Ibid.*, p. 363 [3rd ed., p. 359].
[75] *Ibid.*, p. 929 [3rd ed., p. 939].

command was followed by a severe attack of dysentery, brought on by his neglect of his body, which persisted for six months and threatened his life.

Ramākrishna's biographers present a clear picture of this advaitic realization as the primary determinant of his spiritual world-view and teachings and the culmination of the spiritual quest of Rāmakrishna and the whole human race. Describing the day on which he first experienced *nirvikalpa samādhi*, the biographers say with great feeling:

> The day dawned. It was a glorious day for India and indeed for the world, pregnant with immense possibilities for the future. The ancient religion of the Vedanta found a new apostle and the world saw the appearance of a new man filled with the all-embracing love of Buddha and endowed with the keen intellect of Sankara.[76]

Swami Saradānanda says,

> Firmly established in the plane of the non-dual consciousness, the Master . . . came to feel in his heart of hearts that the realization of nonduality was the ultimate aim of all kinds of sadhanas. For, having performed sadhanas according to the teachings of all the main religious denominations prevalent in Bharata, he had already been convinced that they all took the aspirants towards the non-dual plane. Asked about the non-dual state, he, therefore, said to us over and over again, "It is the finale, my child, the acme, which comes of itself in the life of all aspirants, the ultimate development of the love of God. Know it to be the last word of all faiths . . .[77]
>
> It is, therefore, superfluous to say that non-dual knowledge, which is always of a uniform nature, was the standard by which the Master judged everything.[78]

In criticizing these understandings, I do not intend to deny that Rāmakrishna was a non-dualist. Nor do I intend to maintain that his position and teachings were not influenced by the experiences gained through his practice of *jñāna yoga* or by the insights gained through his instruction in Śaṅkara's *advaita*. I do not believe, however, that Rāmakrishna's non-dualism can be understood accurately when it is presented as being fully in accord with Śaṅkara's *advaita*, as Swami Saradānanda explicitly argues it to be.[79] This contention will

[76] *Life of Sri Ramakrishna*, p. 260 [2nd ed., p. 188].
[77] *The Great Master*, pp. 262-63 [3rd ed., p. 258]. I have not been able to find in Mahendranāth's diary the words quoted.
[78] *Ibid.*, p. 602 [3rd ed., p. 598].
[79] *The Great Master*, p. 392 [3rd ed., p. 388].

be supported fully in the next section. Furthermore, to present Rāmakrishna's advaitic realization as the culmination and turning point of his entire spiritual life would seem to impose an artificial and tendentious structure upon the progress of his sādhana.

One example of the misconception of Rāmakrishna's sādhana that is possible through this approach is found in Swami Nikhilānanda's introduction to his *The Gospel of Sri Ramakrishna.* He says:

> Thus, after nirvikalpa samādhi, Sri Ramakrishna realized māyā in an altogether new role. The binding aspect of Kālī vanished from before his vision. She no longer obscured his understanding. The world became the glorious manifestation of the Divine Mother... Sri Ramakrishna discovered that māyā operates in the relative world in two ways, and he termed these "avidyāmāyā" and "vidyāmāyā." Avidyāmāyā represents the dark forces of creation... It must be fought and vanquished... But Vidyāmāyā is the higher force of creation... elevates man to higher planes of consciousness.[80]

While Rāmakrishna may have adopted the terms *māyā*, *vidyā* and *avidyā* from *advaita* in order to describe his insight, it is clear that the vision of the world as "the glorious manifestation of the Divine Mother" did not come to Rāmakrishna "after nirvikalpa samādhi." As we have seen, Rāmakrishna saw the world as such during his tantric sādhana. Moreover, there is no indication that he personally ever felt that Kālī in any of her aspects "obscured his understanding." Rather, from the very beginning he felt that the Divine Mother had been guiding him to "higher planes of consciousness."

Another possible example of artificial structuring is the biographies' placing of all of Rāmakrishna's Vaiṣṇava sādhana before the *advaita*, thus making the highest of dualistic realizations lead directly into the non-dualistic experience. The sketch of Rāmakrishna's life which appears in F. Max Müller's *Ramakrishna: His Life and Sayings* is, as we have shown earlier, both an early source and one which is independent of our major biographies, coming as it did from Swami Vivekānanda; and Vivekānanda reported to Müller that Rāmakrishna "began to practice and realize the Vaiṣṇava ideal of love for God" *after* his experience of *nirvikalpa samādhi.*[81] J. N. Farquhar accepts this chronology,[82] and two other early sources—one again from Vivekānanda—make allusions which would be consistent

---

[80] *S. Nikhil.*, p. 30.
[81] Müller, *Ramakrishna, His Life and Sayings*, pp. 49-50.
[82] Farquhar, *Modern Religious Movements in India*, p. 192.

with such an ordering.[83] While it is clear that Rāmakrishna was engaged in certain aspects of Vaiṣṇava sādhana before engaging in *jñāna yoga*,[84] it is also definite that, after his *advaita* experiences under Totāpurī, he engaged in Vaiṣṇava practices in 1868 while on a pilgrimage to Vṛndāban, the site at which the cowherd Kṛṣṇa is believed to have sported with the gopīs and Rādhā. He tells us that at that time he was "initiated into Vaishnavism," "took the garb of a Vaishnava monk" and "spent three days practicing the Vaishnava discipline." [85] At another place, he tells us that while he was at Vṛndāban he longed for Kṛṣṇa, had visions, became unconscious and went into samādhi.[86] It seems quite likely that it was at this time that Rāmakrishna assumed the *mādhurya bhāva* and experienced a union of love with Kṛṣṇa. Thus it would appear that his biographers transposed this experience of 1868 to just before his entry into the path of *advaita* in order to make his sādhana progress through an ascending succession of "lower" dualistic disciplines towards a climax in the "highest," non-dualistic realization.

My own opinion is that Rāmakrishna's *advaita* sādhana was simply one among the many disciplines that he entered into because of his eagerness to experience all the aspects of his Divine Mother's *līlā*,[87] and that—in comparison with his tantric experiences—it was a relatively passing phenomenon which in the end alarmed and frightened him. Rāmakrishna felt that "this very world is a mansion of mirth" [88] in which a bhakta or lover of God is to enjoy life; and he compared his view with that of a *jñānī* or knower of God who by contrast sees the world as a "framework of illusion" from which one should escape.[89] His six months in *nirvikalpa samādhi* and the ensuing sickness made Rāmakrishna fearful, I believe, that he might never return to his beloved "mansion of mirth" and created in him the anxiety in which he heard the command, "Remain in *bhāvamukha*." At a much later date when Rāmakrishna was again in pain (February 2, 1884), we find this well attested saying:

---

[83] Vivekananda, *My Master*, p. 44; *Madras I*, pp. 5f.

[84] *S. Nikhil.*, p. 687.

[85] *Ibid.*, p. 305. On p. 538, Rāmakrishna mentions 15 days as the period he wore the garb of a Vaiṣṇava monk.

[86] *Ibid.*, pp. 361-62.

[87] *The Great Master*, p 246 [3rd ed , p. 242].

[88] *S. Nikhil.*, p. 139; *Madras I*, pp. 5-6.

[89] *S. Nikhil.*, p. 243, 478, 939.

> O Mother, do not plunge me in the knowledge of Brahman and take away my consciousness!—Do not give me Brahmajnana; I am but Thy child.—I have fears and anxieties! I do want my Mother!—A thousand salutations to Brahmajnana! Give it to him who wants it, O Mother.[90]

At another point, when he seems to feel he will be liberated, he speaks enviously of those who can continue to play the "game" of life—making his coming liberation seem almost a penalty for scoring too many points in the "game." [91] Again he says, echoing an old Bengal Vaiṣṇava preference, "I don't want liberation; I want love of God," [92] and indicated that he would be born again.[93] It would seem from these statements that he was not terribly attracted to *nirvikalpa samādhi*.

Describing his *advaita sādhana* as a whole, Rāmakrishna said,

> Once I fell into the clutches of a jñāni, who made me listen to Vedanta for eleven months. But he couldn't altogether destroy the seed of bhakti in me. No matter where my mind wandered, it would come back to the Divine Mother.[94]

This last sentence provides the proper perspective not only upon his *advaita sādhana* but also upon the whole of his spiritual life—he wandered in many directions but always returned to his attitude of a child before the Divine Mother.

Rāmakrishna's biographers feel that his twelve years of sādhana in effect ended with his *advaita* realization,[95] and we will end our chronological account here. We have seen enough to provide a background for understanding his teachings. His experiments with other religious traditions have not been dealt with here because I feel that they are not of central importance for our task of understanding his distinctively Hindu religious experience and teachings. His own disciples are quite explicit in stating that he did not become well acquainted with the other religions,[96] and that he learned nothing new from his experiences—he simply confirmed what he had already discovered through his Hindu sādhana.[97] Rāmakrishna's visions

---

[90] *Madras II*, pp. 179-80; Cf. *S. Nikhil.*, p. 384; and *Life of Sri Ramakrishna*, p. 575.

[91] *S. Nikhil.*, p. 137; *Madras I*, p. 148.

[92] *S. Nikhil.*, p. 914. Cf. p. 940.

[93] *Ibid.*, p. 829; *Life of Sri Ramakrishna*, p. 343.

[94] *S. Nikhil.*, p. 779.

[95] H. Bhattacharya, ed., *Cultural Heritage*, Vol. IV, p. 674.

[96] *S. Nikhil.*, p. 35.

[97] *Ibid.*, p. 33; Bhattacharya, *Cultural Heritage*, Vol. IV, p. 674.

of Muhammad and of Christ simply repeat the pattern which we noted in his vision of Sītā. As experiential religion they show little or no influence from historic Islam or Christianity. His universalism did not arise out of his experiments with elements from other traditions but rather was developed out of his widely inclusive Hindu experience and teachings. We can understand the basis of his universalism only after we have truly understood his position in its own Hindu terms. It is this task which confronts us in this essay.

## Rāmakrishna's Teachings

Ever since Śaṅkara put forth his system of *advaita*, Hindu philosophical and theological discussion has been a dialectical controversy within the Vedānta school of philosophy between his non-dualism on the one hand and various shades of "qualified" non-dualism (*viśiṣṭa-advaita*) or dualism (*dvaita*) on the other. On the practical religious level the two sides of this discussion have been identified with *jñāna yoga* and *bhakti yoga* respectively. Such categories are considered to be the classical and respectable terms of Hindu discourse. Indologists, after studying the Sanskrit texts, usually describe Indian religious thought in these terms, and modern Hindus in explaining their religious tradition to others have so spoken.

It is not surprising then that Rāmakrishna has been interpreted in such terms. Very typical is F. Max Müller's assessment that Rāmakrishna

> himself distinguishes very clearly between philosophy or Gñāna (knowledge) and devotion or Bhakti, and he himself was a Bhakta, a worshipper of lover of the deity, much more than a Gñānin or a knower.[98]

The general picture of Rāmakrishna which emerges is that on the practical and religious side he was a bhakta of a Personal God (*saguṇa brahman*, *brahman* with qualities) but that on the ultimate and philosophical level he was a *jñānī* of the Absolute (*nir-guṇa*) *Brahman* of *advaita*.[99]

Such a picture is not entirely wrong. Rather it is out of focus and incomplete. Lack of clear focus is of course not unusual in the interpretation of Hindu religion. Indeed to be entirely clear about its multifarious phenomena is to misrepresent it. But the distortion in

[98] Müller, *Ramakrishna, His Life and Sayings*, pp. 93-94.
[99] *The Great Master*, pp. 303-304 [3rd ed., pp. 299-300].

this case is extreme by reason of failure to recognize all of the factors present in the outlook of this complex man. Lacking the tantric element in his world-view, this traditional analysis cannot place Rāmakrishna precisely in the total Hindu heritage nor indicate accurately how the various levels of Rāmakrishna's ideas are integrated into a whole. The incompleteness of the current explanation of Rāmakrishna merely illustrates a *general* problem in our interpretation of Hindu thought—that we have focused too much of our attention on the classical Sanskritic "Great Tradition" without taking adequately into account the more popular, relatively non-literary traditions which we know have had a great impact upon Indian religious life and thought but whose history we scarcely know.

Examples of such popular traditions are the various non-Vedic tantric traditions that are based upon a class of texts, termed *Tantras* or *Āgamas*, of relatively late origin (ca. 400 A.D.). In the case of those śākta tantric traditions involving the worship of goddesses as the śakti, the obstacle posed by our general lack of knowledge has been further intensified by the fact that much of what we did know about them was considered to be disreputable and repulsive. In Rāmakrishna's case, however, both these obstacles to due recognition are penetrable and surmountable. In Mahendranāth's diary we find ample evidence of Rāmakrishna's devotion to Kālī and his involvement in tantric forms of religious practice. Moreover, the sensitive and open-minded reader, while finding some disturbing elements, will also find much that is attractive and worthy of respect. A study of Śrī Rāmakrishna's teachings provides an excellent opportunity for attaining a fuller, more realistic view of Hindu religion and especially of how more popular elements have influenced the classical philosophical traditions.

I have agreed that Rāmakrishna is an *advaitin* but have maintained that his non-dualism must be viewed from the perspective of a tantric *advaita*, not that of Śaṅkara. Speaking of the relationship between śākta philosophy and Śaṅkara's system. T. M. P. Mahadevan says,

> Philosophically, Śākta-darśana is a type of non-dualism. Reality, according to it, is non-dual (*advaita*); it is of the nature of existence-consciousness-bliss (*saccidānanda*). It is *nirguna* in the sense that there are no distinctions in it. Nothing is real apart from it. All things are identical with it. The non-dual reality manifests itself as the world of plurality through the power of *māyā*. So far the Advaita of Śāktism agrees with that of Śankara. But, while for Śankara *māyā* is the principle

of illusion veiling the real *Brahman* and projecting the non-real world, for Śāktism it is a real power really manifesting itself in the form of the variegated universe . . . the one difference between Śāktism and Advaita is . . . that for the former the process of the One becoming the Many is real, whereas it is not so for the latter.[100]

While on an abstract philosophical level this one divergence may be the only one, on the practical level of Rāmakrishna's major concerns the difference is a huge one, expressing itself in many differences of attitudes and actions. Such a system is much more akin to a life and world affirming monism such as Vallabha's *śuddhādvaita* or "pure non-dualism" than Śaṅkara's absolutistic and acosmistic *kevalādvaita* or "absolute non-dualism," as we will hereafter call his system.

We wish to clarify Rāmakrishna's position in its relation to Śaṅkara's *kevalādvaita* and its path of *jñāna*. This issue is a confused one because Rāmakrishna often talks as if he accepted *kevalādvaita*,[101] and his disciples have emphasized his seeming acceptance. The key to understanding Rāmakrishna's formal acceptance of *kevalādvaita* is to note that this acceptance is given under very strict conditions. Rāmakrishna sees two "realms" or frames of reference in which *kevalādvaita* and *jñāna yoga* are valid—realms which in both cases are totally removed from the state of man as he now exists in the world.

The first theoretical context in which Rāmakrishna recognized the validity of *kevalādvaita* was the purer age or *yuga* that existed long ago before the world degenerated to the present corrupt *Kali yuga*.

> The path of knowledge is extremely difficult. One cannot obtain jñāna if one has the least trace of worldliness and the slightest attachment to 'woman and gold.' This is not the path for the Kaliyuga.[102]

In a very interesting and well attested passage, Rāmakrishna tells why the knowledge way is now ineffective.

> To follow jñānayoga in this age is . . . very difficult. First, a man's life depends entirely on food. Second, he has a short span of life. Third, he can by no means get rid of body-consciousness; and the Knowledge of Brahman is impossible without the destruction of body-consciousness. The jñāni says: "I am Brahman; I am not the body. I am beyond hunger and thirst, disease and grief, birth and

---

[100] *Outlines of Hinduism* (Bombay, Chetana Ltd., 1960), pp. 203, 206. Cf. *S. Nikhil.*, pp. 133f, 939.

[101] *S. Nikhil.*, pp. 103, 854f.; *Madras I*, p. 75; *Madras II*, pp. 326-28.

[102] *S. Nikhil.*, p. 150; *Madras II*, p. 39.

> death, pleasure and pain." How can you be a jñāni if you are conscious of disease, grief, pain, pleasure and the like? [103]

Rāmakrishna's statement about our life depending on "food" is sometimes rendered "our mind is extremely attached to material things." [104] Rāmakrishna would seem to be implying that in some past age man's life did not depend upon "food" and that men lived long enough to practice the difficult jñānayoga and rid themselves of body-consciousness. However this may be, Rāmakrishna definitely does not recommend jñānayoga for men in this age. On the contrary, he repeatedly makes clear his own strong preference for and recommendation of bhakti yoga in accordance with the non-Vedic Tantras as the path for the Kali yuga:

> In the Kaliyuga the best way is bhaktiyoga, the path of devotion—singing the praises of the Lord, and prayer. The path of devotion alone is the religion for this age.
>
> The fact is that in the Kaliyuga one cannot wholly follow the path laid down in the Vedas. Once a man said to me that he would perform the puraścharana of the Gāyatri. I said: "Why don't you do that according to the Tantra? In Kaliyuga the discipline of Tantra is very efficacious." [105]

Rāmakrishna's remark above about getting "rid of body-consciousness" points toward the second context or condition in which the teachings of *kevalādvaita* may be regarded as valid. He feels that the teaching that "Brahman alone is real and the world is illusory; I have no separate existence; I am that Brahman alone" is relevant only in and for the moment when one is merged in *nirvikalpa samādhi*. This is the other realm in which he recognized Śaṅkara's teachings. In this state, one is taken beyond all feeling of individuality ("body-consciousness") and all sense of separation from God. Only in this state is it valid for one to view the world as illusion; only in this state is it valid for one to feel that he is Brahman. As soon as the jñānī returns to a level of normal consciousness, as soon as he has enough sense of individuality or "body-consciousness" to utter the word "I" so that he can say aloud "I am Brahman," what he says is no longer true and valid. It is as a matter of fact dangerous for the jñānī and for those who listen to him.

---

[103] *S. Nikhil.*, p. 468; *Madras I*, p. 231; *S. Abhed.*, p. 272.

[104] *Madras II*, pp. 67, 70.

[105] *S. Nikhil.*, p. 143, and *Madras I*, p. 164; *S. Nikhil.*, p. 297. For other expressions of the same sentiments, see *S. Nikhil.*, p. 464, *Madras I*, p. 221; *S. Nikhil.*, p. 452, *Madras I*, p. 210; *S. Nikhil.*, pp. 103, 433, 455.

Let us listen to Rāmakrishna himself:

> Yes, one can find Him along the path of reason as well. This is called Jnana Yoga. The path of reason is extremely difficult. I have told you of the seventh plane where the mind loses itself in Samadhi. This Samadhi, this annihilation of the mind, is possible only when one fully realises that "God alone is true, and the world is false." ... This perception is possible only when the physical consciousness is overcome. Indeed it is a scarcely feasible task in the Kali Yuga ... However hard you may persevere in reasoning it away, your "body-idea" invariably reasserts itself ... Verily the consciousness of the body cannot be killed. Hence in this age, the path of Bhakti is the easiest and the best.
>
> And "I like not to *become* sugar, I want to *taste* it." I never wish to declare that "I am Brahman." I say, "Thou art my Lord, I am Thy servant." It is better to be plying the boat between the fifth and the sixth planes. I do not desire to cross the sixth plane and remain long in the seventh; for I have the longing to chant His holy name and sing His praise. The relation of a servant to the Lord is very good. And you know, it is the waves that belong to the Ganges; none ever say that the Ganges belongs to the waves.
>
> "I am He"—this is not a wholesome attitude. If anyone attains this idea before he has overcome the consciousness of the physical self, great harm comes to him, his progress is retarded and by and by he is dragged down. He deceives others and deceives himself as well, in utter ignorance of his woeful plight.[106]

Thus, on the practical level of the religious life of the embodied individual, he saw that any teaching that identified one's true Self (ātman) with Brahman encouraged an almost inevitable tendency to reduce Brahman to one's empirical self or ego, to identify God with oneself rather than oneself with God. Rāmakrishna saw religion not as "self-realization" but as "God-realization," with the realization of the Divinity of the Self being only one aspect of the realization of the One who is the Divinity of all.

Rāmakrishna did then give a strictly conditioned recognition of the validity of *kevalādvaita*. Yet this recognition is not finally significant for an understanding of his teachings. For the truth of *kevalādvaita* is not expressable in words or teachings, since it applies only to the realm of *nirvikalpa samādhi* which is completely beyond the powers of human comprehension and expression.[107] Therefore, he believed it to be both a bother and unhelpful to attempt to talk about

---

[106] *Madras II*, pp. 70-72; cf. *S. Nikhil.*, pp. 171f.
[107] *S. Nikhil.*, p. 134; *Madras I*, p. 140.

*nirvikalpa samādhi.*[108] Rāmakrishna said, "There is a sign of Perfect Knowledge. Man becomes silent when it is attained." [109]

Moreover, it must be stressed that for Rāmakrishna this "Perfect Knowledge" of the jñānī is not the highest knowledge about God. Here we come more directly to Rāmakrishna's own position. He felt that

> there is a stage even beyond Brahmajnāna. After jnāna comes vijnāna . . . What is vijnāna? it is knowing God in a special way. The awareness and conviction that fire exists in wood is jnāna, knowledge. But to cook rice on that fire, eat the rice, and get nourishment from it is vijnāna. To know by one's inner experience that God exists is jnāna. But to talk to Him, to enjoy Him as a child, as Friend, as Master, as Beloved, is vijnāna. The realization that God alone has become the universe and all living beings is vijnāna.
>
> The vijnāni always sees God . . . He sees God even with his eyes open . . . Brahman alone has become everything. Therefore to the vijnāni this world is a "mansion of mirth." But to the jnāni it is a "framework of illusion" . . . A mere jnāni trembles with fear . . . But a vijnāni isn't afraid of anything. He has realized both aspects of God: Personal and Impersonal. He has talked with God. He has enjoyed the Bliss of God. It is a joy to merge the mind in the Indivisible Brahman through contemplation. And it is also a joy to keep the mind on the Līlā, the Relative, without dissolving it in the Absolute. A mere jnāni is a monotonous person. He always analyses, saying: "It is not this, not this. The world is like a dream." But I have "raised both my hands." Therefore I accept everything.[110]

Another time, Rāmakrishna makes a similar comparison between the *siddha* (the "perfect") and the *siddha* of the *siddha* (the "supremely or super-perfect"):

> He is a Siddha who has realized the Being of God in his own consciousness; as a Vedantic allegory explains, it is as though a man were searching for his sleeping master in a dark room, groping about amongst couches, windows and doors, and rejecting each, saying, "Not this, Not this," till he comes upon him and cries out, "Here is the master." That is to say, he has perceived him as "existing", he has found him, but does not yet know him intimately.
>
> The next class is the Super-siddha. To converse with the master intimately, to realize God more completely through love and devotion, is a higher stage. A Siddha has no doubt attained God, but a Super-siddha has entered into a deeper communion with Him.[111]

---

[108] *Madras II*, p. 38; *S. Nikhil.*, p. 150.
[109] *S. Nikhil.*, p. 148; *Madras II*, p. 33.
[110] *S. Nikhil.*, pp. 287-88, 477-79. Cf. pp. 133-35.
[111] *Madras II*, p. 7; cf. *S. Nikhil.*, pp. 114f.

It is not difficult to see the tantric positivism in Rāmakrishna's open and joyful embracing of all as God nor to see the radical distinction between his emphasis and the renunciation of the world advocated by *kevalādvaita*. However, let us allow Rāmakrishna himself to make explicit this distinction between his tantric *advaita* and that of Śaṅkara:

> The jnāni, sticking to the path of knowledge, always reasons about the Reality, saying, 'Not this, not this'. Brahman is neither 'this' nor 'that'; It is neither the universe nor its living beings. . . . It is the unwavering conviction of the jnāni that Brahman alone is real and the world illusory. All these names and forms are illusory, like a dream. What Brahman is cannot be described. One cannot even say that Brahman is a Person. This is the opinion of the jnānis, the followers of Vedānta philosophy.
>
> But the bhaktas accept all the states of consciousness. They take the waking state to be real also. They don't think the world to be illusory, like a dream. They say that the universe is a manifestation of God's power and glory. God has created all these—sky, stars, moon, sun, mountains, ocean, men, animals. They constitute His glory. He is within us, in our hearts. Again, He is outside . . . .
>
> The jnānis, who adhere to the non-dualistic philosophy of Vedānta, say that the acts of creation, preservation, and destruction, the universe itself and all its living beings, are the manifestation of Śakti, the Divine Power. If you reason it out, you will realize that all these are as illusory as a dream. Brahman alone is the Reality, and all else is unreal. Even this very Śakti is unsubstantial, like a dream.
>
> But though you reason all your life, unless you are established in samādhi, you cannot go beyond the jurisdiction of Śakti. Even when you say, 'I am meditating', or 'I am contemplating', still you are moving in the realm of Śakti, within Its power.
>
> Thus Brahman and Śakti are identical. If you accept the one, you must accept the other. It is like fire and its power to burn. If you see the fire, you must recognize its power to burn also . . . .
>
> Thus one cannot think of Brahman without Śakti, or of Śakti without Brahman. One cannot think of the Absolute without the Relative, or of the Relative without the Absolute.
>
> The Primordial Power is ever at play. She is creating, preserving, and destroying in play, as it were. This Power is called Kāli. Kāli is verily Brahman, and Brahman is verily Kāli. It is one and the same Reality.[112]

Heinrich Zimmer has noted quite clearly the importance of the tantric emphasis within Rāmakrishna's thought and has made several

[112] *S. Nikhil.*, pp. 133f; *Madras 5th*, pp. 165-70. The Madras translation has Rāmakrishna explicitly label the school of Vedānta being criticized as "the Non-dualistic Vedānta Philosophy as explained by Śankara," (p. 168).

insightful comments that deserve development.[113] As he states,

> In Tantra the theistic attitude practically obliterates the abstract ideal of the Formless Brahman (*nirguṇa brahman*) in favor of Brahman-in-the-Gunas (*saguṇa brahman*)—the Lord (*iśvara*), the personal God; and the latter is represented by the Tantrics preferably in the female aspect, since in this the nature of Māyā-Śakti is most immediately affirmed.[114]

Rāmakrishna's tendency to conceive and address the Deity as personal and feminine is conspicuous in any verson of his sayings; but the full extent of this preference is greater than many readers realize because Swami Nikhilānanda—otherwise no doubt the finest translator Rāmakrishna's sayings have found—consistently offers "God" and "He" where the Madras editions (no doubt accurately) read "Mother" and "She." [115] Nikhilānanda, in accommodating to a Western theological bias, has joined in the general obscuration of Rāmakrishna's tantric aspects.

Zimmer has also seen in Rāmakrishna's tantric *advaita* a process of reaffirmation of the world similar to that which occurred in Mahāyāna and tantric Buddhism.[116] From rejecting all as void (*śūnya*), a full reversal took place and all that we actually see and experience came to be revered, accepted and enjoyed as the void. Rāmakrishna has made a similar switch in the *advaitic* affirmation that "All is Brahman." Rather than a negative emphasis upon the *Brahman* as exclusive Reality, we see a positive emphasis upon the All.

Moreover, Zimmer notes a development within Rāmakrishna's thought of a concept of service similar to that of the *Bodhisattva* of Mahāyāna Buddhism.[117] There are indeed hints of such an idea in Rāmakrishna's teachings although a full case cannot be made. We have noted that Rāmakrishna did not wish to be liberated and felt that he would be born again.[118] Moreover, he distinguishes between

> two types of paramahamsas: the jnāni and the premi. The jnāni is self-centered; he feels it is enough to have knowledge for his own self. The premi, like Śukadeva, after attaining his own realization, teaches men. Some eat mangoes and wipe off the traces from their mouths; but some share their mangoes with others. Spades and

[113] *Philosophies of India*, pp. 560-602.
[114] *Ibid.*, p. 568.
[115] See note 66 above.
[116] *Philosophies of India*, pp. 560, 597.
[117] *Ibid.*, p. 561.
[118] *S. Nikhil.*, pp. 829, 914.

> baskets are needed to dig a well. After the digging is over, some throw the spades and baskets into the well. But others put them away; for a neighbor may use them. Śukadeva and a few others kept the spades and baskets for the benefit of others. (To Girish) You should do the same.[119]

At another place he calls such *premīs Īśvarakoṭis* or Divine Messengers who adopt the attitude of a servant before God.[120] Romain Rolland tells us that Rāmakrishna was concerned that if his disciples experienced *nirvikalpa samādhi* they might not return to the world to help others so he discouraged them from seeking this realization. Rolland says that once when Swami Vivekānanda sought *nirvikalpa samādhi*, Rāmakrishna rebuked him,

> Shame on you! I thought that you were to be the great banyan tree giving shelter to thousands of tired souls. Instead you are selfishly seeking your own well-being. Let these little things alone, my child. How can you be satisfied with so one-sided an ideal? You might be *all*-sided. Enjoy the Lord in all ways! [121]

Such a situation is recorded in Mahendranāth's diary, and Rāmakrishna's words do substantiate in a kernel the sense of the above quotation.

> Narendra [speaking]: . . . I replied, 'It is my desire to remain absorbed in samādhi continually for three or four days, only once in a while coming down to the sense plane to eat a little food.' Thereupon he [Rāmakrishna] said to me: 'You are a very small-minded person. There is a state higher even than that. "All that exists art Thou"—it is you who sing that song.' [122]

As history records, the chastened Narendra went on to become the dynamic Swami Vivekānanda, the founder of the Rāmakrishna Mission which has continued to heed its Master's command "You should do the same" as Śukadeva and work "for the benefit of others". It seems clear that the development of this Mission with its great social awareness and involvement owes no little debt to Śrī Rāmakrishna's dynamic and life-affirming śākta tantric world-view.

As we have said, Rāmakrishna is usually interpreted as a bhakta, a lover and devotee of a personal Deity. There is, of course, no conflict between this interpretation and the view of Rāmakrishna

---

[119] *Ibid.*, p. 679.
[120] *Ibid.*, pp. 707-708; *Madras I*, pp. 270-72.
[121] Rolland, *Prophets of the New India*, pp. 203, 55.
[122] *S. Nikhil.*, p. 935; *Madras II*, pp. 360f. Cf. *S. Nikhil.*, p. 939.

as a śākta. Rāmakrishna saw bhakti, as have many of the great bhakta theologians, not as a specific sādhana but as a quality of love and devotion that must pervade all sādhana if it is to be successful. It is "the essence of all spiritual discipline." [123] To Rāmakrishna, "love of God is the one essential and necessary thing" [124] for realizing Her, and, as we have seen, he recommends that all in this Kali yuga follow the way of bhakti yoga.[125] He even specifically asks jñānīs to give up their unnecessary speculation, and follow the way of bhakti—assuring them that the Mother will give them *Brahmajñāna* if they desire it.[126] The only necessary ingredient in the quest for God is a passionate love and longing for Her.

The last aspect of Rāmakrishna's teaching which we will consider is of central importance in that it explains why he is so open to so many diverse types of religious practice and why he believes that all that is necessary for realizing the Divine Mother is a sincere and passionate love and longing for Her. Rāmakrishna is a complete divine determinist. He believes that the Divine Mother is the only actor and that man himself does nothing.

> What is knowledge? And what is the nature of this ego? "God alone is the Doer, and none else"—that is knowledge. I am not the doer; I am a mere instrument in His hand. Therefore I say: "O Mother, Thou art the Operator and I am the machine. Thou art the Indweller and I am the house. Thou art the Driver and I am the carriage. I move as Thou movest me. I do as Thou makest me do. I speak as Thou makest me speak. Not I, not I, but Thou, but Thou." [127]

Rāmakrishna made it quite explicit that he saw man as having no free will, and he agreed that man cannot truly be held responsible for his acts. Only the Divine Mother is responsible for what happens in the world.[128] Here is the reason why Rāmakrishna is hesitant to completely condemn any religious practice. He feels that they are all divinely ordained and that if there are any errors the Mother Herself will correct them.[129] Rāmakrishna does not, however, hold a mechanistic view of the world. Though he feels that the world and men are controlled by divine law, he also feels that the Divine Mother in Her

---

[123] *S. Nikhil.*, p. 123; *Madras I*, p. 125.
[124] *S. Nikhil.*, p. 123; *Madras I*, p. 234.
[125] *Madras I*, p. 221; *S. Nikhil.*, p. 464. Cf. note 105 above.
[126] *S. Nikhil.*, pp. 150, 468; *Madras II*, p. 38; *Madras I*, p. 232.
[127] *S. Nikhil.*, p. 98; cf. pp. 211, 220.
[128] *Ibid.*, p. 460.
[129] *Ibid.*, p. 80; *Madras I*, p. 40.

sporting with the world and men can alter Her control.[130] Man must depend totally upon the loving action of the Divine Mother. Therefore, all that can avail man is bhakti—the longing love of a child for its missing Mother. When the Divine Mother hears the yearning call of Her bhakta, Her heart will be moved and She will graciously grant the realization of Herself.

## CONCLUSION

This essay has argued that Śrī Rāmakrishna's religious experience and teachings can be understood accurately in their own terms only if placed in a pattern determined by his śākta bhakti as transformed by his tantric sādhana and as integrated into a coherent world-view dominated by a tantric form of *advaita*. If my analysis is valid, it would require the revision of certain prevailing views regarding Rāmakrishna, the Rāmakrishna Mission and modern Hindu religion:

(1) This study would necessitate a reassessment of the sources of the dynamic and life-affirming aspects of the Neo-Vedānta thought of the Rāmakrishna Mission and those who are indebted to it. These thinkers self-consciously place themselves in the line of Śaṅkara's *Advaita Vedānta*, seeing his system as the most beautifully consistent ever conceived by man. Yet we find a definite lessening of emphasis upon the acosmic aspects of Śaṅkara's thought and an assertion of views that in varying degrees divinize man and the world and set forth a monistic basis for ethical action. The passive uninvolved Brahman of Śaṅkara's system is replaced by a more truly monistic metaphysic in which Brahman is an active vital evolutionary spirit or force of which all things and beings are manifestations. Critics of Neo-Vedānta have noticed these departures from Śaṅkara's basic positions, have seen the changes as the outcome of the operation of unacknowledged influences, and have supposed Neo-Vedānta to be the outcome of the massive importation of aspects of Western and Christian realism and ethical concern. The Western and Christian presence in India may of course have exerted a powerful impetus toward the reshaping of traditional Vedānta, but it is no longer necessary to see the West as its material source. Our attention to the tantric factors in Rāmakrishna's outlook has shown us, in this determinative person, the extra-Śaṅkarite but traditionally Hindu source of a monist understanding that was dynamic and life-affirming.

---

[130] *S. Nikhil.*, p. 817.

The Hindu roots of the new elements in Vedānta were obscured by late Victorian India, unwilling to acknowledge the extent of its debt to the popular and pervasive but, at that time, "disreputable" tantric traditions. Only in the thought of Śrī Aurobindo do we find an open and self-conscious recognition of a tantric world-view as the essential basis for a coherent synthesis of the diverse Hindu traditions.[131] It is significant that Śrī Aurobindo's attempt at a theoretical synthesis was at least partially inspired by Rāmakrishna's success at a practical one.[132]

(2) With regard to Rāmakrishna's teaching of the universal truth within all religions, the view that emerges from a consideration of Rāmakrishna's own ideas and practice turns out to be more inclusive in its recognition, more genuinely universalistic in its outlook than the theory of comparative religion that one finds in the official biographies. The view of world religions in those works can be compared in its fundamental idea with the classical Christian view of other religions as *praeparatio evangelica*. It has been the characteristic view of the Rāmakrishna Mission that theistic religion does find and must find its consummation and final satisfaction in the trance of *nirvikalpa samādhi* in which all personality, human or divine, vanishes. In this light, those Christian, Jewish, Muslim and Hindu traditions that are based upon the conception of a personal Deity are seen as being of positive but preparatory value. Rāmakrishna was less conditional in his acceptance. Possessed of strong personal preferences himself, he was nevertheless willing to acknowledge all forms of mysticism, theistic and non-theistic, personal and impersonal, as alternative ways to the realization of highest Reality.

(3) Śrī Rāmakrishna's strong personal preferences as set forth in this essay would seem also to call for a reassessment of the relative significance within the Hindu tradition of the two types of religious experience represented, on the one hand, by Śaṅkara's dispassionate and rationalistic quest for union with an impersonal Absolute (*nirguṇa brahman*) and, on the other, by Rāmakrishna's passionate devotional longing for the personalistically conceived (*sa-guṇa*) śakti Kālī. To call for such a reassessment is not to deny the importance, significance or profundity of Śaṅkara and his Vedānta tradition. Rather it is

[131] Śri Aurobindo [Ghose], *On Yoga, I: The Synthesis of Yoga* (Pondicherry, Sri Aurobindo Ashram, 1957), pp. 45-46. On Śrī Aurobindo and Tantrism, see Kees W. Bolle, *The Persistence of Religion* (Leiden, E. J. Brill, 1965).

[132] Aurobindo, *On Yoga*, pp. 45-55, 698-700.

to point out that Rāmakrishna and many other great Hindu bhakta thinkers have stressed certain limitations in Śaṅkara's way and have preferred and recommended other ways as being more appropriate and meaningful for the majority of their fellow men. As the writer of this essay, I should reveal my own personal preference for a religious way based upon the elevation and ultimate transformation of certain of our personal human qualities over a path based upon the ultimate negation and absolute transcendence of all personal qualities and symbols. This personal preference of mine has of course biased my interpretation of Śrī Rāmakrishna. I only hope that my bias has not distorted his experience and teachings but rather has enabled me to be sensitive to and understanding of certain aspects of his teachings that had become obscured.

## ABBREVIATIONS

| | |
|---|---|
| *The Great Master* | Swami Saradananda, *Sri Ramakrishna the Great Master*, trans. by Swami Jagadananda (Madras, Sri Ramakrishna Math, 1952) [3rd edition, 1963]. |
| *Life of Sri Ramakrishna* | *Life of Sri Ramakrishna Compiled from Various Authentic Sources* (Mayavati, Almora, Himalayas; Advaita Ashrama, 1925) [Calcutta, Advaita Ashrama, 2nd revised edition, 8th impression, 1964]. |
| *Madras I* | *Gospel of Sri Ramakrishna (According to M., a son of the Lord and disciple)* or *The Ideal Man for India and for the World*, Part I (Madras, The Brahmavadin Office, 1907). |
| *Madras 5th* | *Gospel of Sri Ramakrishna (According to M., a son of the Lord and disciple)*, Vol. I (Mylapore, Madras, Sri Ramakrishna Math, 1930, 5th edition). |
| *Madras II* | *Gospel of Sri Ramakrishna (According to M., a son of the Lord and disciple)*, Vol. II (Mylapore, Madras, Sri Ramakrishna Math, 1928, 2nd edition). |
| *S. Abhed.* | *The Gospel of Ramakrishna*, revised by Swami Abhedananda from M.'s Original English Text (Boston, Beacon Press, 1947). |
| *S. Nikhil.* | Swami Nikhilananda, trans., *The Gospel of Sri Ramakrishna* (New York, Ramakrishna-Vivekananda Center, 1952). |

# THE RĀMAKRISHNA MATH AND MISSION

## *A Case Study of a Revitalization Movement*

CYRUS R. PANGBORN

Identifications of the decisive action that created a new social movement and the precise moment of its occurrence will differ according to the perspectives of the chroniclers. Swami Vivekānanda would write that he and the several other young disciples of Rāmakrishna who gathered about their beloved Kālī priest in a garden-house in North Calcutta were in effect founding the Rāmakrishna Math in December of 1885.[1] But just as significant, perhaps, was Rāmakrishna's distribution of ochre cloths and rosaries to eleven young male disciples on an evening in January, 1886; or the occasion favored by Swami Gambhirānanda when, after Rāmakrishna's death, eight of the earlier eleven "embraced monasticism by taking the ritual vow of renunciation and changing their original names" [2] on a January day in 1887.

The last of these occasions and times would seem to be the most decisive, but the choice is actually of little consequence except for establishing routine facts. The important issues are those of what kind of movement was thereby launched and what the reasons are that explain one of the liveliest of the several Indian revitalization movements founded in the 19th century. Thus the aims of sociological analysis are to identify the social genre of the movement by its traits, to support the identification by citing exemplary samples of message and program, and to account for the vigor which has marked the movement from shortly after its inception to the present day.

### *The Lineaments of the Movement*

The movement consists primarily of a central Math and Mission located since 1898 at Belur, across the Ganges from Calcutta, and numerous local maths and missions in other Indian cities and several

---

[1] Swami Vivekananda, Letter to Swami Brahmananda, July 13, 1897, *The Complete Works of Swami Vivekananda*, pub. Swami Gambhirananda, VIII (3rd ed.; Calcutta: Advaita Ashrama, 1959), 411.

[2] Swami Gambhirananda, *History of the Ramakrishna Math and Mission* (Calcutta: Advaita Ashrama, 1957), p. 65.

foreign countries. The Math in every instance is the place of training and residence for monks of the Rāmakrishna Order. Wherever there is a Mission, it means that there is a ministry of teaching and service offered to the lay public. The personnel of a Math consists only of *sannyāsins* (ordained monks), beginning novitiates, and *brahmachārins* (initiated novitiates). A Mission usually requires additional facilities. These may occupy the same grounds with a Math or be entirely separated geographically. In either case, business and professional employees may be part of the personnel, but monks retain authority and control. The full constituency, however, is not accounted for until thousands of lay persons of both sexes are included. Those who look to the monks for religious guidance are, in Indian parlance, devotees. But if they support and share in the work of a Mission as employees, as volunteers, or as beneficiaries, they may join the Mission as lay members. It is the laity who make a *movement* of what would otherwise be only a monastic order.

## *The Movement as a Type*

Types of personal constituency tell us little, of course, about the real nature of a movement. That is revealed only by identifying its basic assumptions, the objectives sought, and the means employed to clarify the first and achieve the latter. It can then be compared with various models or characteristic religious phenomena such as the revitalization movements described by A. F. C. Wallace.[3]

The comparison shows that the Rāmakrishna movement is typical of the genre that Wallace analyzed. It seeks to restore vitality to languishing traditions in order to use them in inculcating authentic contemporary spirituality and to encourage social reform. Three subordinate traits further identify this particular revitalization movement. One, already implied, is its *revivalism*—which Wallace defines as seeking the recovery of "customs, values, and even aspects of nature" once thought to have been present and constructively functional in culture but now missing.[4] The second trait, the *vitalistic* element, is the inclusion of alien notions calculated to act as a stimu-

---

[3] See Anthony F. C. Wallace, "Revitalization Movements: Some Theoretical Considerations for Their Comparative Study," *American Anthropologist*, XLVIII (April, 1956), 264-281.

[4] *Ibid.*, p. 267. The additional terms for two other subordinate traits mentioned on the same page, and reference to which follows, are also derived from Professor Wallace's article.

lant to—especially in synthesis with—traditional features of the culture. Finally, the *messianic* motif appears in the form of trust that "a divine savior in human flesh" has been or will be a crucial agent in effecting personal and cultural transformation. In summary then, the Rāmakrishna Order, together with its Maths and Missions, constitutes a phenomenon properly described as a revivalistic, vitalistic, messianic, revitalization movement.[5] Such is the thesis of this essay. The support for it must come from describing the movement's heroes, their ways of working, the institutions that evolved, and the results achieved.

### *The Genius of the Founder*

Rāmakrishna, the priest of Kālī, is the first and perennially most important "ingredient" of the movement bearing his name, but such a statement means very little without an explanation of India's traditional dependence upon leaders of several types. Hinduism owes its transmission and survival mainly to a combination of unexceptionable priests and exceptional *gurus*, and scarcely at all to consciously contrived and administered formal institutions. Even the so-called sects are amorphous groups of devotees. The sharing of ideas and loyalties, not ecclesiastical machinery, provides for cohesion. Consequently, the ideas of a sect depend for their perpetuation almost wholly on a chain of influential gurus whose appeal derives from an observed congruity between their lives and their message. A guru may be a priest, in which case we know he was born a brahman and has been trained and ordained by another priest. The guru who is a monk has studied with and been initiated by another monk or by the several senior monks of one of the relatively few monastic orders. A third type of guru is the layman whose only credentials are the knowledge and the authority imputed to him by his students. In most instances, gurus neither claim nor have ascribed to them a nature and character other than human and mortal. A few, however, may profess—or have devotees who allege—that they are *avatārs* (deity in human form).

---

[5] Two other possible traits of revitalization movements described by Wallace do not characterize the Rāmakrishna movement; i.e., it is neither *nativistic* nor *millenarian*. In the first instance, it does not seek "the elimination of alien persons, customs, values, and/or materiel," or, in the second instance, expect "an apocalyptic world transformation engineered by the supernatural." *Ibid.*

Rāmakrishna was a curious blend of types. Brahman by birth, he was trained by an older brother for priestly office at the Kālī temple in Dakshineśwar near Calcutta. His manner of life, however, was that of the celibate monk, marriage notwithstanding. In fact, because of his celibacy, he could be initiated into *Sannyāsa* as well as the priesthood, and was so inducted by an itinerant monk who had tarried at Dakshineśwar to teach him the philosophy of Vedānta. Finally, on the basis of his admission toward the end of his life that he was an avatār, his disciples and followers in general have felt free to trust that he was this kind of rarer guru as well. But long before that, they had been drawn to him by the authenticity they accorded to his understanding of selected aspects of Indian tradition and to the spirituality nourished in him by his often quite unconventional religious experiences.

Rāmakrishna, or Gadādhar, as he was named, was born on February 18, 1836, in the West Bengal village of Kamarpukur. By the time his biographers would record the event, the memories of kinsmen and early associates would have already undergone that amazing transformation which projects backward in time the "halo" acquired by the revered adult. Thus his birth and events occurring in his early years that might well have never seemed more than ordinary came to be taken for wonders, blessed portents, and signs. For Rāmakrishna in later life was *not* an ordinary person and no one apparently ever said otherwise. Indisputably, he possessed the charisma that made his halo appear—in others' memories—years before its time.

One component of this charisma was the winsomeness of his childlike simplicity in all thought about himself and in the spontaneity of his affection for others. He had no time to be pretentious or complicated, given the one dominating objective he chose for his life. One is reminded of the dictum of Kierkegaard, "Purity of heart is to will one thing." The one thing Rāmakrishna willed was the attainment of "God-consciousness" and its possession forever. This is not to say that he supposed such an attainment really could be willed. He could will only the "conquest of the flesh" and the "renunciation of wealth" [6] which would empty his life of competing desires. God-consciousness itself—which for Rāmakrishna was principally his absorption in Kālī, the Divine Mother, but, as will be seen,

[6] Swami Gambhirananda, *Life of Sri Ramakrishna* (2nd ed.; Calcutta: Advaita Ashrama, 1928), p. 58.

took other temporary forms as well—was not attained even by twelve years of yearning, half of those in allegedly complete sleeplessness.[7] It came instead by revelation, the vouchsafed presence, the gracious bestowal by Kālī of a vision of Herself which, happening once, re-occurred with increasing frequency until it became continuous. Yet despite awareness of the extraordinary measure of his "God-intoxication" as compared with the spiritual experiences of anyone he knew, he is reported to have replied to a well-known pundit who declared him an incarnation of God, "Well, it is you who say so, but believe me, I know nothing about it." [8]

Not content with achieving his states of God-consciousness for himself alone, he made it his vocation and the symbol of his affection to initiate others to such experience. So urgently, in fact, did he commend his vision of the Divine Mother (God with the personal, feminine attributes of Kālī) that even Totāpurī, the itinerant Vedāntic sannyāsin, was led, according to accounts, to his own vision of the Mother. Totāpurī had thought his own experience of *Nirvikalpa Samādhi* (the superconscious state of complete oneness with the impersonal unconditioned *Brahman*, to which he had introduced Rāmakrishna) was the superior state, but he had to admit that the two experiences were of equal validity. They might be distinct, yet they were not different. "'. . . like milk and its whiteness, the diamond and its lustre . . . [the] Divine Mother and Brahman are one.'" [9] Of a piece with this urge to share and persuade was Rāmakrishna's longing for young disciples whom he could train until they would "realize God" for themselves and then, like him, also teach others. His own later recollection of that time in his life was of climbing atop a building on the temple grounds and crying, "Come, my boys! O, where are you? . . . a mother never longs so intensely for the sight of her child, nor a friend for his companion, nor a lover for his sweetheart, as I did for them!" [10]

The "boys" were only a few of the many disciples for whom the most impressive feature of Rāmakrishna's states of God-consciousness

---

[7] *Ibid.*, p. 62.

[8] *Ibid.*, p. 128.

[9] Swami Nikhilananda, *Ramakrishna: Prophet of New India* (New York: Harper & Brothers, 1948), p. 26. The work is an abridgement of the author's *The Gospel of Sri Ramakrishna*, itself an English translation of the Bengali biography, *Sri Sri Ramakrishna Kathamrita*, by Mahendranath Gupta using the pseudonym "M". The quotation is from the oral teaching of Rāmakrishna.

[10] Gambhirananda, *loc. cit.*, p. 296.

was their presumed diversity. Nikhilānanda, in condensing early accounts of Rāmakrishna's *sādhana* (engagement in spiritual disciplines), cites Hanumān (the monkey god) of the *Rāmāyaṇa* epic as the first of the personal deities with whom after Kālī, Rāmakrishna achieved identification. As though with Hanumān's eyes, he beheld in his devotion the deity Viṣṇu in the form of Rāma as avatār. One hardly need add that for one whose human vision had been monopolized by Kālī, becoming a monkey god in order to adore another deity was a variant.

In succeeding periods, he worshipped Rāma as the Divine Child, experienced mystical union with Kṛṣṇa's spouse Rādhā, then with Kṛṣṇa himself (another avatār of Viṣṇu), and ventured finally into the unfamiliar spiritual territory of other religions. For the early saints whom the Jains call their Tīrthaṅkaras and for the ten successive gurus who established Sikhism, he learned "profound respect," and the Buddha, he concluded, had the divinity of an avatār. But if with any of these he experienced mystical union, there are no accounts of it. On the other hand, he not only regarded Muhammad and Jesus as avatārs but also "merged" with each in turn.

Had his devotees been more familiar with Islam and Christianity and their long history of distrust of mysticism, they would have perceived that Rāmakrishna experienced Muhammad and Jesus not on *their* terms but only on his own. His temporary departures from outward Hindu practice did not make of him, even briefly, either a Muslim or a Christian. What might be correct to say is that he made Hindus of Muhammad and Jesus by initiating them posthumously into Vedāntic Sannyāsa! But this fact was obviously lost on the growing number of those whose admiration for him became enthrallment. They were impressed by the seeming diversity of his experiences and by the multi-faceted character of his personality which such experiences appeared to denote.

The earthy, commonplace, and sometimes pungent terms Rāmakrishna used in teaching further enhanced his magnetism. The way in which he explained the experimentation just described aptly illustrates his style:

> . . . He who is called Krishna is also called Siva and bears the name of the Primal Energy, Jesus, and Allah as well—the same Rama with a thousand names. A lake has several ghats. At one the Hindus take water in pitchers and call it 'jal'; at another the Mussalmans take

water in leather bags and call it 'pani.' At a third the Christians call it 'water.' .... The substance is one under different names, and everyone is seeking the same substance; only climate, temperament, and name create differences. Let each man follow his own path. If he sincerely and ardently wishes to know God—peace be unto him! He will surely realize Him.[11]

Neither style nor content, however, would have wrung from admirers the judgment that he already possessed, lying dormant, an avatār's divine wisdom. Perhaps, therefore, it was the amazing contrast between Rāmakrishna's well-known rebellion against schooling and his manifest intimacy with the broad spectrum of Indian religious traditions that surprised people and made many ardent devotees willing to call him Lord. Commenting on his scholastic rebellion, his American disciple, John Yale, concedes that

> ... we must class Ramakrishna as illiterate. He could hardly read or write his own Bengali. And ... [he] never learned to speak more than perhaps a dozen words of ... [English]." [12]

Yet such formal illiteracy Nikhilānanda says was irrelevant, since he had

> ... an encyclopedic knowledge of religions and religious philosophies .... acquired from his contacts with innumerable holy men and scholars. He had a unique power of assimilation .... [and] seemingly inexhaustible knowledge ...[13]

With Rāmakrishna, then, we have a founder whose qualifications sufficed to inspire the launching of a new movement. In subordinating all interests to the one (and traditionally Indian) objective of realizing God-consciousness, he was at the same time persuading others that this remained life's one supremely valid goal, the skepticism of those influenced by alien values notwithstanding. His principal method was likewise traditional. It was the way of *bhakti* (devotionalism) in general and mystical bhakti in particular. He loved in turn the gods and goddesses of Hinduism's *Trimūrti* theism (even if

[11] Quoted by Nikhilananda, *op. cit.*, p. 29. For the preceding summary of Rāmakrishna's several experiences of identification with varied forms of deity, see pp. 16-29. One must turn to Gambhirānanda's earlier cited *Life of Sri Ramakrishna*, however, to learn that Rāmakrishna behaved as would the monkey god Hanumān during his Rāma *sādhana*, and both impersonated and dressed as a woman when he sought union with Kṛṣṇa. See pages 82 and 176, respectively.

[12] John Yale, *A Yankee and the Swamis* (London: George Allen & Unwin, Ltd., 1961), p. 68.

[13] Nikhilananda, *op. cit.*, p. 27.

Kālī remained his preference), and proceeded to go beyond an "I-in-relation-to-Thou" experience of communion with each one to an "I-am-Thou" or "Thou-in-me" experience of *union*. The tradition had its earliest roots in the Vedic hymns, its justification in the *Bhagavad Gītā*, its clarifying formulations in the *Purāṇas* and *Tantras*, and its revitalization in medieval times from a series of notable Vaiṣṇavite and Śaivite reformers. Any revitalization movement so grounded was bound to be of revivalistic type.

In Rāmakrishna's profession of avatarship we find the origin of the motif that would make the movement also messianic. According to our sources, he had already been hailed as an avatār before he himself professed as much. But the experiences he had during the years from 1864 through 1872, when his sādhana led him beyond Kālī, the Mother, to try other Hindu and non-Hindu ways of realizing God, evidently compelled him to the same conclusion. The "ordinary man" needs "a whole life's struggle to realize one or two phases of God," but "he had in a few years realized God in His diverse phases," [14] says Nikhilānanda in explaining what finally convinced Rāmakrishna himself. The devotees might have succeeded alone, of course, in making the claim credible, but Rāmakrishna's ratification rendered their task much easier and gave them the assurance they needed to be persuasive with others.[15] Once, also, the belief in the avatārship of Rāmakrishna became common ideological currency, the way was paved for mythologizing his conception, birth, childhood, and youth. The wonders wrought by the man became prefigured by events illumined by the halo that had always been there for those with eyes to see it. With that development, the component most essential in launching a new movement—a charismatic, wonder-working founder whose story would bear retelling again and again—had been provided.

### *The Genius of the Apostle*

As in the case of most prophets or reformers, however, Rāmakrishna provided only the requisite impulse or inspiration for a new movement. He had neither the interest nor the skills to plan or

[14] *Ibid.*, p. 33.

[15] The Western monotheist may need the warning that his notion of the connection between a messiah and the eschatological end of history differs from the Indian view. The *avatār*, for theistic Hindus, is messiah for no other than that era of history ushered in by his appearance. He is therefore one of many of a series of messiahs, not the only one.

organize a movement for spreading God-realization. What he did have was the intuition to identify a true "Singh" (lion of the faith) when he saw one, and the capacity to captivate the lion who sought him out. The one destined to play Paul to Rāmakrishna as a Hindu Christ was Narendranāth Dutta, the Narendra or Naren who, as a sannyāsin, would be known as Vivekānanda.

Narendra, son of a Calcutta attorney, student of the intellectually most demanding subjects in arts and sciences at Scottish Church College, sweet singer and vigorous debater, a volatile and sensitive youth in search of a guru, found in Rāmakrishna the man who had seen God and could help others see Him. He had already tried the Brāhmo Samāj in the hope that its leader—at that time, Keshab Chandra Sen—could lead him to the vision for which he yearned.[16] When, having heard about the maverick priest of Dakshineśwar, he went to see him for the first time, he seemed still but little closer to his goal. Rāmakrishna confused and puzzled him, strongly attracted him and yet repelled him, so that he felt he must be on his guard against the priest's influence.

No such ambivalence marked Rāmakrishna's attitude toward Narendra. He acknowledged at their first meeting that he knew Narendra to be "'that ancient sage, Nara—the Incarnation of Nārāyaṇa—born on earth to remove the misery of mankind. . .'"[17] Also, in due time, he professed that he had had a vision in *samādhi* (the superconsciousness experienced when realizing God), before ever meeting Narendra, when he saw Nara, the sage, in the transcendental realm and knew that he would descend to earth. " 'No sooner had I seen Narendra,' " he declared, " 'than I recognized him to be that sage' " [18]

But if Rāmakrishna knew and never doubted the outcome of their meeting, as all informants claim, it would take encounters stretching over four years for Narendra to accept this version of his role and destiny. He had first to overcome his resistance to Rāmakrishna's influence, then gain assurance after his father's death that his family would never be in want if he renounced the world, before finally

[16] The Brāhmo Samāj, an eclectic theistic society founded in Calcutta by Rāmmohun Roy in 1828, combined the temper of Indian *bhakti* (devotionalism) with patterns of ritual, organization, and social action usually more associated with Western religious institutions.

[17] Quoted by Gambhirananda, *loc. cit.*, p. 332.

[18] *Ibid.*, pp. 336-337.

making the commitment to the "Master" and to service in his name. But with these barriers hurdled, he ceased being the avocational devotee and became the world-renouncing, Rāmakrishna-affirming disciple, destined for apostleship as Swami Vivekānanda.

Still there were no visible signs or portents that Vivekānanda would become the chief agent for spreading and perpetuating the influence of Rāmakrishna through much of Bengal, to other parts of India, and even to the West. In the normal course of events, in India, he would have kept the several other young male disciples together in an *āshram* for their own lifetimes. But the charisma of Rāmakrishna would have been diluted and weakened by sharing it, as well as depersonalized in whatever measure the āshram represented institutionalization. The fellowship might have survived for a generation or two and the name of Rāmakrishna might even have won a reference in chronicles of 19th century Bengali history. His influence, however, would have been fragmented and diffused in the course of a few decades, with none of its specific features clearly traceable or indisputably assignable to him.

But the normal course of events was not to be taken for the now obvious reason that no normal course and Vivekānanda would ever have been compatible! To be sure, his first steps were conventional and traditional. They could hardly have been planned to increase his visibility. He simply set off as the virtually anonymous and mendicant monk for places in north-central and western India, famous for their association with heroes and holy men, to expose himself to their spirituality-saturated atmosphere. Then, his thirst for meaning and purpose still unquenched, he went on south to the Cape, north again through central and east India—not content until he had etched in his mind a picture of Mother India as a whole, with the image of Rāmakrishna superimposed at the center of it, as India's light and hope.

It was during this pilgrimage that events conspired to put Vivekānanda's feet on a course rarely trod by Indians before his time. Meanwhile, he was evolving an outlook that would prepare him to exploit the events to good purpose. He later identified his visit to Cape Comorin in late 1882 as the occasion for his realizing that the tradition of "so many Sannyāsins wandering about" was "all madness." Metaphysics, he decided could not be taught to the masses whose stomachs were so uniformly empty. The only way to go about the task of spreading religion was to precede the teaching of it with practical programs for social improvement.[19] Unlike Rāmakrishna, whose fear of defilement by money had become legendary, Vivekānanda was eminently practical. He knew that a social program would cost money, and it did not take him long to decide that while his compatriots might have the means and the heart to give for relief, they had neither in an amount sufficient to effect significant social change. That, he concluded, would have to come from the West.

The new social note in his itinerant preaching elicited response as he moved northward again, especially in such education-conscious cities as Hyderabad and Madras. At the same time, in literate circles, the news was spreading that a Parliament of Religions was to be convened in 1893 in connection with a World Exposition in Chicago. The notion that occurred to Vivekānanda's growing circle of admirers, of sending him to the Parliament to speak for Hinduism, fitted perfectly into his evolving plan to raise money in the West. Their raising of the money for the trip, as objective circumstance, had its subjective endorsement in a dream. He dreamed that he saw Rāmakrishna walking out to sea and beckoning him to follow from the shore. He understood it as a divine command. Waiting only long enough to secure encouragement from Rāmakrishna's widow, the "Holy Mother," he booked passage for America.[20]

This is not the place to repeat the saga of Vivekānanda's Western adventures, but a bare summary at least is indispensable. His remarks at the Parliament of Religions were well received and publicized. He stayed on in the United States where, except for brief periods in London and on the Continent, he traveled widely, lecturing and writing, founding the original Vedānta Society in New York, and raising money among well-to-do American disciples to underwrite

---

[19] Vivekananda, Letter to Shashi Chakravarti, March 19, 1894, *Complete Works . . .*, VI (6th ed., 1956), 254.

[20] Hinduism's lack of formal institutional structure could be regarded at this point as fortuitous for Vivekānanda and the future Rāmakrishna movement, for anyone so lacking in official credentials would hardly have been delegated to represent the religion had there been an ecclesiastical hierarchy to make the choice. It is interesting to note that another Indian delegate to the Parliament was P. C. Mozoomdar, leader of one of the societies into which the Brāhmo Samāj had splintered, but which, even though weakened by division, retained its Western style in organization and thus the machinery for choosing and sponsoring an offical delegate. Decades later, in an introduction to Mozoomdar's lectures, his publisher averred that it was Mozoomdar who took pity on Vivekānanda when he arrived without credentials and "sympathetically arranged for him to represent the Hindu Monks." P. C. Mozoomdar, *Lectures in America and Other Papers*, pub. Sati Kumar Chatterji (Calcutta: Navavidhan Publication Committee, 1955), page v.

the cost of providing a new Math as headquarters for the Order, not returning to India until early in 1897. News of his popularity in the West preceded him and while its extent was undoubtedly greatly exaggerated in the minds of his Indian friends, it had its effect in preparing them to give their conqueror of the West an enthusiastic welcome upon his arrival.

Vivekānanda had made his presence felt with his brother monks, even from a distance, by a steady stream of letters explaining and justifying the program of action he expected to launch from the new Math. He had even formulated a set of rules for the Order, presupposing a movement of the size and scope it possesses today but which then seemed utterly visionary. Yet his presence was required to dissipate the brothers' resistance to adopting a new version of monastic life and duty. Rāmakrishna's mission had been purely religious or spiritual. The brothers wished nothing more than to emulate him. Swami Akhandānanda alone had responded to Vivekānanda's letters and undertaken practical work related to education for the poor in a community of western India for a brief period in 1895. The others remained conventional except for agreeing in 1897 to found (as they did, on May 5) the Rāmakrishna Mission as an organization coordinate with the Math. The action apparently served to bring their reservations to focus and expression, for shortly afterward, in an emotionally charged confrontation, Vivekānanda was accused of lack of faith in Rāmakrishna. As Gambhirānanda recounts it,

> He defended himself with vehemence till his voice choked, his frame shook, and with tears streaming from his eyes, he left the room, followed by some others who wanted to pacify him. At long last, he came back and explained that he purposely kept his devotion to the Master in check. He said, "Oh, I have work to do! I am a slave of Ramakrishna, who *left his work to be done by me and will not give me rest till I have finished it!* And how shall I speak of him! Oh, his love for me!" The upshot of all this was that out of love for the leader the brother-disciples decided from that day not to question his interpretation of the Master's life and teachings, nor his method of work.[21] [Emphasis added.]

The events that followed support Gambhirānanda's conclusion. The "beloved disciple," the ranking apostle, had established his credentials and authority. Considering India's penchant for long

[21] Gambhirananda, *History . . .*, p. 124.

deliberation before action, the speed with which development occurred is amazing. Money raised in America secured property in Belur for new and permanent central headquarters for both Math and Mission. Leadership was contributed for the task of halting an epidemic of plague in Calcutta. A new āshram was begun at Māyāvati in the Himālayas as a retreat for the practice of pure *Advaita Vedānta* (non-dualism), and as the publication office for the oldest journal of the Order, *Prabuddha Bhārata* (Awakened India, originally published from Madras in 1896 by an admirer of Vivekānanda). The central Math also launched a local Bengali journal, *Udbodhan* (literally, Opening, or more freely, Awakening). As yet, the Order and its institutions constituted no large, visible movement, but the foundations laid must have been firm. At least they survived without deterioration while Vivekānanda made a second visit to the West to found new centers on both American coasts and to lecture and travel in Europe. His return after sixteen months was the signal for renewing organizational activity on home soil and for new centers to spring up in other northern cities.

When Vivekānanda died in 1902 half a year before his 40th birthday, the quantifiable size of the movement would have seemed negligible to anyone familiar with the larger religious institutions of the West. Nor was it of an age that would augur continuing stability and survival. The Order, after fifteen years, was still adolescent, and the Mission, after only five years, was still a child. Both had consisted chiefly of their headquarters at Belur and the modest hope of more to come until Vivekānanda's second return from the West. In retrospect, Gambhirānanda's paean of praise sounds plausible:

> Thus did the Math and Mission march on to win fresh laurels at every turn. India was raised from her torpor by Swamiji's mighty message of practical Vedanta. .... Swami Vivekananda the man was gone from the human arena. But Swami Vivekananda the spirit lived for ever to consolidate his conquest of the world . . .[22]

But it was an evaluation rendered in 1957, *post*dating by fifty-five years the brief era it praised. Had this been said at the time, it would have been little more than prophecy. It is what happened during those next fifty-five years that permits the prematurity of early laudation to pass almost undetected.

In telling this part of the Vivekānanda story we have emphasized

[22] *Ibid.*, p. 151.

his continuity as apostle with his master, Rāmakrishna. Rāmakrishna, in turn, represented for him a synthesis of all the best of the ancient Indian traditions. Thus he could say, "Now, all the ideas that I preach are only an attempt to echo his ideas," [23] and mean also, "My plan is to follow the ideas of the great ancient Masters. . . . They were the great givers of strength, and of purity, and of life." [24] Consequently,

> The first work that demands our attention is that the most wonderful truths confined in our Upanishads, in our scriptures, in our Puranas must be brought out from the books, .. the monasteries, .. the forests, .. and scattered broadcast all over the land . . .[25]

This is the same revivalistic motif with respect to dependence upon traditional sources of spiritual wisdom that is found in Rāmakrishna. And just as Rāmakrishna had experimented with various disciplines, Vivekānanda too accepted the time-honored Hindu ways of work, devotion, knowledge, and mysticism. He rejected, however, the customary assumption that these ways were of different value, from lowest to highest, and that men must live countless lives before they would be competent to practice the highest of ways. His ideal, instead, was that all persons "down to the very lowest, without distinction of age or sex," be taught how to synthesize "the best point[s] of Yoga, devotion, knowledge and work . . . now so as to form a new society." [26] Steady devotion to Rāmakrishna, the Incarnation for the age, would provide focus and generate the required vigor for so applying religion to society that it would revivify India. Thus he believed that the new in his message consisted of the emphasis upon the centrality of Rāmakrishna, the sharing of all of India's traditional spiritual resources with all persons immediately, and the necessity of a program for doing this that would go beyond mere demonstration of individually achieved and passive states of religious consciousness. The place he gave Rāmakrishna in his scheme provided the notion of the divine deliverer so that messianism was combined with revivalism in the revitalization movement he envisaged. The third trait he saw as necessary in revitalization was to be provided by introducing the "vitalistic" motif, the importation of

---

[23] Vivekananda, "My Life and Mission," *Complete Works* . . . , VIII, 79.

[24] *Ibid.*, "My Plan of Campaign," III (8th ed., 1960), 220.

[25] *Ibid.*, p. 221.

[26] *Ibid.*, Letter to members of the Math (at Alambazar), April 27, 1896, VII (5th ed., 1958), 484.

alien elements as stimulants to effective and faster action. Work, he never tired of repeating, was not an unfortunate necessity to be imposed upon the low born while great souls merely meditated. Rather, work *is* worship, when done for humanity, not for oneself; and it "leads us to the highest realization of the perfection of the soul." [27] But that preachment was already as venerable as the *Bhagavad-Gītā*. What it needed was application. For that, the requisites were method, practicality, organization, and institutions to provide continuity and permanence. These he imported from the West.

### *The Alien, Vitalistic Ingredient*

The first half of any explanation of this third and final ingredient is still Vivekānanda's story as well. Arriving in the United States from India in July, 1893, he was soon commenting, in letters home, upon India's lack of organizational strategy for pursuing its spiritual ideals. "As regards spirituality, the Americans are far inferior to us," he wrote in December of 1893. "We will teach them our spirituality, and assimilate what is best in their society." [28] A subsequent letter shows what he thought was "best." Referring to Westerners as "these children of liberty, self-help, and brotherly love," he declared, "The secret of [their] success . . . is the power of organisation and combination." [29] The impression that this "secret" made upon him is seen in his deciding before even leaving the West to formulate and send a detailed list of suggested rules for the management of the Math—which still had practically no organizational structure whatever. Containing advice about minor matters of personal monastic lifestyle as well as major questions of corporate government, doctrine, and programmatic activities, the list shows how well the observant Vivekānanda had learned his lessons in Western pragmatism. And although he used his mandate from Rāmakrishna—"He gave me the charge of you all . . ." [30]—to press for adoption of the rules, he urged that Brahmānanda should be elected the first President.[31] Both

---

[27] *Ibid.*, "Karma-Yoga," I (11th ed., 1962), 71.

[28] *Ibid.*, Letter to H. Mitra, December 28, 1893, V (7th ed., 1959), 27.

[29] *Ibid.*, Letter to Shri Haridas Desai, November, 1894, VIII, 328-329.

[30] *Ibid.*, Letter to members of the Alambazar Math, April 27, 1896, VII, 479.

[31] Brahmānanda was very nearly as beloved a disciple of Rāmakrishna as was Vivekānanda. He was one of the original group to take the monastic vow and, as noted later, was reputed to have had the Master's commendation for his administrative abilities.

suggestions were astute for reasons to be noted later, even though no official action was taken at the time. Meanwhile, Vivekānanda remained the leader as the Master's designate, both his authority and his suggested rules being tacitly accepted by the brothers.

Rather surprisingly, therefore, Vivekānanda's concern for structure found its first formal expression when the Math's offspring, the Mission Association, was organized (1897) and provided with a charter of resolutions. It was understood that the practical activities of teaching and philanthropy (social service) engaged in by all local maths as they were formed would be the concern of the Mission Association, and to the first presidency of this, Vivekānanda was elected. The election merely extended the meaning of his *de facto* presidency of the central Math. Brahmānanda, at the same time, was elected to the lesser post of President of the Calcutta unit of the Mission Association. Shortly afterward, the new site acquired at Belur for the central Math was dedicated and occupied. Vivekānanda had already dictated a second more detailed set of rules for the Math, to match those of the Mission in their specificity. But the fact that both Math and Mission had the same president and one common site as headquarters made it virtually impossible for anyone to remember that Math and Mission were, on paper, two different agencies. This, then, was the somewhat less than tidy structure of the movement that obtained during Vivekānanda's second trip to the West.

Upon his return, however, we are told that Vivekānanda made Brahmānanda the "virtual executive head of the Order" [32] and turned his own attention to defining more clearly the Order's ends, means, and dual organizational structure. Even though he had made it explicit that his earlier set of rules for the Math were to be accepted by all subsequently organized local maths, that requirement, he realized, could be honored in the breach as much as by observance unless there was a structure which all his monastic brothers endorsed and supported. Moreover, retention of the Belur property in his own name would be incongruent if he succeeded in shifting the locus of power and authority from himself to the corporate Order. Therefore, although the (now so-called) Belur Math Rules would require little change, he executed a Trust Deed providing for both the creation of a Board of Trustees and the transfer to this Board of the property and his previous authority over it. Then, vacating the

[32] Gambhirananda, *History* . . . , p. 155.

presidency, he left to the eleven new Trustees the election of his successor, and Brahmānanda was chosen. The date of the election was February 12, 1901, and Vivekānanda was already showing the strain of his almost constant labor. He died eighteen months later.

We have said there are several reasons why it was astute of Vivekānanda to wish to shift the mantle of leadership to Brahmānanda. Two reasons in one were that Brahmānanda had not only "a remarkable capacity for administration" but Rāmakrishna's blessing also, in a remembered remark about his ability to "rule a kingdom." [33] If to Vivekānanda was given the vision of what to create and how to create it, to Brahmānanda had been given the quiet reasonableness and sturdy character which would compel respect for his judgment and authority. Thus, by having always insisted that his own work had been only the Master's, and by transferring the focus for the brothers' obedience from himself while he was still living to a man whose qualifications were not charisma but practical abilities, Vivekānanda broke with the Indian pattern of dependence upon a succession of living charismatic gurus. Personal devotion was to be focussed on one, the late Rāmakrishna—who was understood to have been more than a guru; nay, an avatār—and the labors which were to be the fruit of that devotion were to be defined and guided by an organization—the rule of law, not men. The sociologist calls this the institutionalization of charisma. The process spreads and thins the charisma. It may domesticate enthusiasm, but that is the price Vivekānanda had learned in the West to pay for the hope that the movement would have a long future and not only a brief past. It should be added that in selecting the first Board of Trustees, he included only those who had been Rāmakrishna's own disciples. By designating none of those who were *his* disciples and recruits for the Order, Vivekānanda gave added emphasis to his strategy. It minimized his role as successor to Rāmakrishna, maximized Rāmakrishna's centrality, and made the Order as an institution the only-and-ongoing successor.

The rest of the story of how the imported vitalistic element fared is the story of what the *Order* did with this legacy from Vivekānanda.

As events were to show, a donor cannot guarantee, or be guaranteed, that beneficiaries will not squander his gift. Fortunately, however, the first generation of Sannyāsins long outlived Vivekānanda, and he had so persuaded them of the equal and indispensable impor-

---

[33] *Ibid.*, p. 154.

tance of worship, work, and organization that they were fully prepared to preserve each emphasis. Only one, in fact, found Vivekānanda's notions of discipline and structure too constricting to tolerate; yet even he, while choosing to find private quarters and to work independently, preserved ties of friendship with the others until, as the last of them to die (in 1939), the old Order had passed away. Thus the institutional crisis that often occurs for a movement after the successive deaths of the inspiring founder and the organizing genius who was his most notable disciple was postponed by the longevity of the latter's less celebrated but faithful brothers.

Nevertheless, the crisis did occur, nor did it wait for the funerals of all the monks of the first generation. The details are not essential to this account, but the motifs of the crisis are. One was that Vivekānanda's brothers lacked the commanding authority to quell the individualism of the strong-willed ones among their recruits for the Order. A few of the younger generation in the 1920's precipitated a struggle when they could not restrain their personal ambitions and notions for the sake of peace and stability. Only by going to court to relieve one young brahmachārin of duties to which he had successfully aspired, then by expelling him and accepting the departure of his several sympathizers, did the Order thwart the first notable challenge which otherwise could have been the precedent for further fragmentation of authority and unity.

A second factor contributing to crisis was the lack of specific regulations defining the relationship of the ever-multiplying local maths and missions to the Belur headquarters. This factor came into play because the lesson of the Order's successful suit against the brahmachārin was not lost on one of his Sannyāsin sympathizers in Bangalore. Anticipating the prospect that the Order would initiate stronger controls over institutions as well as persons, the monk declared independence for the Math in Bangalore and the several other South Indian centers he had organized. Again, the Order chose to fight a precedent-threatening challenge, won its suit, and watched the dissenting monk walk out with all his followers. This time, however, the Order's victory gave rise to second thoughts on the part of many of the dissidents. Some re-affirmed their loyalty to the Belur Math immediately after the court's decision. Others returned, along with their centers, when the leader's death resolved their conflict between maintaining personal fidelity and realizing the futility of clinging to a lost cause.

Both Math and Mission now moved quickly to effect positive reforms by measures that subordinated individualism to the corporate will. The process required almost a decade of moving from proposals to discussion to trial to revision and adoption. By 1937, the structure essentially obtaining today had been devised, and only minor revisions and amendments have since been needed. Also, while this was occurring, and as a result of the Belur Math's victories in court, the many local centers that had been only voluntarily observing Vivekānanda's dictum that their rules should be the same as Belur's, moved either by wish or by a little prodding to regularize the relationship in a formal and binding way. Thus the reforms, once effected, applied to virtually all the centers of India and abroad which had had the inspiration of Rāmakrishna and the aims of his first disciples as their *raison d'être*.

The needed changes were neither numerous nor revolutionary, but they were important. The training of monastic recruits was made more rigorous and systematic. The central authorities were given power to monitor the training standards and performances of the local maths. Eight years of training were made mandatory for the eventual Sannyāsin, with two of the first four to be spent at Belur. The Belur Math Board of Trustees was enlarged by adding younger sannyāsins to a Board previously consisting of a few senior monks. The result was that new ideas were given a hearing and evaluated openly from within the power structure. Viable innovation became possible because new proposals were not forced underground, there to fester as subversive dissent. The structure of the Governing Board of the Mission also was revised (and made applicable to the local missions), but—one might say—in the opposite direction. Missions had lay members with privileges of representation capable of overriding all too easily the wisdom and will of fulltime officers and staff. Therefore, a number of devices were employed to limit lay membership on the Boards, the power of members, and the possibilities of their seeking ends or using means antagonistic to the Order's ideals and objectives. Perhaps the most important changes were those of requiring all centers henceforth to separate their accounts if they had both maths and missions, to be accountable to the central Math for math accounts and to both the central Mission and to the public wherever there was a local mission, and to undertake no expansion or new projects unless the Belur authorities could be shown that both long-range support and monastic administrative manpower were available. Finally, in order to assure opportunity for periodic evaluation of the effectiveness of greater centralization and for making further changes, if needed, before desires for them could become contentions, it was decided that a Monks' Conference would be held normally every three years. The great majority of the Conference membership would consist of all the Sannyāsins of the Order with fifteen or more years of service to its centers.[34] If it appears that the more junior members of the Order would lack direct voice in such policy-determining convocations, it should be remembered that there is close and intimate association of the monks in residence at a given math. The elders can hardly be unaware of the opinions of the younger monks, and it is unlikely that any decisions reached by a Conference might be conceived without thought for their general acceptability and enforceability. In any case, there have not been, so far as this writer knows, any threats to institutional unity since 1937. Individual monks, if dissatisfied, have left the Order quietly and without trying to take any of the institution with them. Twenty years after, Gambhirānanda would write that

> . . . the spectre of disruption that stared one in the face even in the early thirties was finally disposed of. The organization now stood on the solid rock of goodwill and constitutional coherence.[35]

His judgment seems to have been as predictively accurate as it was then historically factual.

## *In Conclusion*

The steady growth of the movement brought the number of its institutions—chiefly maths and missions—to more than 150 in the 1950's and 60's, with nearly one-fifth of them in countries other than India. Membership in the Order numbers well above 750, and at least as many salaried lay persons serve under the Monks' direction. Thousands of others are part-time volunteers of time and service, and thousands again are lay members of the missions. Except for training novitiates and providing the means for the monastic members to cultivate spiritual disciplines in the maths, the work of the Order is for the benefit of the lay public. Names of the departments according to which the work is organized make the types self-explanatory:

[34] *Rules and Regulations of the Ramakrishna Math*, as Revised in 1958 and Issued by the General Secretary, Belur Math, Howrah, pp. 4-5.

[35] Gambhirananda, *History* . . . , p. 340.

medical service, education, work for women, rural uplift and work among the labouring and backward classes, relief, foreign work, spiritual and cultural [activities]. The principal institutions, representing impressive outlays of capital funds, are schools and colleges, student hostels, libraries, experimental farms, dispensaries, and hospitals both general and specialized.

Public trust in the integrity of the Order and its insistence upon excellence in construction of its institutional buildings and in quality of services rendered have given it marked access to philanthropy. Nevertheless, the tempo of expansion has slowed in recent years because monasticism is not a popular vocation. The increase of democracy in society since India won independence, the departure of the English from positions of authority, and the technological revolution are interrelated causes of a spiraling popularity for vocations in the civil services, the sciences, and technology. Since the Order holds firmly to the principle of entrusting policy, administration, and supervision of its work to its monks only, expansion is presently limited notwithstanding the presence of crucial needs to be met or the availability of financial resources. One might think that the contemporary attraction of Indian "spirituality" for Westerners would offer promise of an increase in recruits for monasticism, particularly if it could be assumed that India's own youth as well were attracted. It is one thing, however, to be a devotee, and quite another to spend eight years in training for, and the rest of one's life in, the state of celibacy, personal poverty, and selfless service.

Yet if the quantifiable expansion of the Order is at least temporarily unspectacular, that does not mean that there is lack of movement on other fronts. Imagination has been notably active in exploiting opportunities to let history enrich the movement and increase its appeal. Centenary celebrations of the respective births of Rāmakrishna and Vivekānanda were utilized for increasing the public's awareness of the movement. The 1963 celebration for Vivekānanda, especially, resulted in his becoming hardly less known as a national hero than the renowned Gandhi. There is, as well, the practice of observing in all centers the annual birthdays of these men and of such lesser luminaries as, for example, Rāmakrishna's wife, the "Holy Mother." Also, the annual *pūjās* (devotional rites) for Hindu gods and goddesses are held according to whatever fashion is traditional in any given region of the country, and the celebration of Christmas is common. In other words, obstructions to one kind of advance have not deterred the Order from increasing and enriching its treasure of historical events, of myth and legend, and ritual.

India is a large country, and it is safe to say that millions of Indians have not yet heard of Rāmakrishna or the movement bearing his name. The prognosis is good, however, for a gradual and continuing increase in public awareness of the movement's presence and probable permanence. That much at least one may aver when so many traits identified by sociological analysis are those that have marked some of the world's most enduring religions. Beginning with a known "savior for this age," the movement spread from a small band of disciples whose means and ends were orchestrated by the most apostolically-gifted one of them all, Vivekānanda. He gave the movement its enduring substance, shape, and structure. The substance was traditional Hindu wisdom, recast as the Gospel of Śrī Rāmakrishna. By making Rāmakrishna the personal symbol of this nativistic element, devotion could be used to power a revival. The notion that work is worship defined the form or shape of the movement. And imported Western patterns of organization or structure constituted the vitalistic element needed for preserving unity, ensuring continuity, and promising a future. Now that some of what was once its future is now its history, the substance is much increased. The movement has a literature of its own—a "gospel," the "acts of its apostles," the "epistles" of Vivekānanda—as well as its "Old Testament," the Vedas. Its myths have been given their shape; its legends multiply. The rituals celebrating anniversaries and birthdays supply color, beauty, and not infrequently, pageantry.

The popular gurus who arise in India from time to time may perform some revitalizing function relevant to the preservation of Indian traditions. But their appearance is unpredictable and their spiritual authenticity not always reliable. It may be, of course, that what Indians call "the corrosive acids of secular modernity" will prove so overwhelming that even institutional organization can not guarantee the transmission of traditional wisdom in vital and relevant forms. But the way in which the Rāmakrishna Order has given revivalistic, vitalistic, and messianic traits to the movement for which it is the soul, and has provided by organization some sustenance for its vision, informs us that it is one revitalization movement wholly dedicated to trying.

# MIXING IN THE COLOR OF RĀM OF RĀNUJĀ

## *A Folk Pilgrimage to the Grave of a Rājpūt Hero-Saint*

Mira Reym Binford

From distant countries the pilgrims come
The *melā* is jammed full of people.
From different lands the pilgrims come
The *melā* is chock full of people.
The unhappy are made happy—
Rāmdevji showers radiance over their homes.
Ting-a-ling, the bells tinkle
The horse's hooves sound—
King Rāmdev comes riding on the blue horse.

Blue horse like a swan, saddle stitched with pearls.
Rāmdev sits on his horse, like the shooting rays of the dawning sun.
Rāmdev sits on his horse, like the shooting rays of the morning sun . . .[1]

Rāmdev, a 15th century Rājpūt martial hero-saint, is regarded by his devotees as an incarnation of Kṛṣṇa. They sing of his many miracles, his powers so great that even Muslims worship him. This 'Hindu Pīr Rāma' is the 'savior of the poor' and special protector of untouchables. He can grant his devotee's desire for a son, cure his illness, keep his ship from sinking . . . He is 'time's shepherd' who 'stays forever with those who believe.'

[1] Song excerpts are from Rāmdev *bhajans* recorded in 1972 during filming of AN INDIAN PILGRIMAGE: RĀMDEVRĀ. This essay grew out of the film, one of six in the University of Wisconsin's Civilizations of South Asia Film Project. The films were made by Michael Camerini and myself. The project, under the overall direction of Joseph W. Elder, Departments of Sociology and South Asian Studies, received financial support from the National Endowment for the Humanities; the Office of Education, U.S. Department of Health, Education, and Welfare; and the University of Wisconsin. This project has given me the extraordinary opportunity of working with Joseph Elder and Michael Camerini, for which I am grateful. AN INDIAN PILGRIMAGE: RĀMDEVRĀ was made with the invaluable help and guidance of anthropologist Baidyanath Saraswati, Indian Institute of Advanced Study, whose insights and generous spirit not only guided the film's development, but made the fieldwork a memorable experience. Ethnomusicologist Komal Kothari, Rupaiyan Institute of Folklore, shared with us his perceptive observations as well as sensitive translations of bhajans. The film was made with the help of anthropology graduate student James MacDonald, cameraman Yagya Sharma, and interpreter Bhadrakant Zhaveri. Like pilgrimage to Rāmdevrā, this work was a collective effort. I am deeply thankful to all those who were part of it and, especially, to the pilgrims themselves.

Rāmdev's grave, in the desert of western Rajasthan, yearly draws several hundred thousand pilgrims. Their presence reflects the flexibility which has enabled the Rāmdev cult to survive for five centuries among his traditional devotees (primarily untouchables), and also to grow in importance among the higher castes, successfully adapting with them to a new urban life.

In a preliminary attempt to trace the roots and evolution of this medieval miracle cult as well as its present relevance and meaning, this essay describes the cult of Rāmdev, the sacred complex of Rāmdevrā, and one particular pilgrimage to Rāmdevrā. Limited as both historical sources and modern field studies are,[2] an examination of pilgrimage in the context of this folk cult can suggest a basis for understanding how and why the cult has developed and survived.

## *The Cult of Rāmdev*

It is said that Rāmdev was born in 1404 A.D., the son of a Toṅwar Rājpūt king, and took *samādhi* in 1458, revered as a saint.[3] But there is almost no historical knowledge about Rāmdev at all. 'Rāmdev,' as used here, refers to the mythical figure central to the Rāmdev cult.[4]

Tod described Rāmdev as "a name famed in Marudesa ... in whose honour altars are raised in every Rajput village in the country," to which Crooke, in the 1920 edition of Tod's *Annals and Antiquities of Rajasthan*, added that Rāmdev was a "Tonwar or Tuar Rajput, of the family of Anangpal of Delhi, now worshipped under the name of Ramsah Pir." [5] Tod depicted the statue of Rāmdev which can still

---

[2] Sudesh Thareja very graciously shared with us what we believe to be the first field study of the Rāmdev cult, her M.A. thesis, "Divine and the Devotee—A Sociological Study of the Religious Tradition of 'Ramdev' of Western Rajasthan," submitted to Jodhpur University in 1973. Portions of the thesis were translated from Hindi by Sudha Bhatt.

[3] Census of India, 1961, Volume XIV, *Fairs and Festivals*, "Rajasthan," Part VII-B.

[4] The tradition of Rāmdev's historicity, evidently important to his devotees, is kept alive through devotional pictures that include his birth- and death-dates, through stories linking his miracles to specific locations in the Rāmdevrā area, and through his descendants. In the village of Rāmdevrā, for example, one is told that a man called Ravrirmal Singhji is the twenty-sixth generation direct descendant of Rāmdev.

[5] James Tod, *Annals and Antiquities of Rajasthan*, Ed., William Crooke, Oxford University Press, 1920, Vol. II, p. 843. Elsewhere Crooke identified Rāmdev as "a well-known warrior, killed in a battle at Ranuja." Rānujā is one of the traditional names for Rāmdevrā village. William Crooke, *Popular Religion and Folklore of Northern India* (London: A. Constable, 1896), p. 200.

be seen in Jodhpur, and related with enchantment his clan's claims tracing its lineage to one Anangpāl who, in the eighth century, rebuilt Delhi on the site of the ancient Indraprastha, a city founded by another heroic ancestor, Yudhiṣṭhira, one of the five Pāṇḍava brothers.[6]

The traditional area of Rāmdev-worship has been western India, from Madhya Pradesh, Gujarat and Rajasthan to as far west as Sind in Pakistan. In recent times, as devotees in search of work have moved to cities, sometimes as far away as Calcutta and Madras, they have taken Rāmdev with them. Rāmdev-worship has traditionally been most important to untouchables, chiefly to Meghvāls, Bhāmbīs (Camārs) and Kāmaḍs, castes associated with leatherwork. Meghvāls, now the largest 'scheduled caste' group in Jaisalmer District, have been the ones who built the village temples to Rāmdev. They and Kāmaḍs have been Rāmdev's village priests and the singers of his *bhajans*.[7] In *Tribes and Castes in the Central Provinces* Russell described the Kāmaḍs as travelling singers from Rājputānā who "worship the footprints of Ramdeo, a saint of Marwar." [8] Enthoven reported that Gujarati and Mārwāṛī Meghvāls living in Cutch at the beginning of this century held "in great estimation a saint called Ramdev Pir, whom they consider their patron saint . . . (and who) became deified by the performances of miraculous deeds." [9]

In Mālwā, Madhya Pradesh, in the mid-1950's K. S. Mathur found that the name of Rāmdev, 'a vegetarian and teetotal deity,' appeared on lists of deities worshipped by 'unclean' castes, but not on lists drawn up by 'clean' caste informants.[10] In the Marwaṛ villages Carstairs studied, also in the 1950's, he found that "the most celebrated of local Gods is Ram-Devji, or Rama-Pir; and tradition has it that he, like the poet Kabir, sought to unite Mohammedans and

[6] James Tod, *op. cit.*, Vol. 1, p. 104.

[7] Words such as *bhajan*, *darśan*, *prasād*, *avatār*, and *dharamśālā*, which are in common use among Rāmdev devotees, have been transliterated according to *their* usage, in their modern Indic and not Sanskrit forms. Although the difference in most of these cases is only a short vowel, the difference in connotation—between *darśan* and *darśana*, for example—is substantial. To use *darśana* would give a Sanskritic implication not appropriate to this tradition.

[8] R. V. Russell and R. B. Hiralal, *The Tribes and Castes of the Central Provinces of India* (Oosterhout, Netherlands: Anthropological Publications), 1969, p. 371.

[9] R. E. Enthoven, *The Tribes and Castes of Bombay* (Bombay: Government of Bombay), 1922, p. 50.

[10] "The Meaning of Hinduism in Rural Malwa" by K. S. Mathur, in L. P. Vidyarthi (ed.), *Aspects of Religion in Indian Society* (Meerut: Kedar Nath Ram Nath, undated), pp. 118-119.

Hindus in one form of worship." [11] The priests of a village Rāmdev temple had 'magical remedies' and the *melā*, or fair, held there annually attracted tens of thousands of people. These pilgrims belonged primarily to the lower castes.

The link between Rāmdev and untouchables remains very strong—both in the minds of non-devotees [12] and as seen in the continuing preponderance of 'ex-untouchable' devotees, at the Rāmdevrā pilgrimage site.[13] Rāmdev's devotees sing that "even the brahman and the Baniyā will say 'Jai' to Bābā Rāmdev." Non-devotees in the traditional Rāmdev areas say that high-caste people do not go to Rāmdev temples—except for women, of course . . . and men, in times of distress. It appears that in the traditional areas of Rāmdev-worship some brahmans, Rājpūts, Baniyās, Jains and others who have not wanted to be identified as Rāmdev devotees have 'resorted to Rāmdev' when they felt in need of his 'specialist' powers. It is among some of these occasional devotees, particularly people of Baniyā and artisan castes who have migrated to cities, that Rāmdev-worship appears to be growing in importance.

There are now Rāmdev temples in most towns and cities of western Rajasthan as well as in Delhi, Madras, Ahmedabad and Bombay. In Bombay we visited some of the Rāmdev temples and met groups of Rāmdev devotees. Regular *bhajan* sessions unite and define each of these groups. The groups are composed of residents of certain housing colonies (such as a group of municipal sweepers from Saurāshtra) or consist of the followers of a particular *guru* (such as the diverse group that meets monthly with Dula Bhagat, an affluent and influential guru).[14] All the bhajan groups we observed in Bombay

---

[11] "Pattern of Religious Observances in Three Villages of Rajasthan" by G. M. Carstairs, in L. P. Vidyarthi, *op. cit.*, p. 67.

[12] Rāmdev's name is even now popularly linked with untouchables. In Western India one can still hear a saying, the Hindi version of which is, "Rāmdevjīkō jō bhī mile, Ḍheḍ hī Ḍheḍ mile"—literally, "Whomever Rāmdevji found, he found mostly Ḍheḍ (untouchables)." The saying is used to comfort a person who reaches for a high goal and, after great effort, achieves very little—as, "After all, for all Rāmdevji's miracles, his followers were only Ḍheḍ."

[13] As Dr. Baidyanath Saraswati has pointed out in a personal communication, the predominance of untouchables in the Rāmdev cult is understandable in view of the reluctance of the higher Hindu castes to perform grave-worship.

[14] Certain singers and composers of Rāmdev bhajans attract a following and are regarded as gurus by their devotees. They play a much more important role as leaders than do the *pujāris* of the urban Rāmdev temples. Serving as the nucleus around whom a new group of devotees forms, a guru may also establish new temples, organize group pilgrimages and start local Rāmdev melās. He propagates

are of mixed caste. The devotees are predominantly first-generation city-dwellers, and it is striking that most of the 'ex-untouchables' among them brought Rāmdev to the city as their family deity whereas the artisans, Baniyās and Jains, knew him as a minor God with special powers. For the latter, Rāmdev has become more important in day-to-day life only after they came to the city, and it is among them that his cult seems to be spreading. Being uprooted, they perhaps find strength by reaching deeper into a part of their own tradition—through a cult flexible enough to mix a miraculous Rājpūt hero with *bhakti* egalitarianism and the binding experience of the bhajan sessions.[15]

The cult of Rāmdev, as B. N. Saraswati has pointed out, is fundamentally different from movements founded by poet-saints like Kabīr, Dādū or reformers like Nānak. He has indicated one basis of difference in describing "the saint-based *bhakti* cults (as) well-organized institutions with objectives clearly defined by their respective founders and subsequently elaborated by the corps of ascetic specialists." [16] As far as we know, Rāmdev did not leave behind a fixed body of scripture, a set of rituals or a system of belief. The cult has grown around the mythical figure of the heroic Rāmdev and not around his teachings. It has not developed into a sect with an exclusive identity;[17] there is no central cult leader or organization. Rāmdev's descendants have inherited his temple as a property, not a spiritual legacy. Thus we cannot know what Rāmdev's teachings may have been. Today's devotional pamphlets and bhajans present standard

the cult's teachings through his bhajans and his preaching. At least some of the gurus receive financial support from their followers. We saw no clear evidence of formal *guru-śiṣya* relationships or initiations.

[15] Our time with these urban groups was long enough only to provoke questions, for future study, regarding the Rāmdev cult as an urban phenomenon. It would be interesting to examine the cult's apparently successful adaptation to the pressures generated by urban life and its role in upward social mobility and group assertion in general. Also, Rāmdev's appeal must be understood in the context of the widespread upsurge in the popularity of gurus and 'god-men' in post-independence India.

[16] Personal communication.

[17] As is generally true of Hindu worship, there do not seem to be any groups or castes that worship Rāmdev to the exclusion of other Gods. The Meghvāls, for example, also worship Gaṇeśa, Śitalā, Mātās and Kṣetrapāls. The Bombay artisan-caste devotees also worship Ambāmā and Śiva. The minstrels of Rāmdev bhajans also sing compositions by Mīrābāī and Kabīr. Such non-exclusiveness may help to keep the cult open to other influences as Rāmdev devotees probably carry over some of the devotional practices and attitudes from one to another of the deities they worship.

homilies and injunctions to do good and live simply. Concern about the nature of ultimate reality, the soul, or salvation is not marked.

In the absence of fixed institutional structures, there appear to be two vehicles which have provided for the cult's transmission: the Rāmdev bhajans and his *samādhi* site. The bhajans were not composed by Rāmdev; they tell of him and his miraculous deeds. They combine the heroic and devotional, depicting Rāmdev as God-king, all-powerful father, compassionate savior, heroic conqueror, miracle-worker, problem-solver, and solace.[18] The existence of Rāmdev's grave site has made pilgrimage itself a force for the propagation of the cult.

The bhajans continue to be composed; the miracles, or *parcās* continue to happen. That the parcās continued after Rāmdev's death was taken as an important proof of his sainthood by his Muslim devotees. The parcās provide devotees with Rāmdev's 'life-story,' from his birth as Kṛṣṇa incarnate into the royal house of Pōkaran, to his final samādhi at Rāmdevrā.[19] They tell of a life devoted to rescuing people in distress; vanquishing dacoits, demons and Mughul armies; teaching the vanity of pride and falsehood; and winning a great many followers. Rāmdev performed parcās for the members of his own family, for kings and women, peddlers and merchants, untouchables and Muslims, devotees and doubters. Some of the miracles have a distinct practical bias, as when Rāmdev helped a merchant grow rich, made a bullock-less bullock cart move, or transformed his ugly bride into 'a most beautiful lady.' There are stories of Rāmdev bringing the dead back to life, turning dacoits into saints, and endowing pond-water with curative powers. Most striking are the tales of miracles Rāmdev performed to demonstrate his superior spiritual prowess to the Muslims. One story recounts a controversy between Rāmdev's devotees and the Hindu followers of a Muslim *pīr* (saint). The son of the latter group's leader suddenly falls ill and dies. The entire town is stunned. When Rāmdev arrives

---

[18] In the last decade or two, as records, radios and printed songbooks have become more widely available, new Rāmdev songs have proliferated. A few singer-composers have attained fame, performing in cities as distant as Madras and Bombay where devotees have opened new Rāmdev temples. Two feature films on the life of Rāmdev, produced in the mid-1960's, have reportedly made good profits.

[19] To his devotees, Rāmdev is an avatār of Kṛṣṇa not of Viṣṇu—a common theme in the bhakti tradition, but a bone of contention for orthodox brahmans who know the next incarnation of Viṣṇu, Kalki, is yet to come. Today the followers of certain gurus claim that these gurus are themselves avatārs of Rāmdev.

at the cremation ground, he declares that the boy is only sleeping and brings him back to life. The people turn away from the Muslim pīr and the boy's father becomes a devotee of Rāmdev. The ending is typical; in another story, the Muslim king of Delhi, having had his ears poisoned against Rāmdev, finds himself humbled by a demonstration of Rāmdev's superior spiritual power, promptly repents and becomes Rāmdev's devotee.

Because specific historical sources are lacking, it is not possible to do more than speculate about the role of Islam in the origin of the Rāmdev cult. Current cult tradition portrays Rāmdev as a great synthesizer of Hindu-Muslim differences. The cult, however, shows no blending of Islam and Hinduism at a doctrinal level. What remains today of the encounter with Islam are the stories of Rāmdev's spiritual triumphs over Muslim saints and kings; his Islamic appellations; the presence of Rāmdev's and his descendants graves in and around the temple and, above all, the fact of grave-worship. At Rāmdevrā, the central object of worship is a cloth-covered grave to which a silver mask of Rāmdev is sometimes affixed. The adjoining grave, said to be that of Rāmdev's mother, is inscribed with a Qur'ānic verse: "All that is done is the work of God—nothing lies in the hands of man." These Islamic elements are taken in stride by Hindu pilgrims and do not seem to play a significant role in their *darśan* experience. They suggest, however, that at one time the cult presented enough of a blend to make it possible for Muslims, especially the recently converted on whom Islam still sat lightly, to worship Rāmdev.

During the years when Rāmdev is said to have lived, Mārwāṛ was an independent Hindu kingdom, ruled from Mandōr by Chundā, Rinmul and Jōdhā of the Rathoṛ dynasty.[20] A year after Rāmdev's death, Jōdhā laid the foundation of Jodhpur which then became his capital. It was not until a hundred years later that an invasion from Delhi succeeded in Mārwāṛ, but invasions and battles with neighboring vassals of the Mughul emperors had been a fact of life for many years. The adjoining kingdom of Ajmer had first passed into Muslim hands at the end of the twelfth century, and *ṣūfīs* had begun making converts in Rājputānā not long after. Thus, although it remained under Hindu rule until a century after Rāmdev, during his time Mārwāṛ must have experienced the critical cultural challenge posed by Islam. In response to this challenge, various movements

[20] Markand Nandshankar Mehta and Manu Nandshankar Mehta, *The Hind Rajasthan*, Amritlal G. Shah, 1896.

developed in Rājputānā around heroes and saints, some of whom tried to bridge Hindu-Muslim differences, and some of whom conquered Muslims in battle.[21] In Rāmdev's case, whatever the actual coming-to-terms between Hindu and Muslim may have been, it seems to have been based in the parcās, the miracle tales narrating what amounts to Rāmdev's answer to the challenge of Islam.

It is revealing that the Rāmdev tradition refers to his miracles as *parcā*, a word that also means 'piece of paper, examination, evidence, power, proof.' [22] The miracle stories give evidence of Rāmdev's divine nature, proof of his superior spiritual power. The parcās thus suggest how a culturally beleaguered people may have tried to defend themselves, to 'prove' the power and validity of their faith. If they could 'prove' that even the threatening conquerors believed in their Rāmdev, that even the pīrs from Mecca bowed down to him, that he too was a pīr, then the pull of the magnet of Islam might diminish and those already converted might see a way of remaining within the Hindu fold. Perhaps it was in this way that Rāmdev became 'the God of Hindu and Muslim.' [23]

---

[21] Some of the many deified heroes have over the years developed highly specialized functions as, for example, the snakegods Gugā and Tejā. Some of these *pīrs*, hero cults and syncretic movements are discussed in Aziz Ahmad, *Studies in Islamic Culture in the Indian Environment* (Oxford: Oxford University Press, 1964), Chapter V; also Yusuf Husain Khan, *L'Inde Mystique au Moyen Age-Hindous et Musulmans* (Paris: Librairie d'Amérique et d'Orient, 1929); and William Crooke, *Religion and Folklore of Northern India*, edited by R. E. Enthoven (Oxford: Oxford University Press, 1926), Chapter V.

[22] Ramcandra Varma, *Manak Hindi Kos*, Hindi Sahitya Sammelan, Prayag, 1964; and Sitaram Lal, *Rajasthani Sabad Kos*, Caupasdin Shiksha Samiti, Jodhpur, V. S. 2026. *Parcā* is derived from the Persian *paracaḥ* and the Sanskrit *paricaya*. In Rajasthani, *parco* has the meanings given above, whereas in Hindi, Urdu and Gujarati, the meaning of 'miracle' is absent, and the current meanings are 'test, examination, piece of paper, proof.' However, two Hindi idioms have used *parcā* as the Rāmdev tradition does: *parcā denā*, 'to provide a hint or clue by the help of which people may know' and *parcā māgna*, 'to persuade a God or Goddess to reveal him or herself, his or her influence or power.' Colloquially, *parcā denā* also means 'to show one's strength or true colors.' (The bhajans and pamphlets about Rāmdev in circulation at Rāmdevrā are primarily in Rajasthani-Mārwāṛī, Gujarati and Hindi. Some are said to be in *Ḍingal*, an old literary dialect of Mārwāṛī, but this has not been verified.)

[23] Historically, the distinction between Muslim and Hindu custom has not been a rigidly demarcated one in Rājputānā. The self-consciously defined new Muslim identity is a relatively recent phenomenon. Because the new identity, purified of what are now considered to be Hindu influences, makes such religious expression as Rāmdev-worship less acceptable, and because of the emigration of Muslims to Pakistan and the closing of the border to pilgrim traffic in 1965, the progressive decline in Muslim attendance at Rāmdevrā is understandable. Para-

If today Rāmdev is no longer as much 'the God of Hindu and Muslim' as he once was, he is still the special God of the untouchables. The Rāmdev cult in its present form shares certain characteristics with the bhakti movement—the importance of a direct relation between the devotee and his God with a minimum of ritual and of specialist functionaries, the role of bhajans and of bhajan-meetings, and the commitment to egalitarian ideals.

It would be difficult to determine whether the cult of Rāmdev grew out of the bhakti tradition or simply out of the same historical circumstances that gave rise to bhakti, or whether it began merging into the bhakti stream only much later in its evolution. However, it seems reasonable to conclude that having started in response to the challenge of Islam, the Rāmdev tradition evolved as a deified-hero cult, with little or no structural or philosophical foundation. Instead of remaining a local, specialized phenomenon, as did many other hero cults, it seems to have taken on some of the coloration of the syncretic bhakti cults, as well as of the orthodox Hindu mainstream.

Compared to bhakti influence, the influence of brahmanic orthodoxy on the Rāmdev cult is sparse and, probably, much more recent.[24] Devotees can now buy pamphlets setting out the 'teachings' of Rāmdev and the rituals for special Rāmdev *pūjās*. There is a half-Sanskrit *mantra*, to be recited 108 times, in order to free the devotee from sin and ensure that Rāmdev grants his desires. In the Rāmdevrā bazaar, the legends of Rāmdev are sold under such titles as *Rāmdev Rāmāyaṇ*, *Śrī Rāmdev Brahmā Purāṇ*, *Śrī Rāmdev Gītā*. *Śrī Rāmdev Cālīsā*, and *Śrī Rāmdev Līlāmrit*. Brahmans are hired as *pujārīs* for the Rāmdev *samādhi* and they claim to use his parcās as a text during *ārati*. It is too early to tell what results such efforts towards Sanskritization are having on devotees' behavior, but they may be early signs of Rāmdevrā's transformation from an oral tradition site to a site with

---

doxically, whereas the boundaries delineating Muslim and Hindu practices become more sharply fixed, the myths of synthesis flourish.

[24] The link to Kṛṣṇa functions as a link to mainstream Hinduism in general, not necessarily to the Vaiṣṇavite rather than Śaivite branch. Though identified as an avatār of Kṛṣṇa, and depicted with the Vaiṣṇav mark, Rāmdev was also the disciple of a Śaivite guru. According to the tales of Rajasthani villagers, Rāmdev joined a *tantric panth* called 'mahādharam' with his devotee Ḍālībāī as partner. (G. M. Carstairs, *op. cit.*, p. 67). Similarly, Thareja cites the explanations given in current devotional pamphlets that Rāmdev joined a *tantric kuṇda panth* in order to abolish caste differences. (S. Thareja, *op. cit.*, Chapter II, p. 26). But no evidence of tantric influence in the present-day Rāmdev cult has become apparent.

its own '*sthala purāṇa*,' someday perhaps to become part of an all-India pilgrimage tradition.

Perhaps the evolution of the Rāmdev cult reveals both ends of a spectrum of flexibility—at its inception, an eclectic openness, reaching out to Muslims and untouchables, and eventually, partly to legitimize itself in a changed context, a reaching out to other castes and to elements of the brahmanic tradition. Thus, it would seem that a cult which developed its strength outside the realm of orthodoxy is now moving in the direction of that very orthodoxy. Borrowings from the brahmanic tradition appear, so far, to be limited to outward forms which do not substantially change the core of cult practices and beliefs.

## *The Sacred Complex at Rāmdevrā*

Rāmdev's gravesite is in the village of Rāmdevrā, Jaisalmer District, Rajasthan, in an area where the annual rainfall is measured in millimeters. Rāmdev is said to have founded the village, or to have died there in battle. There seem to be no written records to establish the origin of the village or the identity of the graves. The temple complex, on a hillock overlooking a small lake, is a short distance from the village and its railway station. The present Rāmdev temple, enlarged by the Mahārājā of Bikaner in 1913, contains fourteen graves.[25] According to the priests tending them, the *samādhis* in the main temple include those of Rāmdev, his sons, parents and other family members, his guru and some of his disciples.[26]

The temple pūjā is performed to Rāmdev's samādhi and it is to this grave that pilgrims come for darśan, bringing their offerings of small cloth horses, flags, coconuts, sweets, rice, flowers and money. A silver umbrella hangs above Rāmdev's cloth-covered grave and, on occasion, a silver mask of his face is attached to one end of the grave. Sitting in front of the grave, two priests accept the pilgrims'

[25] It was presumably at this time that some of the graves were realigned. Dr. Baidyanath Saraswati, in a personal communication, has suggested that the change in grave alignment may be an indication of the development of a 'brahmanic aesthetic standard' and of the blending of brahmanic and non-brahmanic elements in the 'ritualization of grave-worship' at Rāmdevrā.

[26] The priests say that the temple also holds the graves of several saints of Rāmdev's time, leading to questions about whether pilgrims still come specifically for darśan of these other saints or whether Rāmdev has eclipsed them, and how it came to pass, if indeed it did, that other saints came to be buried under Rāmdev's roof.

offerings and dispense *prasād* and water taken from Rāmdev's miracle well. The sanctum, like the temple itself, is accessible to all, regardless of caste or religion.

After Rāmdev's samādhi, the most important focus of pilgrims' devotions is a nearly life-size cloth horse of vivid colors, whose legs have darkened from the touch of many hands pressing them in worship. Crowded around the Rāmdev temple are graves, hero-stones and small shrines: shrines to Śiva, Hanumān, Hinglāyat Devī, Śrī Kailāś-Jabreśwar, and to Rāmdev's wife; shrines containing his relics; and a small temple to his female disciple Ḍālībāī, a Meghvāl foundling whom Rāmdev adopted.

The temple complex is a private enterprise, a complex patchwork of individual and group rights. The bulk of the collections from Rāmdev's samādhi (plus a share from some of the other shrines) is divided equally among the 300 families of Toṅwar Rājpūts of Rāmdevrā village who are considered Rāmdev's descendants and proprietors of the temple. The remaining portion of the samādhi collections is set aside for the support of the temple and its charitable work. The coconuts brought by pilgrims are shared by the Toṅwars with the Bhīls and Bhāmbis of the village.

The Toṅwars hire brahmans as 'temple servants' rather than Meghvāls or Kāmaḍs who are traditionally *pujārīs* of village Rāmdev temples. This gesture toward orthodoxy does not seem, however, to have resulted in an elaboration of ritual, nor to have created a need for more mediation by 'sacred specialists' between the pilgrims and Rāmdev. We observed no significant distinction between the hired brahman priests and the hereditary low-caste priests who tend the lesser shrines.[27] None of the priests seem to follow any prescribed form of behavior, nor do they wear the *tilak* or any other distinguishing mark or apparel. To the extent that they accept offerings and distribute prasād, priests of course play a role in the pilgrim's experience, but it is not an essential role. At the lesser-known *samādhis*, where no prasād is given and only the occasional devotee puts down a very small coin, priests are often absent, letting one man look after several graves.

The only important priestly ritual is the *āratī* performed five times

---

[27] The hereditary priests are descendants of Rāmdev's disciples, or of others who served him or were in their own ways devoted to him, such as potters, drummers and tailors.

daily to Rāmdev's samādhi during which the priest simply waves camphor, incense and the 'eternal flame' before the grave.[28]

For the participants in this pilgrimage, the primary experiences do not revolve around rituals. Even when rituals such as *muṇḍan* (haircutting) are involved, the primary experiences grow out of the vows and prayers that pilgrims bring with them. And central to all they experience is darśan, both of Rāmdev's grave and of the temple complex as a whole. Particularly important in the activities of pilgrims are the lake and the well, known for the miraculous curing power of their water, and the large old *jāl* tree in front of Rāmdev's temple, which wears the signs of its sacred power most colorfully. Its branches are hung with many-colored threads, blouses and scraps of cloth, tied there by women desiring a child and by men attesting to the fulfillment of a vow.[29]

Near the sacred complex are some small permanent buildings run by the temple trust. The trust provides for educating the village's children, caring for lepers, feeding *sādhus* and beggars, and providing drinking water for pilgrims—but not, it seems, for propagating the cult of Rāmdev. Around the charitable institutions and resthouses, many hundreds of tents and huts spring up each year at melā time.

In one of the Rāmdev bhajans the devotee sings:

> "Oh Bābā, my soul is captivated by the *melā*
> Oh people, go and mix in the color of Rām of Rānujā . . ." [30]

At melā time pilgrimage offers the chance to mix both in the color of Rāmdev and in diverse colors of people and sights not a part of ordinary life. At melā time Rāmdevrā village is transformed into a thriving bazaar town. From the villages and towns of Rajasthan,

---

[28] Although the priests said that there was a text for the *ārati*, they did not seem to use it during the crowded melā days. Clearly, texts and ritual were of minimal importance and could be treated casually. The blurring of distinction between sacred and non-sacred functionaries was demonstrated one day when the 'eternal flame' at Rāmdev's samādhi suddenly went out and was relit, not by the *pujārī* but by the policeman posted there to keep the stream of pilgrims flowing swiftly past the grave. Similarly, at Bombay Rāmdev temples, *pujārīs* are not specialists—in fact, anyone can fill the role. At one Bombay temple, the right to perform the *āratī* at the monthly pūjā is auctioned among the devotees, and the *pujārīs* at this temple include women.

[29] The relationship between Rāmdev and the power of this tree calls for more investigation. However, the tree appears to be viewed as a physical link to Rāmdev, a vehicle for transmitting his power.

[30] Rāmdevrā and Rānujā are names of the village in which Rāmdev's grave is located.

from as far as Agra and Hardwar, come craftsmen, peddlers and shopkeepers with all manner of wares—colorful sweets, painted clay pots, woven blankets, bangles, prayer beads, plastic lockets containing Rāmdev's image, stone carvings of his footprints, wooden and cloth horses. There are preachers, puppet shows, dramas, musicians, family planning films . . . and woven through it all (by the strolling bhajan-singers and the hawkers of Rāmdev's 'pictures') are the sounds and images of Rāmdev.

The melā's most vivid colors are mixed by the pilgrims themselves. Waiting in long lines at the temple and wandering through the bazaar are the villagers who come to Rāmdevrā on foot, on camelback, in bullock carts, trains and buses. Townspeople loaded with valises, briefcases and transistor radios make their way to the resthouses through dense crowds . . . a group of tribal women, each carrying an infant, pauses on its way out of the temple to listen to a bhajan . . . a sophisticated city girl in sunglasses stops to place flowers at a shrine . . . a famous devotee from Bombay rests after darśan while her car and chauffeur wait . . . The rush of running feet and shouts of 'Jai bolenge' signal the joyous arrival of a group of over a thousand pilgrims, men and women from Bikaner who had vowed to make the 140-mile pilgrimage on foot. After darśan of Rāmdev, the Bikaner pilgrims spend the day resting and celebrating their arrival at a mammoth *bhang* party.

Such pilgrimages provide many chances for social mixing and sharing. Rāmdevrā in general, compared to the large pilgrimage cities like Kāśī (Benares) and Madurai, offers considerable opportunity for social interaction. Mixing is encouraged by the absence of caste or religious restrictions anywhere in the sacred complex,[31] including the resthouses,[32] by the festive melā atmosphere, and by the shared faith in Rāmdev that brings pilgrims to this desert village where they are all strangers.

---

[31] I am grateful to Dr. Baidyanath Saraswati for his observations about the opportunities for social mixing at Rāmdevrā.

[32] According to S. Thareja, of the 50 resthouses at Rāmdevrā, 20 were built by shudra groups or individuals, 9 by vaishyas, 5 by kshatriyas, and 2 by brahmans. There are no restrictions at the resthouses—pilgrims of any caste may be accommodated, but generally upper-caste pilgrims do not stay in resthouses built by lower-caste groups. (S. Thareja, *op. cit.*, Chapter V, pp. 7-10.)

*A Pilgrimage to Rāmdevrā*

Bābā of Rānujā, remembrance of you comes to me,
My Bābā of Rānujā, remembrance of you comes to me,
Remembrance of you comes, Beloved, there is no sleep in the eyes,
My Bābā of Rānujā, remembrance of you comes to me.

Your temple is pleasing to my eye, the white flag flutters.
Your temple is pleasing, the white flag flutters.
From distant lands pilgrims come for your *darśan.*
My Bābā of Rānujā, remembrance of you comes to me.

Good rice, *halvā* and *pūrī*, sweet *cūrmā* are offered.
Good rice, *halvā* and *pūrī*, sweet *cūrmā* are offered.
Sitting in your court, everyday you eat *laḍḍū*,
Bābā of Rānujā, remembrance of you comes to me.
Remembrance of you—Oh, you with the flag, with the face I love,
Bābā of Rānujā, remembrance of you comes to me.

The main Rāmdevrā melā is held each year from the second to the eleventh of the bright half of the month of Bhadon (August-September). The last day is the anniversary of Rāmdev's samādhi. Over 100,000 pilgrims come to Rāmdevrā during this auspicious ten-day period.

To reach the melā, the group of pilgrims whose *yātrā* was the subject of the film, *An Indian Pilgrimage: Rāmdevrā*, travelled for twenty-four hours by third-class train from Bombay to Jodhpur, and then for about ten hours by a special bus which brought them directly to the melā grounds.[33] From Bombay they carried the requirements for their ten-day journey—bedding, clothing, cooked and uncooked food, and offerings for Bābā Rāmdev. They were thirteen women, three children and three men, and they had become a group for the purpose of this *yātrā*. In Bombay, they are part of a larger group of devotees who gather at a monthly bhajan session led by Dula Bhagat, a popular Rāmdev devotional singer whom they consider as their guru.[34]

Rāmdev was a familiar deity to the ancestors of these pilgrims, but

[33] The Government provides extra trains and several hundred buses to Rāmdevrā at melā time. The provision of such facilities, and the attendance at ceremonial functions of political figures (such as Members of Parliament, or the Cabinet Minister and harijan leader, Jagjīvan Rām) are sometimes interpreted as politically-motivated and related to the presence of large numbers of 'ex-untouchables' at Rāmdevrā.

[34] See Footnote 14.

not of central importance. A few of them are Jains; most belong to artisan castes and come from families that still perform their caste work.[35] Their economic level ranges from middle-class to quite poor, but most of the group is lower-middle-class. Two of the women are quite well-off — Sōnāben, who is married to an auditor, and Mīrāben, whose husband is the owner of a small workshop. The poorest person in the group, Trivenīben, came to Rāmdevrā with her only son and an infant daughter in order to discharge a vow she had made more than ten years earlier when she promised Bābā Rāmdev that if he granted her a son, she would bring the boy to him for darśan.

The pilgrims in this group are Gujaratis living in the Greater Bombay area, in widely scattered localities. This was the first Rāmdevrā *yātrā* for all except two, Nānīma and Sōnāben, who were also the most ebullient and indefatigable of the pilgrims. Nānīmā was more than 90 years old, a Jain of the *Sōnī* caste, and a long-time devotee of Rāmdev. During the last five years she had visited Rāmdevrā several times; once she saw a vision of Rāmdev. This time she wanted to request Bābā's blessings for her grandson's business. The grandson, who made inexpensive costume jewelry, was in his thirties, and accompanied her on this pilgrimage.

Some members of the group did not discuss their specific objectives for the pilgrimage. They included Hīrāben, a widow who runs a small tailor shop to support her family; Mīrāben, the workshop owner's wife, a woman of fervent devotion who, despite poor health, spends much of her time at temples and bhajan sessions; and two middle-aged childless couples. One of the middle-aged men, Dhanjībhāī, a flower-seller, acted as leader, or coordinator, for the *yātrā*, although he was not in any way the group's spiritual leader.

They reached the melā grounds early on the morning of September 14th, 1972, five days before Rāmdev's samādhi-anniversary. They were assigned a small room at a *dharamśālā* (resthouse) in which they changed clothes, locked up their belongings before going out, and where they retreated now and then for a private argument or exchange of confidences. At night, bedding was unrolled in the verandah near

---

[35] These pilgrims' caste occupations included tailor, carpenter, goldsmith, utensil-maker. All, except one fisherman family, were artisans. Among the pilgrims Thareja interviewed at the 1972 melā, more than one-quarter identified themselves as belonging to 'artisan, Jain or other business communities,' and about one-quarter came from urban areas. (S. Thareja, *op. cit.*, Chapter III).

this room, or on the roof of the dharamśālā. During the day, the verandah provided a place for cooking, resting, getting to know each other better, and mixing with pilgrims from other places.

Soon after arriving in Rāmdevrā, they dressed in their best clothes and prepared for the main group event of the pilgrimage, a procession to the temple where they would have darśan of Rāmdev's samādhi and make a collective offering. From Bombay they had brought a small silver statue of Rāmdev on horseback. In addition, they borrowed from the temple a much larger silver horse for which they made a donation of Rs. 100. The silver horses, along with small cloth horses, flags, incense and a clay lamp, were placed on a large brass platter and carefully decorated with a profusion of flowers which Dhanjībhāī had brought from his flower stall in Bombay.[36] After a brief pūjā, they sprinkled auspicious red powder on the horses and on each other, and set out for the temple. Their procession was accompanied by hired musicians. At its head were men carrying elaborately decorated flags to be offered to Rāmdev and then hoisted to the top of his temple. The silver horses rode on a tray on the head of Sōnāben, who was on her eleventh pilgrimage to Rāmdevrā. The majestic temple horse, riderless, dominated the procession.[37]

By the time their procession reached the temple, the weight of the brass platter on the sweating woman's head, their concern for protecting her burden as they made their slow way through the waiting

---

[36] The chief symbols of Rāmdev are the horse, flag and his footprints. The small silver statue the pilgrims brought from Bombay showed Rāmdev as he is most commonly depicted, astride his horse. The larger silver horse they borrowed from the temple was riderless. When Rāmdev's horse is worshipped riderless, his invisible presence is said to be understood. His horse was the inseparable companion of his miracle deeds, and itself possessed some miraculous attributes. The horse's ubiquitous presence in Rāmdev-worship may reflect the popularity and power of the horse image in Rājputānā as well as specific recognition of Rāmdev's horse as an embodiment of some of his power.

The flags which pilgrims bring as offerings range from tiny banners to grand silk and spangle creations that flutter in the desert wind from the top of Rāmdev's temple. But they all hark back to the medieval warrior's banner fluttering atop his lance. The lance and banner are called *nejā* and Rāmdev is 'the God with the powerful *nejā*.' The red footprints on Rāmdev's banner signify that he is an avatār of Kṛṣṇa. Rāmdev is often shown with the *nejā* in his left hand while his right is raised as in the *abhaya mudrā*. The assurance of protection given by his right hand is reinforced by the left, holding the emblem of both earthly and spiritual power.

[37] When the offering had been made, one of the priests, returning the borrowed silver horse to safekeeping in a storeroom, sauntered out of the temple nonchalantly carrying the horse by its ear, in striking contrast to its ceremonial entry a short while earlier.

line of pilgrims outside the temple, their anxiety that none of their group be left behind in passing through the narrow temple entrance, the extreme heat and crowding of the dark, confined space around the samādhi—all combined to make their approach to the moment of darśan arduous and tense. Reaching Rāmdev's samādhi at last, they were hurried by the priests through the horse-offering, pushed and jostled by other pilgrims as they quickly performed their pūjā and tried to reach for prasād—and they were outside. Their moment at Rāmdev's samādhi had passed very swiftly. During the remainder of their stay, most of them returned two or three times daily for darśan of Rāmdev.

Every night some of the Bombay pilgrims sat up until dawn beside the miracle lake of Rāmdev, singing his bhajans. If they stay awake for three consecutive nights beside Rāmsarovar, singing bhajans, they may see a vision of Rāmdev, or receive his *jyōt darśan*, experiencing his presence through a bright light in the sky. Then their desires may be granted. Pilgrims who can afford it also honor Rāmdev by paying to have bhajans performed by professional singers. All day, singing groups from the traditional castes of Rāmdev-devotees wander around the melā grounds and the dharamśālās, looking for new arrivals. Except perhaps during the afternoon lull for rest after the noon meal, the sound of cymbals and singing voices is always in the air—at Rāmdevrā the pilgrim can worship Rāmdev, by singing or by being still and listening, throughout the day and night.

On their first day at Rāmdevrā, right after offering the silver horse, the women went to an open field near the temple and joined another group of women in singing Rāmdev bhajans. In the hot afternoon sun they formed a circle, clapping their hands in rhythm to the song, and began to dance. Very soon the wife of the workshop owner, Mīrāben, went into trance and was taken by the other women to the shrine of Rāmdev's female disciple, Ḍālībāī. Mīrāben fell onto the ground and prostrated herself in front of Ḍālībāī's samādhi. The other women put prasād into her mouth and, as she rose and began to dance again, they continued clapping and chanting in a protective circle around her. Not long after Mīrāben's darsan the spirits of Rāmdev had 'entered' her.[38] The other women supported and protected her, enabling her in

[38] Later we learned that in Bombay Goddess Ambāmā also occasionally 'enters' Mīrāben. At this time, in Rāmdevrā, Mīrāben did not speak. In Bombay, at some bhajan sessions, when a devotee becomes possessed by Rāmdev, the others ask questions and request guidance from the one possessed.

A stone carver who sells images of Rāmdev in the Rāmdevrā bazaar.

A picture of Rāmdev decorates a sweet shop in the Rāmdevrā bazaar.

One of the many hereditary singers of Rāmdev *bhajans* who come to Rāmdevrā at the time of the *mela*.

The graves of Rāmdev and his mother, inscribed with Qur'anic verses, with a collection box, coconuts, sweets, and other offerings in the foreground.

Pilgrims returning home. Most pilgrims come to Rāmdevrā from surrounding rural areas.

Mīrāben, in trance, after the spirit of Rāmdev had 'entered' her.

Photographs, by Michael Camerini, Yagya Sharma and Mira Binford, were taken during the filming of *An Indian Pilgrimage*: *Ramdevra*, produced and distributed by the South Asian Area Center, University of Wisconsin, Madison, Wisconsin.

this crowded place to sustain a very personal experience of her God.

That same crowded first day at the melā some of the women accompanied Trivenīben for her son's *muṇḍan* (haircutting) ceremony, completing the vow she had taken when, after six daughters, she asked Rāmdev to grant her a son. She vowed then that she would not wear her marriage necklace until she had brought the boy to Rāmdevrā. Now, after taking her son for darśan, Trivenīben put on the *mangalsūtra* she had not worn for eleven years.[39]

For the privilege of making their flag and horse offerings, the pilgrims had to pay a collective fee to the temple. In addition, they took individual small offerings whenever they went to the temple for darśan. Although many pilgrims at Rāmdevrā no doubt cannot afford to make an offering of money, the total collected during the 1972 melā was estimated at Rs. 300,000.[40]

Wherever they moved on the melā grounds, they were reminded that almsgiving is one of the basic 'meritorious acts' of pilgrimage. Preachers in their tents held forth on the subject, others roamed about soliciting donations for their charities. Beggars waited in the bazaar lanes and lined the long uphill approach road to the temple. Huge cauldrons of rice and lentils were prepared daily for beggars and sādhus by the Rāmdev Annakṣetra, for which donations were also solicited. Some of the pilgrims gave money for the enlarging of Lake Rāmsarovar. For one rupee, twenty donkey-loads of sand were removed. Donkeys could be seen slowly trudging up and down the banks of the lake day after day. In the desert heat, in Rāmdevrā where no rain had fallen for ten years, this seemed meritorious work indeed.

[39] For Trivenīben, Rāmdev's powers seem to have been confined to traditional concerns. Rāmdev could grant her a son, but this son was her seventh living child and, when Trivenīben subsequently gave birth to yet another daughter, she started saving money for a tubectomy. She did this before saving for the pilgrimage to fulfill her vow to Rāmdev, and seems not to have appealed to Rāmdev to help her stop having children.

[40] The figure of Rs. 300,000, estimated by the civil authorities in 1972, compares with Rs. 90,000 collected twelve years earlier, as reported in the Census of India, 1961 (*op. cit.*). There does not seem to have been a corresponding increase in the number of pilgrims attending the melā. Figures in this realm are notoriously unreliable but a guess that collections may be growing along with an increase in the proportion of relatively more well-to-do urban pilgrims may be supported by the spurt in dharamśālā construction during the same period. Of the fifty rest-houses at Rāmdevrā, only three were built in the decade of the fifties, whereas twenty-six were built during the sixties. Outside of Rāmdevrā, new temples have been constructed and new melās started, also suggesting the flow of new money toward Rāmdev.

On the second day of their five-day stay at Rāmdevrā, the Bombay pilgrims embarked on a trip away from the sacred complex. Their destination was a series of sites associated with Rāmdev, and the excursion as a whole revealed the ease with which tourism or adventure can be integrated into any pilgrimage. They visited the shops in the nearby town of Pōkaran and stopped at the samādhi of Rāmdev's guru and at his ancestral castle.[41] Pōkaran Fort is said to have been the seat of Rāmdev's father. It is a sprawling old castle, run-down but grand, with a commanding view of the surrounding countryside. Visitors with some imagination should be able to reconstruct more heroic Rājpūt days. A group of village pilgrims saw more. Walking through room after room full of photographs of recent generations of the castle's occupants, posed stiff and dignified, with proper martial moustaches, the villagers would pause and point out to each other: "This is a picture of Rāmdev and his brother . . . this shows his father . . . this is Rāmdev on his horse . . ." and so on.

Outside the shrine of Rāmdev's guru, the Bombay pilgrims learned a tradition new to them. They found other pilgrims squatting down to arrange piles of small stones into 'bungalows,' thereby assuring themselves of fine homes in heaven. Some of the Bombay pilgrims laughed at first, but not one failed to build his or her 'bungalow,' making it as tall as possible. When they finished, another group of pilgrims came along, dismantled their constructions and started building anew.

On the fourth day in Rāmdevrā, a few members of the group left to return to Bombay. The rest had the chance to make another small yātrā which reflected their fluid definition of pilgrimage. Sōnāben, the energetic veteran of ten Rāmdevrā yātrās, tried to stir the group's interest in going to the place where Rāmdev performed miracles for the *Pāñc Pīr* from Mecca,[42] a place she remembered from a long-ago

---

[41] The Bombay pilgrims omitted another part of the Rāmdev pilgrimage which is performed by some devotees—a twenty-five mile walk around the city of Jodhpur, stopping at a cave where Rāmdev's guru meditated, and a park with life-size statues of Rāmdev and a dozen other Rājpūt heroes on horseback. However, the pilgrims found it natural to combine what was basically a 'Rāmdev pilgrimage' with stops at Mt. Ābū and Ambājī, shrines that are sacred to other deities and have no connection to Rāmdev.

[42] The five Muslim saints heard about Rāmdev's powers and, full of jealousy, they came to test him. After performing several miracles, including reviving a servant who had died of snakebite, Rāmdev asked the *Pāñc Pīr* to sit on a carpet so small there was only room for one. But as soon as they sat down, there was room for all of them. Rāmdev offered them food. They refused, saying they had

visit. Somehow they could not get clear directions, and the rest of the group was reluctant. Sōnāben recalled seeing five sacred *nīm* trees, testimony to the miracles Rāmdev worked to dispel the skepticism of the five Muslim saints. Her enthusiasm was persuasive. Eventually, two bullock carts were hired, at exorbitant rates. One of the drivers said he knew the way. They set out in the afternoon glare, trying to hold on to each other to keep from falling off the flat-bed carts while also holding above their heads a thick blanket to ward off the sun's rays . . .

After bumping through the desert long enough for all to become thoroughly desiccated, the drivers admitted that they were lost. That the group finally reached its destination was due to a *deus ex machina* introduced by the film team—a jeep. Making several trips, it at last brought the group to what was—clearly—the right place. A small shrine stood in the dense shade of ancient trees, a few wealthy pilgrims, who had arrived by car, rested under a tree, and a group of shepherds, Muslims and Hindus, chatted together under another tree while herds of sheep and camels drank at the water-hole. They had reached an oasis. Although none of the pilgrims had much 'information' about it, they knew that this was a sacred place, and its darśan was desirable. The link to Rāmdev made it an integral part of their pilgrimage. They would tell other pilgrims about the place of the *Pāñc Pīr*, and of the five sacred *nīm* trees.[43]

---

left their vessels in Mecca, whereupon Rāmdev miraculously summoned their bowls from Mecca. The *Pāñc Pīr* realized the error of their doubts, addressed Rāmdev as '*pīr*' and requested his blessings. He presented them with a tree branch which flew them straight to Mecca, and there took root and grew into a huge shady tree.

[43] The oasis is near the village of Malasar. A group of five saints is worshipped in many parts of India under the name *Pāñc Pīr*, although the identity of the five varies from place to place, sometimes including both Hindu and Muslim saints. Crooke's theory about the *Pāñc Pīr* may be improbable, but it is nevertheless suggestive of the way the popular mind links different levels of the tradition. He writes that in western India, the title of *Pāñc Pīr* is "sometimes given to five Rājpūt heroes, Ramdeo, Pabu, Harbu, Mallinath and Guga, and it is at least a plausible theory that the five Pirs may have originally been the five Pandu brothers, whose worship has . . . become degraded, been annexed by the lower Musulmans, and again taken over by their menial Hindu brethren." (William Crooke, *The Popular Religion and Folklore of Northern India*, *op. cit.*, p. 206). To clinch the parallel with the five Pāṇḍavas, Crooke points out that Rāmdev is "now known as Deva Dharma Raja, which is one of the titles of Yama, the god of death, and Yudhishthira, his putative son." (W. Crooke, *ibid.*, p. 200). As pointed out on page 122 of this essay, the Toṅwar Rājpūt clan to which Rāmdev belonged traced its lineage to Yudhiṣṭhira.

Obviously, pilgrimage is a flexible form of religious expression which allows the pilgrim considerable creativity. Pilgrimage to Rāmdevrā illustrates the ways in which new symbols, new saints, heroes and Gods, and new reasons for making the journey can be accommodated within the larger structure of pilgrimage. At Rāmdevrā one can see the process whereby a local oral-tradition site becomes integrated into the all-India pilgrimage tradition. In his essay on pilgrimage sites in the Indian tradition, Bharati [44] shows the wide range of alternatives Hindu pilgrimage encompasses—in its variety of types of sacred sites and their functions and, most strikingly, in the variety of the pilgrims' objectives.[45] Elsewhere, Bharati states: "Every pilgrimage has a strictly defined purpose and scope; and the procedure is exactly prescribed, with rather little leeway for the individual's ingenuity in matters relating to travel." [46] In making this observation he cannot have in mind this level of folk pilgrimage, in which nothing is prescribed as it is at *purāṇic* sites such as Gayā or Kāśī (Benares).[47] Prescriptions are oral, optional and can be disregarded without damaging one's chances of attaining the goal of the pilgrimage. The pilgrim is guided not by texts or priests, but by the experience of previous pilgrims, by his own imagination and ingenuity, and by his needs. He may receive Rāmdev's blessing regardless of whether he stays up singing for three nights or makes a particular offering in a particular way.

Since nothing is prescribed, observances become desirable or

[44] See "Pilgrimage Sites and Indian Civilization" by Agehananda Bharati, in Joseph W. Elder (ed.), *Chapters in Indian Civilization*, Vol. 1 (Dubuque: Kendall/Hunt, 1970), pp. 83-126.

[45] For an extensive bibliography of sources on Hindu pilgrimage, see S. M. Bhardwaj, *Hindu Places of Pilgrimage in India* (*A Study in Cultural Geography*). (Berkeley: University of California Press, 1973). This essay was written before I had seen Bhardwaj's field-study of pilgrims' attitudes and behavior. However, with the exception of Ujjain in Madhya Pradesh, his research was conducted exclusively in the Himālayan region.

[46] "Pilgrimage in the Indian Tradition" by Agehananda Bharati, in *History of Religions*, Vol. III, I (Summer 1962), Part I, p. 137.

[47] Even the auspicious time for pilgrimage is not rigorously observed at Rāmdevrā. The pilgrims in the Bombay group left Rāmdevrā before the samādhi anniversary day, as did most other pilgrims. Because of the shortage of water and accommodations and the extreme heat and crowding during the melā days, many devotees prefer to plan their pilgrimage for another time. Attendance figures for the melā period thus no longer reflect the increase in the total number of pilgrims coming to Rāmdevrā. However, the emerging attendance pattern may mark a qualitative shift as Rāmdevrā moves from being primarily a melā-site to an all-year-round site.

necessary largely in proportion to the pilgrim's need, and a strong element of uncertainty must remain. Ranjan, a young girl suffering from leucoderma, and her mother had tried a severe regime of fasting in Bombay without obtaining the hoped-for cure. They had heard that at each melā Bābā Rāmdev works a small number of miraculous cures and, with great difficulty, they managed to meet the cost of the journey. Ranjan's mother anxiously sought suggestions from other pilgrims about what was to be done at Rāmdevrā. At the *Pāñc Pīr* site she collected the bark of a tree said to have curative powers, planning to apply it to Ranjan's skin.

Although most pilgrims come to Rāmdevrā with specific desires, these are inextricably mixed with the darśan experience and with the sense of spiritual well-being that comes from engaging in a 'meritorious act.' The range of motivation in the Rāmdevrā pilgrimage is indicated by two of the Bombay pilgrims. Sōnāben, coming back year after year out of gratitude for a prayer answered, seems to find in her annual pilgrimage a way of reaffirming Rāmdev as a strong and vital center in her life. She seeks out and relishes group devotional activities, whether bhajan-singing, bearing the horse-offering to the temple, or drawing the entire group into the adventure of rediscovering a half-remembered sacred place. In Mīrāben one senses an overflowing fervor which might be difficult to contain in the confines of her middle-class existence without the kind of exchange of energy that must take place when she becomes possessed by Bābā Rāmdev. Focused on Bābā Rāmdev in a way that is impossible in ordinary life, pilgrims open themselves to this kind of intense devotional experience. For some few days they put themselves in a time out of time in which the primary experience is bhakti. They hear other pilgrims tell of their encounters with the divine power of Rāmdev, they hear of miracles that happened long ago and those that happened yesterday.[48] Again and again, standing in line outside the temple with thousands of others, they are part of a great mass of people, all of whom worship Rāmdev. Cumulatively such experiences result in a kind of confirmation. Although it is an interior process, it has an exterior dimension too—for whether the pilgrim comes to Rāmdevrā to give thanks or to appeal for Rāmdev's intervention in present problems, his coming is a public declaration of his devotion.

[48] Before boarding the train at Rāmdevrā station on the first leg of their return journey to Bombay, the pilgrims had heard that "one lame girl from Bikaner and one blind man from someplace else regained their lost strength and eyesight during this *melā*."

Mixing 'in the color of Rām of Rānujā,' spending days and nights in worship, and, above all, passing through the experience of darśan—being in the presence of Rāmdev in this his most sacred place—pilgrims emerge with a renewed sense of devotion. Even if none of the miracles of this melā happened to them, they return to mundane life more deeply confirmed in the faith of Rāmdev. At their local Rāmdev temple, at an all-night bhajan session, they may again sing:

"Bābā of Rānujā, remembrance of you comes to me . . ."

# THE MEDIEVAL BHAKTI MOVEMENT IN HISTORY

## *An Essay on the Literature in English*

ELEANOR ZELLIOT

Historians of India, perhaps more than those of any other area, feel the need for an understanding of the historical implications of religious developments. The questions are many, and they come both early and late in a review of Indian history. Almost all we know about the Aryans comes from the sacred Vedas; we ponder the relationship of Buddhism to the rise of the Indian state; fifteen hundred years later, we look to see how renascent Hinduism and revived Islam intertwine with nationalism. And, between the ancient and the modern lies the *bhakti* movement, the spread of a personal devotional faith. Its roots are in the far past, its flowering is still apparent today, its place in history is puzzling and fascinating.

Here I should make clear that I am speaking of bhakti not as a religious *concept* of devotional worship but as a *movement*, the phenomenon of a set of religious ideas and structures first seen in the South in the 7th century and slowly sweeping up to the North by the 15th century. The very use of the word "movement," which does not appear in a discussion of any other facet of Hinduism until the modern period, implies an historic place. Bhakti has been credited with securing the final triumph of Hinduism over Jainism and Buddhism, with bringing the vernaculars into being as literary languages, with spreading the concepts of the Great Tradition of brahmanical Hinduism to the common man, with reconciling Hinduism and Islam, with reviving Hinduism in the face of the Muslim threat, with providing the ethos for the last great Hindu kingdom in India, that of the Marāṭhās. The saint-poets of the bhakti movement have been compared with Christian mystics, who, however, left behind them no movements. The bhakti movement has been seen as the Indian counterpart of the Protestant Reformation, with one or another of its poet-saints, usually Kabīr, sometimes Caitanya, filling the role of Luther.

It is also possible to write the bhakti movement small, or so broad it loses its historicity. It is true that many of its regional groups can be seen as Mandelbaum (1970, p. 523) described religious sects, i.e., "movements to reorganize society," but "equality rather than hierarchy among all believers was a common theme, and in almost all these movements the devotees finally came to sort themselves into jatis [endogomous castes] and to act like other jati members in their local order." Contemporary saints and religious figures, especially Mohandas K. Gandhi, have been described as *bhaktas*. As Louis Renou wrote, "There is no sect [or, indeed, Hindu movement] without some element of Bhakti" (quoted in Mandelbaum, p. 533).

I will not attempt to substantiate any of these claims or to deal with bhakti in its broad context. My essay will review the medieval bhakti movement in the various language areas in rough chronological fashion and with great brevity, noting the basic literature in English available and raising a few questions along the way in an attempt to see where we stand in viewing this many-faceted, multi-language movement as a whole. My excuse for this audacious attempt is that a wealth of literature has appeared in English, current scholarship is rich, and my curiosity moves me. Recently, three of my students have written undergraduate papers on the Sikh Gurus, the Liṅgāyats, and Śaiva bhakti in the South, and we were forced to ask together: if bhakti in Punjab became the militant Sikh nation, if bhakti in Karnataka became a non-conformist caste-like sect within Hinduism, if bhakti in Madras was thoroughly interwoven with brahmanical religion and orthodox temple worship, then what exactly is the place of the bhakti movement in history?

The elements of each medieval bhakti group generally are these: saint-poets, known by name and surrounded by legendary history, singing songs of devotion to Kṛṣṇa, Rāma or Śiva in the common language of their area; a companionship among these saints, knowledge of one another and at times of poet-saints in other areas; inclusion of all castes and of women among the saint-poets; an anti-ritual or non-ritualistic attitude, sometimes iconoclastic, sometimes deprecating of orthodoxy, with full trust only in devotional experience; and, a continuance of structure from the original saint-poets: a succession of poets or *gurus*, an order, a lay community, a pilgrimage, a festival, a caste-like group, a community devotional singing of the songs called a *bhajan* or a *kīrtan*. There seem to be exceptions to all these bench marks. Each regional bhakti movement shares something in common with others, but no two seem to have identical structures, attitudes, influences, or histories.

My brief notes on the various regional forms of the bhakti movement concentrate on three of these areas, all related to my basic interest in the historical aspects of bhakti: (1) the vernacular literature of the saint-poets; (2) the linkages between various bhakti saints and movements; and (3) the new or different forms emerging in each bhakti movement.

The first area, that of literature, seems more and more important as I look at each successive wave of poet-saints. Shashibhushan Dasgupta (1946, pp. xxxi, xxxiii), the Bengali historian of "obscure religious cults," wrote: "The origin and growth of the modern Indian literatures (we mean the modern Indo-Aryan literatures) was closely associated with the origin and growth of some religious sects . . . Bengali, along with other Indo-Aryan languages, grew up with the tenets of some minor religious sects, which rose mostly outside the circle of the high class people and were characterized by a general tendency of protest against current orthodox religious systems." A close relationship of bhakti saint-poets and the growth of vernacular literature holds true for all movements except that of Tamilnādu, where didactic and heroic poetry existed in Tamil long before the 7th century bhakti saint-poets wrote. Everywhere else, either a founding saint-poet or his immediate disciples created poetry which was among the first literature in the tongue of the area. The association of the bhakti movement with the literary use of the regional languages is a tempting field of exploration in terms of regional development.

New translations of bhakti poetry by *poets* have added to my interest in this area. Their work has released bhakti literature from the banality and sententiousness to which it had long been condemned, making far more understandable the influence of bhakti poetry upon literary development. Those which have been especially meaningful to me are Kolatkar's brief selection from the Maratha poet Tukārām (1966), the Dimock-Levertov *In Praise of Krishna* (1967) from the Bengali, Ramanujan's *Speaking of Śiva* (1973) from the Kannada, and Arvind Krishna Mehrotra's fragments of Kabīr (1971). Paul Althaus' *Mystic Lyrics from the Indian Middle Ages* (1928) is without scholarly apparatus and does not reach the heights of the poets above, but the double translation (Hindi and Marathi through German to English) has produced a moving simplicity. Tagore's *Songs of Kabir* (1915) is to my mind lovelier than any other poetry he wrote in English, but it is more Tagore's bhakti than Kabīr's. Other translations are often competent, but few give the reader a sense that he is reading literature, the great poetry of a people.

My second interest, the inter-relationships of the bhakti saint-poets, works both in the direction of the development of regional identities and in the exploration of cross-region cultural contacts in medieval India. Many saint-poets mention other saints in their work; each saint is surrounded with legendary history; in three language areas, collected lives of the saints were written shortly after the high point of the movement. We have neither name nor legend for the author of the great bhakti Sanskrit text, the *Bhāgavata Purāṇa*, which was written no earlier than the 10th century, nor for much other religious literature in Sanskrit. The historicity of the bhakti saint-poets might well be used for history. Many saints travelled widely, most acknowledge the other saints who influenced them. The 10th century *Periya-Purāṇam*, lives of the Tamil Śaiva saints, by Sekkilār; the early 17th century Hindi *Bhakta Mālā* (garland of devotees) by Nābhāji and its 18th century gloss; and the 18th century Marathi *Bhaktavijaya* and *Bhaktalīlāmṛta* by Mahīpati not only collect the legends that exist around every saint but indicate who was considered to be within the general bhakti religious tradition. Legend both reveals and obscures the relationships of the medieval saints, but I think a close reading of the material available might produce some new theories about medieval culture contacts.

The third area, that of specific changes, of new structures which arose from the bhakti movement, is an attempt to get beyond general intellectual influence to see the mechanics of change. Mahadeo Govind Ranade (1900) claimed that the circle of saint-poets in the Marathi-speaking, area produced the spirit of the Māraṭhā Kingdom, and one can actually see that the structure which developed in Maharashtra, that of pilgrim bands journeying at a specific time through the countryside to one point, might well have been a force for unity. Burton Stein has shown for the medieval Tamil-speaking area how very specific changes in temple ritual brought shudras for a time into the temple. But historians generally have not dealt with institutional changes but rather with intellectual history.

Here again, new directions in scholarship add to our image of the *actuality* of the bhakti movement. One cannot work backward from contemporary portraits of bhakti in action, but the pictures created by the scholar who is also participant-observer allow us to speculate more clearly on possible ways of influence in the past. Irawati Karve began this trend with "On the Road," a moving essay on her participation in the Maratha bhakti pilgrimage to Paṇḍharpur.

Dimock (1967) not only describes a Bengali village kīrtan but arranges his song translation in kīrtan order so that his book becomes a service of praise in the Bengali tradition. Milton Singer gives something of the flavor of Rādhā-Kṛṣṇa bhajans in Madras City as well as their social significance. Surajit Sinha describes the Bengali religious tradition in its missionary endeavours with tribal cultures, a phenomenon credited to Bengali and Assamese bhakti several centuries ago.

Other issues I would like to deal with but cannot here are the relationship of the bhakti saint-poets to the State, the connections of the bhakti circles with various sects (Gorakhnāth, Mādhva, etc.), and the modern use of bhakti song-literature and sects in reform movements.

It will be noted that I have left out all references to Sufism and to the Muslim followers of the Rāmānanda panth in this essay. The relationship of Muslim and Hindu mysticism in thought and practice presents complexities beyond the scope of this already too complex essay and deserves a more thorough study than I am able to give it. The interaction of Sufism and bhakti is of undeniable historic importance, and I leave this area neglected with great reluctance.

The other vast area omitted is that of philosophy, metaphysics, the bhakti tenets of belief.* Interested readers will find, however, that most of my reference concentrate on belief rather than historical consequences.

Literature in English on the bhakti movement begins with H. H. Wilson's vastly prejudiced and astonishingly knowledgeable study of religious sects, first published in *Asiatic Researches* in 1828 and 1832. He did not recognize a bhakti *movement*, but described the sects of the North in such detail that the reader may glean some history and linkages. Wilson understood all sects, bhakti and otherwise, to be similar entities, but noted that "the terms Bhakta, or Bhagat, usually indicate any individual who pretends to a more rigid devotion than his neighbours" (1862 ed, pp. 15-16). Considerations of bhakti chiefly as sects appear also in Pai (1928), with wondrous illustrations, in Ghurye (1953) and in Bhandarkar (1913), who felt Vaiṣṇava religious reform soon became sectarian.

Bhakti on a regional basis was first discussed by missionary-

* For a bibliography on the doctrines of bhakti, see Norvin J. Hein, "Hinduism," in *A Reader's Guide to the Great Religions*, edited by Charles J. Adams (New York: The Free Press, 1968), pp. 60-69.

scholars who found in it the religion closest to Christian morality and devotion. Brief articles began to appear in the mid-19th century, with translations of "hymns" and "psalms" and thorough studies of bhakti schools following in the 20th. Recently, Jesuit scholars (Deleury, 1960 and Dhavamony, 1971) have done unbiased scholarly work on the cult of Viṭhobā in Maharashtra and Śaiva Siddhānta in the South.

Indian scholars began some critical work in the 19th century, but the great tomes on bhakti and the competent surveys of literature which put bhakti in its literary context appeared chiefly in the 1930's and '40's. Bengal, Madras, Gujarat and Maharashtra were covered with considerable thoroughness during this period, and it is on these works and translations that the historian must concentrate for the investigation of bhakti as history. To my mind, the most stimulating volume available is Shashibhushan Dasgupta's work on early Bengali cults.

Recently, a few over-all considerations of the bhakti movement have appeared, the most useful being V. Raghavan's *The Great Integrators*, which contains the broadest range of translations. The National Book Trust and the Sāhitya Akademi have begun a series of biographies which are not original scholarship but competent summaries of available material and translations of selected poetry. The Maharashtra Information Centre has performed a similar service for Jñānadeo, Eknāth and Tukārām.

J. N. Farquhar's painstaking *Outline of the Religious Literature of India* and James Hastings' magnificent *Encyclopaedia of Religion and Ethics* are dated but invaluable reference sources for almost every bhakti figure mentioned in this essay. Selections from saint-poets are available to the general reader in the anthologies edited by William Theodore de Bary and Ainslee Embree. A new approach to bhakti is represented by *Krishna: Myths, Rites and Attitudes*, edited by Milton Singer, which combines theology and anthropology in a creative way.

The bibliography which follows each section is limited to sources in English available in the United States. Much material is also available in French and German, from sectarian headquarters, and in other general histories of regional literature.

## GENERAL BIBLIOGRAPHY

*Translations*:

Alphonso-Karkala, John B., ed. *An Anthology of Indian Literature*. Middlesex: Penguin Books, 1971. (See "Age of Bhaktas," pp. 481-570.)

Althaus, Paul, tr. *Mystic Lyrics from the Indian Middle Ages*. Rendered into English [from German] by R. T. Gribble. London: George Allen and Unwin, 1928.

de Bary, William Theodore, ed. *Sources of the Indian Tradition*. Vol.1. New York: Columbia University Press, 1964 (1958). (See "The Songs of the Saints of Medieval Hinduism," pp. 345-360.)

Embree, Ainslee T., ed. *The Hindu Tradition*. New York: Modern Library, 1966. (See "The Traditions and the People's Faith," pp. 227-270.)

*Other Works*:

Behari, Bankey. *Minstrels of God*. Bombay: Bharatiya Vidya Bhavan, 1970.

——. *Sufis, Mystics and Yogis of India*. Bombay: Bharatiya Vidya Bhavan, 1971. (Includes translations of Jñāneśwar, Nānak, Kabīr, Nāmdev.)

Bhandarkar, R. G. *Vaiṣṇavism, Śaivism and Minor Religious Systems*. Varanasi: Indological Book House, 1965 (1913).

*Cultural Heritage of India*. Vol. IV. Calcutta: Rama Krishna Missions Institute, 1956. (Includes several articles by various authors.)

*Cultural Heritage of India*. Vol. II. Calcutta: Sri Ramakrishna Centenary, no date. (A different series from above; also includes several articles.)

Carpenter, J. Estlin. *Theism in Medieval India*. London: Constable, 1926 (1921).

Dasgupta, S. N. *Hindu Mysticism*. New York: Frederick Ungar, 1959 (1927). (See "Popular Devotional Mysticism," pp. 141-168.)

Farquhar, J. N. *An Outline of the Religious Literature of India*. Delhi: Motilal Banarsidass, 1966 (1920).

Ghurye, G. S. *Indian Sadhus*. (With the collaboration of L. N. Chapekar.) Bombay: Popular Depot, 1953.

Hastings, James, ed. *Encyclopaedia of Religion and Ethics*. 12 vols., plus Index. Edinburgh: T. and T. Clark; New York: Scribners, 1908-1927. (See entries under bhakti, sect names and names of individual poet-saints.)

Majumdar, A. K. *Bhakti Renaissance*. Bombay: Bharatiya Vidya Bhavan, 1965.

Mandelbaum, David C. *Society in India: Change and Continuity*. Vol. II. Berkeley: University of California Press, 1970. (See "Social Regrouping through Indigenous Religions," pp. 523-545.)

Pai, D. A. *Monograph on the Religious Sects in India among the Hindus*. Bombay: The Times Press, 1928. (Includes photographs and drawings.)

Raghavan, V. *The Great Integrators*: *The Saint Singers of India*. Delhi: Publications Division, Government of India, 1966. (Includes translations, many original, of over fifty saint-poets.)

Raychaudhuri, Hemchandra. *Materials for the Study of the Early History of the Vaishnava Sect*. Calcutta: University of Calcutta, rev. ed. 1936.

Sen, Kshitimohan. *Medieval Mysticism in India*. Oriental Reprints, 1974 (1936).

Shivapadasundaram, S. *The Śaiva School of Hinduism*. London: G. Allen and Unwin, 1934.

Singer, Milton, ed. *Krishna*: *Myths, Rites and Attitudes*. Chicago: University of Chicago, 1968 (1966).

Wilson, H. H. *Religious Sects of the Hindus*. Edited by Ernst R. Rost. 2nd ed. Calcutta: Susil Gupta, 1958. (Edition used here: *Essays and Lectures Chiefly on the Religion of the Hindus*. Vol. I: A Sketch of the Religious Sects of the Hindus. Col. and edited by Reinhold Rost. London: Trubner, 1862.)

## TAMILNĀDU

Bhakti in its medieval form of a circle of saint-poets singing of God in the tongue of their area emerged in the Tamil country in the 7-9th centuries. The Tamil Śaiva saints, called the Nāyaṉārs, numbered sixty-three and included court aristocrats, brahmans, peasants, an untouchable, and a woman. The circle of Vaiṣṇava saint-poets of the same petiod, the twelve Āḻvārs, although far fewer in number included the same range of classes. Tamil was already a literary language by the time the saint-poets appeared, but the content of that literature was didactic, romantic and heroic. The saint-poets added a vast quantity of more specifically Hindu poetry. They are credited with aiding the demise of Jainism and Buddhism in the South by bringing both king and commoner into the Vaiṣṇava or Śaiva folds.

A major saint in each group, Appar among the Nāyaṉārs and the Vaiṣṇava Nammāḻvār, was from the agricultural Veḻḻāḻa caste; the legends of their lives suggest strongly that it was during this period that peasants became more closely associated with the Hinduism of the brahmans. The amount of contact between the saint-poets and the courts and the clear association of the saints with Pallava, Pāṇḍya, Cōḻa or Cēra territories suggests also that the bhakti religious development played a part in the polity of the early kingdoms.

The poetry of the Southern saints is similar in its stress on the validity of personal experience to later bhakti, and it includes critical passages such as Appar's questions:

> Why chant the Vedas? hear the Shastras' lore?
> Why learn daily the books of right conduct?
> Why know the six Vedangas again and again?
> No release except to those who constantly meditate on the Lord.
> (Dhavamony, p. 152)

Nevertheless, both Śaiva and Vaiṣṇava bhakti movements were soon legitimized (perhaps engulfed would be a better word) by larger schools of Hinduism, the Āḻvārs into the Śrī Vaiṣṇavas and the Nāyaṉārs into the Śaiva Siddhānta. Four thousand hymns of the twelve Āḻvārs were canonized in the *Prabandham* by Nāthamuni, head of the Śrī Vaiṣṇava community centered at the temple of Śrīrangam, and he "made arrangements for their use in temple worship" (Hooper, p. 10). The Āḻvārs were followed by a series of *āchāryas*, brahman theologians whom V. Rangacharya calls the equivalent of the Popes in the Christian Church. They interpreted the Āḻvārs as incarnations of

Viṣṇu's weapons, and attempted successfully to reconcile bhakti with other ways to salvation, i.e., knowledge and ritual, and to blend the Vedas, the Upanisads, the *Gītā* and the Tamil *Prabandham*. It was the greatest of these āchāryas, Rāmānuja of Śrīrangam (1050-1137), who created the theological works and set in motion the sectarians which eventually made their way north to influence Kabīr and northern bhakti in general.

In his article "Social Mobility and Medieval South Indian Hindu Sects" Burton Stein gives a factual account of the way in which non-brahmans were introduced into temple functions at Śrīrangam and Tirupati temples. It is one of the rare attempts at illustrating the integrative function of bhakti in terms of historical institutions. We also have contemporary descriptions of the continuing integrative function of Vaiṣṇava bhakti in the work of Milton Singer and V. Raghavan on the bhajans of Madras City and the methods of religious instruction in the South.

There is less of this explicit or contemporary sort of study for the Śaiva bhakti tradition, but a great deal of material exists on the philosophy of the Śaivas and on the saint-poets. The last and greatest of the Nāyaṉārs, Māṇikkavāśagar, is the only saint, however, whose full work seems to be available in English. His *Tiruvācakam* ("Holy Sayings") was translated in 1900 by Pope and is the subject of Vanmikanathan's study. Shortly after the death of Māṇikkavāśagar, the work of all sixty-three Nāyaṉārs was collected by Nambi Āndār Nambi at the request of the Cōḻa king, Rāja Rāja I, in the 10th century. The canonization resulted in 12 books, the last being the *Periya-Purāṇam*, the lives of the saints, by Sekkilār. These twelve books, called the *Tirumuṟai*, came in time to be regarded as "the Tamil Veda" in popular writing, and are recognized as one of four categories of sacred canon by the Śaiva Siddhānta, the major Śaiva school in the South.

Although bhakti clearly dominated Śaiva worship in the days of the saint-poets, it appears to have evolved into a way of worship underlying and integrated into a far more complex system of philosophy. It seems that no separate non-conformist strain of bhakti remains in the South. All four major sects or schools pay homage to the saint-poets, and while bhakti remains to some degree a way of integrating various castes at the religious level it is fully within the orthodox tradition.

*Translations*:

Hooper, J. S. M. *Hymns of the Ālvārs*. Calcutta: Association Press, 1929.

Kingsbury, F. and G. E. Phillips. *Hymns of the Tamil Śaivite Saints*. Calcutta: Association Press, 1921. (Includes Sambandhar, Apparswāmi, Sundaramūrti, and Māṇikkavāsagar.)

Māṇikkavāśagar. *Tiruvācagam*. ("Sacred Utterances.") Tr. by G. R. Pope. Madras: University of Madras, 1959 (1900).

*Other Works*:

Dhavamony, Mariasusai. *Love of God According to Śaiva Siddhānta*. Oxford: at the Clarendon Press, 1971.

Krishnasvami Aiyangar, S. *Some Contributions of South India to Indian Culture*. Calcutta: University of Calcutta, 1942.

Mahadevan, T. M. P. *Ten Saints of India*. Bombay: Bharatiya Vidya Bhavan, 1965. (Lives of Tirujñāna Sambandhar, Tirunāvukkarasu, Sundaramūrti, Māṇikkavāśagar, Nāmmālvār, Āndāl.)

Narayana Ayyar, C. V. *Origin and Early History of Śaivism in South India*. Madras: University of Madras, 1936.

Nilakanta Sastri, K. A. *Development of Religion in South India*. Bombay: Orient Longmans, 1963.

Raghavan, V. "Methods of Popular Religious Instruction in the South," in *Traditional India: Structure and Change*. Milton Singer, ed. Philadelphia: The American Folklore Society, 1959, pp. 130-138.

Rajamanickam, M. *The Development of Śaivism in South India*. Madras: Dharmapuram Adhinam, 1965.

Rangacharya, V. "The Historical Evolution of Sri Vaishnavism in South India," in *The Cultural Heritage of India*. Calcutta: Sri Ramakrishna Centenary Committee, no date. Vol. II, pp. 66-103.

Singer, Milton. "The Great Tradition in a Metropolitan Center: Madras," in *Traditional India: Structure and Change*. Milton Singer, ed. Philadelphia: The American Folklore Society, 1959, pp. 141-182.

——. "The Rādhā-Krishna *Bhajanas* of Madras City," in *Krishna: Myths, Rites, and Attitudes*. Chicago: University of Chicago, 1968 (1966), pp. 90-138.

——. *When a Great Tradition Modernizes: An Anthropological Approach to Indian Civilization*. New York: Praeger, 1972. (See Chapter 5, "Urbanization and Cultural Change: Bhakti in the City.")

Stein, Burton. "Social Mobility and Medieval South Indian Hindu Sects," in *Social Mobility in the Caste System in India*. James Silverberg, ed. The Hague: Mouton, 1968. (Comparative Studies in Society and History, Supplement III.)

Varadachari, K. C. *Ālvārs of South India*. Bombay: Bharatiya Vidya Bhavan, 1966. (Includes prose translations.)

Vanmikanathan, G. *Pathway to God through Tamil Literature*. I: Through the Thiruvaachakam (by Māṇikkavāśagar.) New Delhi: Delhi Tamil Sangam, 1971.

Venkateswaran, T. K. "Rādhā-Krishna *Bhajanas* of South India," in *Krishna: Myths, Rites, and Attitudes*. Milton Singer, ed. Chicago: University of Chicago, 1968 (1966), pp. 139-172.

## KARNATAKA

The Śaiva bhakti-poets of the Karnatak reached their height two centuries after the death of the last of the canonized Nāyaṉārs of the Tamil area. The Viraśaivas of the Kannada-speaking region use the same term for their poems to Śiva, a word meaning "sayings, or having said," *vācana*, as is found in the title of Māṇikkavāśagar's work, the *Tiruvācakam*. The greatest of the Kannada saint-poets, Basavaṇṇa (1106-1167) was like Māṇikkavāśagar in that he too was prime minister to a king. But here the nature and history of the movements diverge. King Bijjala of Kalyāṇa was assassinated, and the sect was blamed, persecuted and scattered. In the years at Kalyāṇa, however, Basavaṇṇa had written his poetry, attracted many followers, founded a "religious hall of experience" in which men and women from all walks of life gathered for religious discussion, and instructed thousands of *jangamas* or mendicant devotees. The sect was able to endure until another period of toleration, even patronage, under the Vijayanagar kings. So strong was their identity in the 19th century that the British listed them as a caste in the census, and although the Viraśaivas (Liṅgāyats) contain several social levels, they function now as a caste-like group. Still anti-brahman, still non-conformist to some degree, they form an important political block of sixteen percent of the population in the State of Karnataka.

In a remarkable book entitled *Speaking of Śiva* A. K. Ramanujan allows four of the 10th to 12th century Viraśaiva saints to speak in English poetry. The devotion, the social criticism, and the literary genius of Basavaṇṇa, Dēvāra Dāsimayya, Mahādeviyakka and Allama Prabhu are revealed so strikingly that we can understand both the power of their religion and their literary contribution. An earlier set of translations by Ramanujan and M. G. Krishnamurthi contains some poetry not found in the larger book. The new literature on the Liṅgāyats also includes a contemporary study of their relationship with other castes, politically, socially and religiously, in a northern Karnataka village. (See C. Parvathamma.)

Vaiṣṇava bhakti in the Kannada-speaking area seems not to have emerged in literary form until Purandaradāsa Viṭṭhala (1480-1564), a poet-singer of the Hari-dāsa sect. Said to be of the Mādhva tradition, he carries in his name a relationship to the God Viṭṭhala, whose chief temple at Paṇḍharpur is in Marathi-speaking territory. Purandaradāsa sang of a pilgrimage to Paṇḍharpur, but there seems to have been no connection with the Maharashtrian saint-poets.* Purandaradāsa is honored as the founder of the Southern (Karnatic)

* There may be a stylistic link with Eknāth, q.v. Purandaradāsa wrote as a Bairagi with a dose of bhang and as a street vendor of sugar candy (see Raghavan, pp. 38-39), just as Eknāth put poetry into the mouths of the street folk around him.

style of music. He did have disciples (Raghavan gives two songs of the shepherd Haridāsa Kanakadāsa and two of Vijayadāsa), but the musical creativity of Purandaradāsa passed to the later Telugu-speaking saint-singers. It culminated in Tyāgarāja (1767-1847), known as the greatest of all Karnatic composers, who acknowledged his debt to Purandaradāsa.

*Translations—Viraśaivism*:

Ramanujan, A. K., tr. and introduction. *Speaking of Śiva*. Baltimore: Penguin, 1973. (Includes an article by William McCormack.)

Ramanujan, A. K., and M. G. Krishnamurthi, trs. *Some Kannada Poems*. Calcutta: Writers Workshop, 1967.

*Other Works—Viraśaivism*:

Desai, P. B. *Basavesvara and His Times*. Dharwar: Karnataka University, 1967.

Hunashal, S. M. *The Lingāyat Movement: A Social Revolution in Karnatak*. Dharwar: Karnatak Sahitya Mandira, 1947.

McCormack, William. "The Forms of Communication in Viraśaiva Religion," in *Traditional India: Structure and Change*. Milton Singer, ed. Philadelphia: American Folklore Society, 1959, pp. 119-129.

——. "Liṅgāyats as a Sect," *Journal of the Royal Anthropological Institute* 93; Part 1 (1963), pp. 59-71.

——. "On Liṅgāyat Culture," in Ramanujan (see above), pp. 175-187.

Nandimath, S. C. *A Handbook of Viraśaivism*. Dharwar: Lingayat Education Association, 2nd ed., 1953.

Parvathamma, C. *Politics and Religion: A Study of Historical Interaction Between Socio-Political Relationships in a Mysore Village*. New Delhi: Sterling, 1971.

Venkatesa Iyengar, Masti. *Popular Culture in Karnataka*. Bangalore: Bangalore Press, 1937. (Also includes the Vaiṣṇava Haridāsas.)

*Vaiṣṇava*:

Ramachandra Rao, S. K. *Sri Purandaradāsa*. Tr. by K. Sampathgiri Rao. Bangalore: Sri Purandaradasa Fourth Centenary Celebrations Committee, 1964. (Includes some translations.)

Sitaramiah, V. *Purandaradāsa*. New Delhi: National Book Trust, 1971. (Includes translations in prose paraphrase).

## MAHARASHTRA

A bhakti movement began in Maharashtra toward the end of the 13th century and continued to produce saint-poets of exceptional strength and creativity until the 17th century. Its founder was Jñāneśwar (Dnyānadeo), a brahman outside respectability because his father had been a *sannyāsi* (celibate religious wanderer.) Jñāneśwar's major work, a Marathi version of the *Bhagavad Gītā*, is one of the earliest and greatest Marathi literary works. The saint, or another bearing his name (see Edwards below), also wrote *abhaṅgas*, poems to the God Viṭṭhala (Viṭhobā) of Paṇḍharpur. There is a dual strain in Jñāneśwar, and in the later saint-poet Eknāth—a tie to the *Nāth* cult of the North and a link to the Viṭṭhala temple in southern Maharashtra which seems to be of Karnatak origin. A multitude of saint-poets followed Jñāneśwar, many of them non-brahman and all devotees of Viṭhobā, a Vaiṣṇava God usually identified with Kṛṣṇa but stylistically unique. The best known of the early circle is Nāmdev, who travelled in the North and whose poems appear in the Sikh *Granth*.

The next major saint-poet was Eknāth (1548-1600), a brahman from the old capital of Paithan who not only translated Sanskrit works to make those available to the common man and edited Jñāneśwar but also wrote a remarkable series of poems which as yet remain untranslated. These put the message of bhakti into the mouths of the non-Sanskritic world around Eknāth: untouchable Mahārs and Māṇgs, prostitutes, rope-dancers, the blind, the deaf, the worshippers of demons. I know of no Western religious mystic who uses the vocabulary and the characteristics of the lower orders to speak of the meaning of the divine.

The last of the great saint-poets, the Marāṭhā Tukārām, lived in Dehu, a village near Poona, in the 17th century. A full range of his poetry is available, from the hymn-like renditions by Fraser and Marathe to the avant-garde translations of Kolatkar. R. D. Ranade, himself a mystic, has arranged the *abhaṇgas* of Tukārām in prose versions to show both the pattern of his life and his religious thought.

In the 18th century, the brahman Mahīpati wrote four volumes on the lives of the saints, much of which has been translated by Justin E. Abbott. Mahīpati included not only those who were *vārkaris*, pilgrims to Paṇḍharpur, in his volumes, but also Kabīr, Rohidās (Rai-dās) and Sūrdās from the North and Maharashtrian saints outside the Paṇḍharpur tradition such as Rāmdās.

The ties North and South (and there is in Bengali literature a reference to Caitanya having visited Maharashtra*) reflect the area's position as a crossroads region. The movement, however, is remarkable for its purely Maharashtrian character. A chapter in Mahadeo Govind Ranade's *Rise of the Maratha Power* (1900) states a commonly held view: the saint-poets were innovators of Marāṭhā ethos which underlay the 16th century Marāṭhā Kingdom; they instituted a revolt against social inequality and so unified a people. It is true that almost every Marathi-speaking caste can claim a saint-poet:

* This may stem from a reference in Bahinā Bāī (q.v.) to a Caitanya who may not have been the Bengali saint.

Nāmdev was a tailor; Cokhāmeḷā was an untouchable Mahār; Gorā was a potter; and there are nearly fifty more. It is also true that the organized form of the movement, a twice-yearly pilgrimage to Paṇḍharpur in village bands of devotees, brings into one grand moment of community devotion vast numbers from all over the Marathi-speaking area. (See Irawati Karve.) However, although the *pālkhis* (a group formed around a palanquin bearing the footprint of the saint honored by that group) are composed of all castes, the smaller *dindis* within that group are of one caste, and when the procession reaches Paṇḍharpur the untouchables (until Independence) could not go into the temple. Deleury, in the major work on the structure of the bhakti cult, notes that some *pālkhis* have been started within the last fifty years. Nevertheless, it seems to me that the unifying possibilities of this bhakti movement are too strong to be ignored. The presence of the greatest saint-poet, Tukārām, at the moment of Śivājī's rise to power and the creation of the last great Hindu state in India seems to be not a coincidence but a fusion of two kinds of dynamic.

*Translations*:

Abbott, Justin E., tr. *Stotramālā*: A *Garland of Hindu Prayers.* A Translation of Prayers of Maratha Poet-Saints, from Dnyaneshvar to Mahipati. Poona: Scottish Mission Industries, 1929. (Poet-Saints of Maharashtra, 6.)

Bahinā Bāī. *Bahinā Bāī.* A Translation of Her Autobiography and Verses by Justin E. Abbott. Poona: Scottish Mission Industries, 1929. (Poet-Saints of Maharashtra, 5.)

Jñāneśwar. *Jñāneshvari.* Tr. by V. G. Pradhan; ed. and with introduction by H. M. Lambert. 2 vols. London: George Allen and Unwin, 1967-1969.

Macnicol, Nicol. *Psalms of Maratha Saints*: *One Hundred and Eight Hymns Translated from the Marathi.* Calcutta: Association Press, 1919.

Mahipati. *Bhaktalīlāmṛit* (*Nectar from Indian Saints*). Chapters 1-12, 41-51. Tr. by Justin E. Abbott, N. R. Godbole and J. F. Edwards. Poona: J. F. Edwards, 1953. (Poet-Saints of Maharashtra, 11.)

——. —— *Eknāth.* Chapters 13-24. Tr. by Justin E. Abbott. Poona: Scottish Mission Industries, 1927. (Poet-Saints of Maharashtra, 2.)

——. —— *Tukārām.* Chapters 25-40. Tr. by Justin E. Abbott. Poona: Justin E. Abbott, 1930. (Poet-Saints of Maharashtra, 7.)

——. *Bhaktavijāya* (*Stories of Indian Saints*). Chapters 1-30. Tr. by Justin E. Abbott and Narhar R. Godbole. Poona: N. R. Godbole, 1933. (Poet-Saints of Maharashtra, 9); Vol. II, Chapters 31-57, Poona: United Theological College of Western India, 1934. (Poet-Saints of Maharashtra, 10.)

Tukārām. *The Poems of Tukārām.* Tr. by J. Nelson Fraser and K. B. Marathe. 3 vols. London, Madras: Christian Literature Society, 1909-1915.

——. "Tukaram," Tr. by Arun Kolatkar, in *Poetry India* 1:1 (1966), pp. 21-29.

——. "Tukaram: Twenty-five poems," Tr. by Prabhakar Machwe, in *Mahfil* V: 1 & 2 (1968-9), pp. 61-69.

——. *Village Songs of Western India.* Translations from Tukārām by John S. Hoyland. London: Allenson, 1934.

*Other Works*:

Behere, N. K. *The Background of Maratha Renaissance in the 17th Century: Historical Survey of the Social, Religious, and Political Movements of the Marathas.* Bangalore: Bangalore Press, 1946.

Belsare, K. V. *Tukaram.* New Delhi: Maharashtra Information Centre, 1967.

Dandekar, S. V. *Dnyānadeo.* New Delhi: Maharashtra Information Centre, 1969.

Deleury, G. A. *The Cult of Vithobā.* Poona: Deccan College Postgraduate and Research Institute, 1960.

Deming, Wilbur Stone. *Eknāth, a Maratha Bhakta*, Bombay: Karnatak Printing Press, 1931.

Deshpande, Kusumavati. *Marathi Sahitya.* New Delhi: Maharashtra Information Centre, 1966.

Edwards, J. F. *Dnyānesvar, the Outcaste Brāhmin.* Poona: United Theological College of Western India, 1941. (Poet-Saints of Maharashtra, 12.)

Fraser, J. Nelson and J. F. Edwards. *The Life and Teaching of Tukārām.* Madras: Christian Literature Society for India, 1922.

Karve, Irawati. "On the Road," in *Journal of Asian Studies*, XXII:1 (1962), pp. 13-29.

Kulkarni, Shridhar. *Eknath.* New Delhi: Maharashtra Information Centre, 1966.

Machwe, Prabhaker Balwant. *Namdev*: *Life and Philosophy.* Patiala: Punjab University, 1968.

Ranade, M. G. *Rise of the Maratha Power.* Delhi: Publications Division, Ministry of Information and Broadcasting, Government of India, 1961 (1900). (An edition published by the University of Bombay in 1960 carries a critical introductory essay by R. V. Oturkar.)

Ranade, R. D. *Pathway to God in Marathi Literature.* Bombay: Bharatiya Vidya Bhavan, 1961 (1933).

Sardar, G. B. *The Saint-Poets of Maharashtra* (*Their Impact on Society*). Tr. by Kumudini A. Mehta. Bombay: Orient Longmans, 1969.

## KASHMIR

Śaiva bhakti, strong only in the South, found a new voice in the 14th century in Kashmir. Lal Ded, a woman saint, sang:

> I, Lallā, went out far in search of Śiva, the omnipresent Lord;
> having wandered, I found Him in my own body, sitting in His house.
> (Raghavan, p. 144)

Her songs or sayings are known all over Kashmir. Here again, Śaiva bhakti uses the word for "having said" for its poetry, and Lal Ded's work is known at the Lalleśvari Vākyāni. Temple's major work seems to have superceded other translations, although it is far from poetic. A new popular biography of Lallā has been published by the Sāhitya Akademi.

*Kashmiri*

Lal Ded. *Lallavakyani.* (The Word of Lalla the Prophetess. Being the sayings of Lal Ded, or Lal Diddi of Kashmir. Done into English verse from Lallavakyani or Lal Wakhi by Richard Carnac Temple.) Annotated. Cambridge: Cambridge University Press, 1924.

Kaul, Jayalal. *Lal Ded.* New Delhi: Sahitya Akademi, 1973.

## NORTH INDIA

The North Indian bhakti tradition contains at least three distinct groupings: Kabīr and the Rāmānandis, the Vallabhāchāryas, and the solitary, influential figure of Tulsī Dās. Within the Rāmānanda-Kabīr tradition, Kabīr himself, Raidās, Guru Nānak and Dādū must be discussed separately in view of the different histories of their followings. The cult led by Vallabha arose in Benaras but became a popular movement in Gujarat and is treated in the section on that region except for its best-known poet, Sūrdās, who is discussed here as a major Hindi poet.

### *Kabīr and the Rāmānandis*

Kabīr (15th century) and his school are not only the northern bhaktas of greatest interest to social historians, but Kabīr is also the link with the southern tradition of bhakti. His guru, according to legend, was Rāmānanda, fifth generation in the line stemming from the great Rāmānuja. Rāmānanda was far less orthodox in practice than the Śrī Vaiṣṇavas of the South, and among his disciples were shudras, untouchables, Muslims and Hindu-Muslims such as Kabīr. Kabīr, in turn, left disciples of varying castes. The movement around Kabīr is rather like the bhakti movement in Maharashtra in that the saint-poets were aware of one another and their lives were joined in the *Bhakta Mālā* (garland of devotees) written by Nābhāji around 1600. No single movement, however, emerged from Kabīr, but rather a group of sects, limited either on a caste or territorial basis.

Kabīr was certainly no Luther in terms of establishing an inclusive organized challenge to the established religion, but he was a protestant. Dasgupta (1946, p. 400) estimates that at least one-third of the literature of Kabīr was devoted to criticism against orthodox Hindus and Muslims. Although Kabīr's devotion was in the Rāma tradition, his poetry indicates that the name of God, and sometimes God himself, is not of first importance. As in the case of other Hindu-Muslim syncretists, Dādū and Guru Nānak, a Book has replaced images in the worship centers of the sect. While Kabīrpaṇthis are found all over the North, particularly in Uttar Pradesh and the old Central Provinces, but also in considerable numbers in Gujarat, they are usually low in caste. Protestant though it may have been, powerful though Kabīr's poetry is, Kabīr's movement has been accommodated in various ways into Hinduism.

Kabīr's basic work, the *Bījak*, has been translated into English by the Rev. Ahmad Shah, but is not available to me. Much of Kabīr, however, does appear in translation. In addition to those listed in the bibliography, see Althaus (1928) and Behari (1971) in the general bibliography and the translations of the *Ādi Granth* and Macauliffe below. Rabīndranāth Tagore and Evelyn Underhill introduced the idea of Indian mysticism to the Western literary world in *Songs of Kabir* (1915), but F. E. Keay notes that only five of these one hundred poems can be said to be authentic Kabīr.

*Rai-dās*

Rai-dās (Rav-dās, Ravi-dās, or Rohidās), the 15th century cobbler-saint disciple of Rāmānanda, was perhaps the guru of Mīrā-bāī, felt at one with Nāmdev and Kabīr, has been incorporated into the *Granth-Sāhib*, and sang ecstatically of the blessings of the Lord on the poor and the polluting. His followers, however, are exclusively from his own caste of Camārs (or, Cambhārs in Maharashtra). Much of the anthropological work on the Camār caste indicates a reverent attitude toward Rai-dās and notes the efforts of some of the caste to rise in social status through reference to his sanctity. Four of Rai-dās' poems appear in Althaus (1928), two in Raghavan (1966), and others in translations of Sikh scriptures.

*Guru Nānak*

Guru Nānak (1469-1539) began his teaching much in the same way as other Kabīr-related bhaktas. By 1708, however, the time of the last of the ten gurus who successively inherited his leadership position, the tradition had changed from a belief in the goodness of his faith to a militant assertion for the right to that faith by the now numerous members of the movement. Various changes came slowly but surely: the creation of a successor, not necessarily in direct descent from the founder of the sect; the establishment of one center for the faithful and a number of designated centers for worship; a community kitchen; one Book of Scripture; appointed spiritual leaders; regular contributions from the faithful to the sect; a separate script; an annual gathering; an army; and, toward the end of the formative period, a set of five outward symbols denoting the separate identity of the Sikhs (disciples) from both Hindus and Muslims. The last five gurus were not only spiritual leaders but martyrs and heroes, caught in political maneuvers that brought them into conflict with the previously tolerant Mughal overlords. Although there are still families of mixed Sikh-Hindu loyalties, there is no doubt but that the Sikhs are highly conscious of themselves as a people. Guru Nānak's bhakti had far more significant political consequences than that of any other saint-poet.

The *Granth-Sāhib*, the holy book of the Sikhs, reveals a broad bhakti heritage. Curiously enough, Jayadeva, the 12th century poet from eastern Bihar, is represented in the writings, along with Nāmdev from Maharashtra, Kabīr and Rai-Dās from the Uttar Pradesh area, and in the Bhai Banno collection of the *Granth-Sāhib* the rājpūt princess Mīrā Bāī is given a place. The great bulk of the *Granth*, however, consists of the songs of Guru Nānak and his successors. Macauliffe's six volumes on the Sikhs and their literature seems to contain the most complete history for the purposes of this study. Of the enormous amount of literature on the Sikhs, the most useful studies of the place of religion in their history are by Archer, Grewal and Bal, McLeod, Gurmukh Nihal Singh, and Harbans Singh.

## *Dādū*

Dādū (1544-1603), born in Ahmadabad, lived most of his life in Rajasthan and it is from that area that most of his followers come. Like Guru Nānak, he was strongly influenced by Kabīr and was associated with both Hindus and Muslims. The *Bāni*, a large body of hymns and poems serves as scripture for the sect. The Dādū-paṇthis form three groups: celibate religious leaders, lay members, and militant Nāgas who until very recently served the government of Jaipur State as mercenaries. W. G. Orr's book on Dādū supercedes the fragmentary earlier studies and contains translations of portions of the *Bāni*. A poem by Sundar-dās, a disciple of Dādū, may be found in Dasgupta (1946, p. 416). A worthy successor of Kabīr in terms of castelessness and protest against both Hindu and Muslim ritualism, Dādū in the end seems to have created only one more Hindu sect.

*Translations*:

*Ādi-Granth, or the Holy Scriptures of the Sikhs*. Tr. by Ernest Trumpp. London: W. H. Allen, 1877.

*Ādi-Granth: Selections from the Sacred Writings of the Sikhs*. Tr. by Trilochan Singh and others. London: G. Allen and Unwin, 1960.

Kabīr. "The Bhakti of Kabir: Three Poems." Tr. by Barron Holland, in *Literature East and West* XIII:1 & 2 (1969), pp. 95-98.

——. *Bijak*. Tr. by Ahmad Shah. Cawnpore, 1917.

——. *Kabir*. Tr. by Arvind Krishna Mehrotra, in *Delos* 6 (1971), pp. 136-137.
——. *Some New Translations of Kabir*. Tr. by Charles S. J. White, in *Mahfil* I:1 (1964), pp. 19-21. (Includes bibliography of sources in English.)
——. *Poems of Kabir*. Tr. by David Canalos, in *Mahfil* VI: 2 & 3 (1970) pp. 63-69.
——. *Songs of Kabir*. Tr. by Rabīndranāth Tagore with the assistance of Evelyn Underhill. New York: Macmillan, 1915.

*Other Works*:

Archer, John Clark. *The Sikhs*. Princeton: Princeton University Press, 1946.
Grewal, J. S. *Guru Nanak in History*. Chandigarh: Panjab University, 1969.
Grewal, J. S. and S. S. Bal. *Guru Govind Singh*. Chandigarh: Panjab University, 1967.
Jindal, K. B. *A History of Hindi Literature*. Allahabad: Kitab Mahal, 1955.
Keay, F. E. *Kabir and His Followers*. Calcutta: Association Press, 1931 (The most useful of several studies, includes translations.)
Macauliffe, Max Arthur. *The Sikh Religion: Its Gurus, Sacred Writings and Authors*. Six volumes in three. Delhi: S. Chand, 1963 (1909). (Includes translations.)
Machwe, Prabhakar. *Kabir*. New Delhi: Sahitya Akademi, 1968. (Includes translations.)
McLeod, W. H. *Guru Nanak and the Sikh Religion*. Oxford: At the Clarendon Press, 1968. (Includes full bibliography.)
Orr, W. G. *A Sixteenth Century Indian Mystic: Dadu and His Followers*. London: Lutterworth Press, 1947. (Includes translations.)
Singh, Gurmukh Nihal, ed. *Guru Nanak: His Life, Times and Teachings*. Delhi: Guru Nanak Foundation by National Publishing House, 1969.
Singh, Harbans, *Guru Nanak and Origins of the Sikh Faith*. Bombay: Asia Publishing House, 1969.
Vaudeville, Ch. *Kabir*. Vol. I. Oxford at the Clarendon Press, 1974.
Westcott, G. H. *Kabir and the Kabir Panth*. Calcutta: Susil Gupta, 1953 (1907). (Includes translations.)
White, Charles S. J. *Bhakti as a Religious Structure in the Context of Medieval Hinduism in the Hindi-speaking area of North India*. Unpublished Ph.D. Thesis, University of Chicago, 1964.

## *Sūrdās*

Sūrdās, the blind 16th century poet of Agra was one of the eight poets associated with the first years of the Vallabha sect. However, his songs to the child Kṛṣṇa and the lover Kṛṣṇa are sung all over North India and he has a popularity beyond the confines of the Vallabha group (see Gujarat). His only specific following, however, is one of professional minstrels, often blind, who consider themselves Sūrdāsis.

*Translations*:

Sūrdās. "As Krishna Awaits His Lover," Tr. by Barron Holland, in *Mahfil* IV:2 (1968), pp. 30-32. (Five poems from Sursāgar.)
——. "Six Poems from Surdas," Tr. by S. M. Pandey and N. H. Zide, in *Mahfil* I:2 (1964), pp. 24-26.
——. "Surdas: Twelve Poems," Tr. by Karla McMechan, in *Mahfil* V: 1 & 2 (1968-9), pp. 55-60. (From Sursāgar.)

*Other Works*:

Pandey, S. M. and Norman Zide. "Surdās and His Krishna-bhakti," in *Krishna: Myths, Rites and Attitudes*. Ed. by Milton Singer. Chicago: University of Chicago, 1968 (1966), pp. 173-199. (Includes bibliography.)

### *Tulsī Dās*

Tulsī Dās (1543-1623) is the best known bhakti figure in North India and certainly the dominant literary influence in Hindi. His version of the *Rāmāyaṇa*, entitled *Rāma-carita-mānasa* (holy lake of the acts of Rāma), was so popular that the *Bhakta Mālā* called him Vālmīki born again for the redemption of mankind, and it seems that Tulsī Dās' *Rāmāyaṇa* has replaced Vālmīki's Sanskrit *Rāmāyaṇa* as "the Bible of the North." Tulsī Dās' influence cannot be denied, but he left no school, no sect, no well-known disciples, no structure. His concept of Rāma, however, is carried not only in his writing and his songs but in the widespread Rām Līlā dramas of the North which are based on his *Rāmāyaṇa*. (see Hein.)

*Translations*:

Tulsī Dās. *Kavitāvali*. Tr. by F. R. Allchin. London: George Allen and Unwin, 1964. (Includes good critical introduction.)

——. *Rāmacaritamānasa* (*The Holy Lake of the Acts of Rāma*) Tr. by W. Douglas P. Hill. Bombay: Oxford University Press, 1971 (1952). (Includes introduction.)

——. —— (*The Rāmāyana of Tulsi Dās*). Tr. by F. S. Growse. Allahabad, 7th ed., 1937 (1877-81).

——. *Vinaya-Patrika* (*The Petition to Rām: Hindi Devotional Hymns of the 17th Century*). Tr. by F. R. Allchin. London: George Allen and Unwin, 1966. (Includes good critical introduction.)

*Other Works*:

Hein, Norvin. "The Rām Līlā," in *Traditional India: Structure and Change*. Ed. by Milton Singer. Philadelphia: American Folklore Society, 1959, pp. 73-98.

The *Bhakta Mālā*, written by Nābhā Dās around 1600 and enlarged by a commentary by Priya Dās in 1722, is a catholic work which has no sectarian bias but includes the lives of many North Indian saints and some notes on Marāṭhā bhaktas. Nābhāji was a Rāmānanda who was asked by a Vallabha disciple to write this "Garland of Devotees"; the author of the gloss, Priya Dās, was a follower of Caitanya. The work, which has not been translated into English, reflects this inclusiveness. See Farquhar (general bibliography) for a few notes and further references.

## GUJARAT

Bhakti in Gujarat may be described under three headings: Narsiṃha Mehtā and a group of lesser saint-poets; the Vallabhāchārya sect; and the Rājpūt princess Mīrā Bāī. Although Vallabhāchārya (1479-1531) was a Telugu brahman born in Benaras, his chief lay following is in Gujarat. Mīrā Bāī is included here also because she was closely associated with Dwarka, is even more popular in Gujarat than in the North, and is claimed by Gujarati historians of literature.

Narsiṃha Mehtā (1414-1481, or 1500-1580) seems to be a solitary figure. He knew of Jayadeva and Kabīr, and was followed by a number of other poet-saints, but there seems to be no bhakti group surrounding these Gujarati figures. Raghavan (1966) quotes from two persons widely separated in time: Akho of Ahmadabad in the 17th century and Bapu Saheb Gaekwad of Baroda, who lived into the 19th century (pp. 82-84 141.) Raghavan also gives one of Narsiṃha Mehtā's poems (p. 139), and quotes the hymn widely used by Mohandas K. Gandhi in his song meetings (pp. 59-60). Narsiṃha Mehtā was a Nāgār brahman from Junagadh who, legend tells, dined with untouchables and refuted caste. His songs, however, were incorporated into the services of the Vallabha sect, and are not generally used in other Vaiṣṇava bhajans or kīrtans, although they are sung in Gujarati homes. K. M. Munshi claims that the use of Narsiṃha Mehtā as a vehicle for Vallabha teachings means that no songs in Narsiṃha's original language are available.

The Vallabha cult represents still another development of the bhakti movement. Vallabhāchārya was not a poet himself in a vernacular language, but among his disciples and those of his son-successor, eight poets, including Sūrdās, provided the sect with a song-literature. Vallabha preached in Gujarat, and there among merchants and landowners found the great lay response to his teaching. The movement continued to produce poets, including Haridās of Baroda who wrote on Narsiṃha Mehtā and Dayārām (1762-1852), a critic of the Vallabha cult from within, but its great stress is on the guru, the appointed Mahārājas of the cult, and on formalized services in the home or in temples owned by the Mahārājas (the designated spiritual leaders of the sect). A Mahārājah Libel Suit in Bombay in 1862 made highly public some of the less puritan practices of the Mahārājas. The sect may not have deserved all the opprobrium it received from reformers, but it is clear that the absolute control of the sect by the Mahārājas reaches heights not found in other bhakti cults.

Mīrā Bāī, the 16th century royal saint-poet, is beloved all over North India as well as among Gujarati speakers and Sindhi Hindus. She sings of Rai-dās in two or three poems as her guru, legends tell of her contact with Caitanya and Vallabha ascetics, her songs are incorporated into one edition of the Sikh *Granth* and into the scriptures of the Kabīrpaṇthis; but she is a solitary figure with no organized following. She exists as a reincarnated Rādhā, in love with Kṛṣṇa. Her place in Rājpūt history, confused though it is in legend, does allow us some view of politics and orthodoxy in her time, and a biography by Goetz is chiefly devoted to the history surrounding Mīrā Bāī. Behari (1961) offers over 100 translations of her songs along with a brief life, and Nilsson (1966) translates fifty songs and synthesizes the English and Hindi literature on Mīrā Bāī into a popular biography. A new translation of Mīrā's poetry by Prakash Kurl has recently been published, but I have not seen this.

All these facets of bhakti in Gujarat receive attention in two competent studies, those of K. M. Munshi and N. A. Toothi.

*Translations*:

Mīrābāī. "Six Padas of Mirabai," Tr. by S. M. Pandey and Norman Zide, in *Mahfil* I:4 (1964), pp. 23-26.

*Other Works*:

Behari, Bankey. *Bhakta Mira*. Bombay: Bharatiya Vidya Bhavan, 1961. (Includes translations of 100 songs.)

Bhatt, Govindlal Hargovind. "The School of Vallabha," in *Cultural Heritage of India*, Vol. III. Ed. by Haridas Bhattacharya. 2nd rev. ed. Calcutta: Ramakrishna Mission Institute of Calcutta, 1953ff, pp. 343-359.

Goetz, Hermann. *Mira Bai; Her Life and Times*. Bombay: Bharatiya Vidya Bhavan, 1966. (Includes full bibliography in English.)

Mulji ,K. (Vadunathaji Vrajaratnagi). *History of the Sect of Mahārājas or Vallabhāchāryas in Western India*. London: Kegan Paul, Trench, Trubner, 1865.

Munshi, K. M. *Gujarata and Its Literature*. Bombay: Longmans, Green, 1935.

Nilsson, Usha S. *Mirabai*. New Delhi: Sahitya Akademi, 1969. (Includes translations.)

Pandey, S. M. "Mirābāi and Her Contributions to the Bhakti Movement," in *History of Religions* V:1 (1965), pp. 54-73.

Toothi, N. A. *The Vaishnavas of Gujarat*. Calcutta: Longmans, Green, 1935.

## BENGAL

Rādhā-Kṛṣṇa bhakti in Bengal began with Jayadeva, whose 12th century masterpiece, *Gīta Govinda*, is in Sanskrit but who also wrote songs in Maithili which have been appropriated by Bengali Vaiṣṇava bhakti devotees. Several singers using the name Chandidās around the 15-16th centuries and the poet Vidyāpati continued the song tradition, carrying a *sahaja* (easy, natural, not suppressive of the senses) doctrine from earlier Buddhist and Hindu cults. The giant figure of Caitanya (1486-1533) then dominates the bhakti movement. A convert from brahman orthodoxy to the bhakti mode, Caitanya was both an ascetic of the Daśnāmi (Śaṅkarāchārya) order and an active innovator of the popular kīrtan of the street and village. The Caitanya sect (called Mādhva Gaudīya) continues as an orthodox group based in Vṛndāban, with an interesting offshoot known as the Krishna Consciousness Movement in the West. (The chant heard on American streets, "Hare Krishna, Hare Krishna, Krishna, Krishna, Hare Hare; Hare Rāma, Hare Rāma, Rāma Rāma, Hare Hare," was sung by Caitanya himself in his 16th century kīrtans.) Another phase of the movement developed a song literature in Bengali which is used in the bhajans described by Dimock (1967). Caitanya himself wrote no Bengali songs, but the bhajan always begins with an invocation to Caitanya as Gaurachandra. The bards of Bengal known as Bauls seem loosely connected to the whole movement, especially the early Sahaja emphasis, although they form an unconventional and distinct professional group. (See Dimock, 1966, and Bhattacharya, 1969.)

Of all the literature on Bengali Vaiṣṇavism, Shashibhusan Dasgupta's *Obscure Religious Cults* is the most thought-provoking for a historian concerned with beginnings. Similarities with Buddhism, comparisons of Sahajis with non-Bengali medieval saints, the origin and growth of the vernacular literature in connection with the movement, and the lines of Sahajiyā and Nath influences are some of the issues he discusses. Other monumental studies of Vaiṣṇava faith and literature are those of S. K. De, Dinesh Chandra Sen, and Sukumar Sen. There are some translations of Vaiṣṇava songs in many of these volumes. One song by Jayadeva appears in Althaus and a few poems from Rāmprasād (1718-1775) may be found in de Bary and Raghavan (1966). Dimock discusses the erotic mysticism of the Vaiṣṇava-Sahajiyā cult (1966) and Bhattacharya has felicitous if rather secular translations of Chandidās and Vidyāpati, the latter with comments by W. G. Archer.

The literature on Caitanya himself begins with a translation of a 16th century biography by Goswāmin and includes work by D. C. Sen, a study by the missionary scholar M. T. Kennedy, two enthusiastic volumes by Nisikanta Sannyal, a life by S. K. Ghose who was editor of the newspaper *Amrita Bazar Patrika* as well as a devotee, a critical biography by A. K. Majumdar, and a popular biography by Dilip Kumar Mukherjee.

The finest translations are by Edward Dimock assisted by the poet Denise Levertov. *In Praise of Krishna* includes some nine poets and a description of a contemporary village kīrtan. Other works which note the modern life of Vaiṣṇavism in Bengali include Dimock (1968) and Surajit Sinha, the latter on current Vaiṣṇava influence on a tribal culture, a phenomenon not unknown in the Caitanya movement of the past.

I have included in this section a work by Mukhopadhyaya on Orissa, which I have not seen but presume deals with the long period Caitanya lived and taught in Purī.

*Translations*:

Bhattacharya, Deben, tr. *Songs of the Bards of Bengal.* New York: Grove Press, 1969. (Includes illustrations.)

Chandidās. *Love Songs of Chandidās: The Rebel Poet-Priest of Bengal.* Tr. and introduced by Deben Bhattacharya. New York: Grove Press, 1970 (1967).

Dimock, Edward C. Jr. and Denise Levertof, tr. *In Praise of Krishna: Songs from the Bengali.* Introduction and Notes by Edward C. Dimock Jr. Garden City, New York: Doubleday, 1967.

Goswāmin, Krishnadāsa Kavirāja. *Sri Sri Chaitanya Charitāmrita.* Tr. by Nagendra Kumar Roy. 3 parts. Puri: translator, 2nd ed., 1959.

Thompson, Edward J. and A. M. Spencer, tr. *Bengali Religious Lyrics: Vaishnava.* Calcutta: Association Press, 1925.

Vidyāpati. *Love Songs of Vidyāpati.* Tr. by Deben Bhattacharya, ed. by W. G. Archer. New York: Grove Press, 1970 (1963).

*Other Works*:

Bhaktivedanta Swami Prabhupada, A. C. *Teaching of the Lord Chaitanya: The Golden Avatar.* New York: Bhaktivedanta Book Trust, 1972 (1968).

Dasgupta, Shashibhusan. *Obscure Religious Cults.* Calcutta: Firma K. L. Mukhopadhyay, 1962 (1946).

De, S. K. *Early History of the Vaiṣṇava Faith and Movement in Bengal.* Calcutta: Firma K. L. Mukhopadhyaya, 2nd ed., 1961 (1942).

——. *Bengal's Contribution to Sanskrit Literature and Studies in Bengal Vaiṣṇavism.* Calcutta: Firma K. L. Mukhopadhyaya, 1960.

Dimock, Edward C. Jr. "Doctrine and Practice among the Vaiṣṇavas of Bengal," in *Krishna: Myths, Rites and Attitudes.* Ed. by Milton Singer. Chicago: University of Chicago, 1968 (1966), pp. 41-63.

——. *The Place of the Hidden Moon: Erotic Mysticism in the Vaiṣṇava-Sahajiyā Cult of Bengal.* Chicago: University of Chicago, 1966. (Includes translations.)

Ghose, Shishir Kumar. *Lord Gauranga.* Bombay: Bharatiya Vidya Bhavan, 1961. (Condensed from an earlier two volume edition.)

Ghosh, Jyotish Chandra. *Bengali Literature.* London: Oxford University Press, 1948.

Kennedy, Melville T. *The Chaitanya Movement.* Calcutta: Association Press, 1925.

Majumdar, Asoke Kumar. *Caitanya, His Life and Doctrine: A Study in Vaiṣṇavism.* Bombay: Bharatiya Vidya Bhavan, 1969.

Mukherjee, Dilip Kumar. *Chaitanya.* New Delhi: National Book Trust, 1970.

Mukhopadhyay, Prabhat. *The History of Medieval Vaishnavism in Orissa.* Calcutta: R. Chatterjee, 1940.

Sanyal, Nisikanta. *Sree Krishna Chaitanya*. 2 vols. Royapettah, Madras: Tridandi Swami Bhakti Hridaya Bon, Sree Gaudiya Math, 1933.
Sen, Dinesh Chandra. *Chaitanya and His Companions*. Calcutta: University of Calcutta, 1917.
——. *History of the Bengali Language and Literature*. Calcutta: University of Calcutta, 1954 (1911).
——. *The Vaiṣṇava Literature of Medieval Bengal*. Calcutta: University of Calcutta, 1917.
Sen, Sukumar. *History of Bengali Literature*. New Delhi: Sahitya Akademi, rev. ed., 1971 (1960).
——. *History of Brajabuli Literature*. Calcutta: University of Calcutta, 1935.
Sinha, Surajit. "Vaiṣṇava Influence on a Tribal Culture," in *Krishna: Myths, Rites, and Attitudes*. Ed. by Milton Singer. Chicago: University of Chicago, 1968 (1966), pp. 64-89.

## ASSAM

Bhakti in Assam was initiated as a movement by Śaṅkaradeva (1449-1568?) in the closing decades of the 15th century and according to its historians effected a religious, literary and artistic renaissance throughout the Brahmaputra Valley. Neog's book on Śaṅkaradeva and Sarma's study of the Vaiṣṇava movement and its chief institution, the *satra*, are thorough and careful works of scholarship which lack only translations of the song literature. (Three poems are available in Raghavan.) Much of the Assamese movement is similar to the bhakti movement in general: Śaṅkaradeva's pilgrimages; references to other bhakti saints, chiefly Kabīr; equality in spiritual matters; devotion to a personal god; and songs in the vernacular (an Assamese form of Brajabuli). Differences include a wide range of devotional practices, including a dance-drama-music form initiated by Śaṅkaradeva himself and the institution of the *satra*. The word itself is a corruption of a Sanskrit word denoting a lengthy sacrifice, and evidently was first used for sittings during which holy works were read. A 16th century definition of *satra* was "an assembly of holy persons where bhakti in all its aspects is preached" (Sarma, p. 104). The institution grew to be rather like a Buddhist math, with a specific architectural shape, a religious head (not necessarily a brahman), lay-members, a full panoply of teaching, crafts for the accessories of the drama and later for worship images, performances, and manuscript preparation. The movement has suffered a number of schisms, but the *satra* seems common to all.

Barua, Birinchi Kumar. *History of Assamese Literature*. Honolulu: East-West Center Press in cooperation with Sahitya Akademi, 1965 (1964).
Neog, Maheswar. *Sankaradeva and His Times*. Gauhati: Gauhati University, 1965.
Sarma, S. N. *The Neo-Vaisnavite Movement and the Satra Institution of Assam*. Gauhati: Gauhati University, 1966.

ANDHRA

I have been unable to find much satisfactory material on the history of bhakti in the Telugu-speaking territory. Evidently there were saint-poets in a 15th and 16th century school at Tirupati who followed the Kannada tradition of saint-musicians. The height of this tradition was reached by Tyāgarāja (1767-1847), a Telugu speaker living in Tanjore who is widely accepted as the greatest composer of Karnatic music. He often praised music itself as a path to God in his songs, one of which appears in de Bary, and fifteen in Raghavan. (See general bibliography.) The books on Tyāgarāja himself are chiefly concerned with his music.

In Andhra itself, Keshav Swami (1608-1682) seems to have been related to the Marāṭhā tradition. He wrote songs to Viṭhobā of Paṇḍharpur as well as Rāma, Kṛṣṇa and Śiva, and his songs appear in Marathi and Hindustani as well as Telugu. In the conceit of Eknāth and Purandaradāsa, he assumed various roles—dyer, washerman, devotee of Khandoba, juggler—to praise God. (Prasad, p. 97.) The best known bhakti saint of the area is Rāmdās of Bhadrācalam, a 17th century saint who praised Rāma. Prasad notes (p. 121), "Ramdas will be remembered by the Telugu people as his verses and Kirthanas are sung and there is no doubt that they will be sung forever."

Prasad, Dharmendra. *Saints of Telangana.* Hyderabad: Abul Kalam Azad Oriental Research Institute, no date.

NEW INTERPRETATIONS
IN EPIC MYTHOLOGY

# LIFE OUT OF DEATH

## *A Structural Analysis of the Myth of the 'Churning of the Ocean of Milk'*

J. BRUCE LONG

Ancient Indian literature reflects a general concensus among the Vedic sages and Hindu mythographers that in precosmogonic times, before the cosmos had assumed its present form, all things existed in a state of perfect unity and absolute stasis. As yet, no distinctions of any kind (life-death, good-evil, pleasure-pain, etc.) had arisen. Light had not been distinguished from darkness, dry land had not been separated from the waters, and Being had not as yet been differentiated from non-Being.[1]

The sages envisioned the cosmos in its present form as having evolved by means of the fragmentation of that primal unity, the emergence of the basal elements (air, fire, earth, water and space) out of the particles of the original 'stuff' and the distribution of those elements throughout the realm of 'names and forms' (*nāma-rūpa*).[2] This universe of multiplicity-out-of-unity and unity-within-multiplicity presents itself to man's perception as an immensely complex network of intersecting vectors of power which are, at once, complementary and interchangeable. According to various views of the

---

[1] The 'philosophical hymn' in Rig Veda X.129 presents this picture of primordial unity in terms which are at once intellectually provocative and poetically inspiring. This hymn testifies to the fact that from the beginning of the Vedic epoch, the sages were concerned with questions pertaining to the essential origin and nature of the universe, the ontological relation between 'Being' and 'non-Being', death and immortality and all the other 'primitive' oppositions. Cf. BAU I.2.1-7 for a more highly elaborated expression of the same fundamental vision of the cosmogony.

[2] Consult BAU I.1.1, where the most elaborate of all brahmanical sacrifices, the horse-sacrifice (*aśvamedha*), serves as a paradigmatic model for describing the evolution of the various components of the universe from the many parts of the horse. Whether this rite was a sacrifice to the sun, a fertility ceremony or a coronation rite, the horse is a most appropriate cosmogonic metaphor in a culture which viewed the creation of the world both in terms of a primordial sacrifice and an eternal conflict between polar opposites. See also the 'creation of the world from the Self' at BAU I.4.1 ff. where the original 'one', out of loneliness, sub-divided its inner essence to form a 'second' and from that primal pair, the world of multiplicity (*nāmarūpa*). Cf. BAU I.3.1-21; 5.21.

cosmogony portrayed in the Vedic hymns, the entire universe, both in its finite and infinite realms, was projected into being either by the self-immolation of a primeval Superman (*Puruṣa*) or by the dismemberment of a cosmic serpent (*Vṛtra*) at the hands of a divine hero (Indra). The multiple levels of reality were, in turn, constituted by the various parts of the anatomy of this primal creature. Another hymn (X. 121) eulogizes a microscopic golden seed (*hiraṇya-garbha*) as both the material and efficient cause of the cosmos, which exploded the world into existence by means of an inner incandescence.

Disregarding for the moment the ideological distinctions among the various Vedic cosmogonies, they all seem to be in agreement concerning one matter: the world, as we live in and know it, emerged from a powerfully disruptive partition of a precosmogonic unity in accordance with the dictates of the law of necessity (*Ṛta*). The Vedic *Ṛṣis* (sage-singers) and the Hindu *Kathakās* (story-tellers) could subscribe without reservation to the dicta of Heraclitus that, "It is necessary to know that war is common and right is strife and that all things happen by strife and necessity," (frag. 214) and "Out of all things there comes a unity and out of a unity all things." (frag. 206) In India, as in ancient Greece, the world was envisioned as existing in a state of relatively stable but precarious balance, established in the midst of the eternal conflict between the opposing forces of creation and destruction, light and darkness, good and evil.

It is this conflict between opposed but interrelated forces that, at one and the same time, established the world in existence and threatens it with extinction. In more specific terms, it might be said that the act of fragmenting the primal unity and distributing the parts throughout the world along lines of bi-polar opposition, was both a necessary precondition for the emergence of the world-order and a tragic testimony to the world's imperfection. Or again, the murder of the Primordial Serpent (*Vṛtra*) was both the unavoidable prelude to world evolution and a lamentable crime on a cosmic scale.[3]

Given the precarious status of the world, the ancient Indian bards (particularly in post-Vedic times) invested existence in the temporal world (*nāmarūpa*, *vyavahāra*) with a most ambivalent evalua-

[3] While the ambiguity of Indra's triumph over the serpent Vṛtra is never elaborated and, at the same time, is championed without reservation in the early Vedic literature (RV I.32), in the epics and purāṇas Vṛtra is said to be a brāhmaṇa. This fact transmutes Indra's apparently salutary and heroic act of world-redemption into an act of unredemptive culpability.

tion. Hindu literature and spirituality are informed by the conviction that, as man and his world came into being through the disruption of a primal unity and as man is identified essentially (i.e., spiritually and ontologically) with that primordial reality, he will realize his highest ideals only by transcending this world of cosmic conflict and illusoriness and, thereby, reintegrating himself with the source from which he and the cosmos emerged in the beginning.[4]

One of the most remarkable characteristics of the religious vision of the Vedic sages and Hindu mythographers is this puzzling juxtaposition of apparently contradictory ideas (i.e., multiplicity from unity, life through death, order out of conflict, etc.). Sometimes the oppositions are juxtaposed and then reversed in order to demonstrate that they are nothing more than interchangeable terms of the same reality. Sometimes the polarities are posited, reversed and then transposed into or merged with a third, 'higher' principle in order to accentuate the relativity of their status and function. And finally, on occasion, the polarities are simply displayed in a relationship of opposition and left in that state to be dealt with on their own terms. The sages and mythographers seem determined both to assert the unavoidability of the sets of polarities within the realm of mythical thought and, at the same time, to press beyond the level of polar opposition into a sphere of a larger and higher meaning.

Our primary aim in this paper will be to investigate the nature and application of this mode of thought described above, as it is put into service in one of the most popular myths in Hindu literature, i.e., the myth of the Churning of the Ocean of Milk for the Elixir of Immortality (*amṛta-manthana*). We shall attempt to decipher the meaning or 'message' of this myth as it is reflected in the formal components constituting the myth and the structural relationships obtaining between the several parts. In addition, we shall also attempt to put to a provisional test the approach to the study of myths formulated by Claude Lévi-Strauss.[5] The procedure we propose to follow is to subject the myth under consideration to a thorough structural

---

[4] See *Bhagavad Gītā* VI.18-29 where the supreme goal of 'integration' is said to result from seeing 'all things in the Self and the Self in all things', by viewing everything as identical (*samatvam*), and by transcending the opposites through reabsorption in the Eternal, unchanging One. Cf. BG II.48; IX.29; XIII.27.

[5] "The Structural Study of Myth," in *Structural Anthropology*. New York: Basic Books, 1963. (Originally published in *Myth: A Symposium*. T. A. Sebeok, ed. "Bibliographical and Special Series of American Folklore Society," no. 5, Bloomington: Indiana University Press, 1955.)

analysis, adhering where possible to the principles laid down by Lévi-Strauss, but by this procedure to demonstrate that, while many of the formal characteristics of that model are to be found in this myth, the myth itself betrays certain 'complications' which cannot be accommodated by this particular structural model. By demonstrating that Lévi-Strauss' model (at least, as he presents it in his earlier writings) is too simplistic to deal adequately with this myth, we intend to question the validity of one of the primary implications of his use of structural analysis in his early writings (especially, *The Savage Mind*)—that the structure which he found operative in the myths and symbols of the Indians of North and South America is the model of human thought universally.

A brief rehearsal of a few of the basic ideas in Lévi-Strauss' approach to the study of myth is in order before considering the myth itself. Like Sigmund Freud before him, Lévi-Strauss has professed an overriding concern with "the unconscious nature of collective phenomena" (1969: 18). In pursuance of this objective, he has engaged in a search for a universal logic of a nonrational sort which, he believes, is shared by all mankind. One avenue of approach to this universal logic is through the structural analysis of myth.

In keeping with this intention, he has claimed that all myths, from all levels of culture, display certain universal properties, which, when taken as a whole, yield a certain message embedded in a formal structure ('morphos'). Or, contrariwise, the central, underlying meaning of a myth or a group of myths is to be discovered by discerning the way in which mythic themes or mythologems are combined to form a system of meaningful relationships.

Lévi-Strauss claims, furthermore, that, however greatly altered any one version of a myth may be *vis-à-vis* another version taken as the paradigmatic version and however great the disparity may be among the details of any number of versions of the same myth, the essential underlying structural components that these stories possessed in the beginning will be retained in each of the several versions and will be accessible to the analyst even in their most 'distorted' forms. Therefore, the meaning of a myth or a collection of myths, according to Lévi-Strauss, resides not in the specific details of the narrative (e.g., dramatis personae, geographical sites, or particular acts by the mythic characters) but in the network of formal relationships among the constituent parts of the myth.

He asserts "that behind the manifest sense of the stories, there must be another non-sense, a message in code" (Leach, 1970: 56). It is the task of the student of mythology (and, by extension, the student of human culture) to uncover and delineate the central meaning of this latent message by deciphering the structural framework underlying the details of the narrative.

This hidden message, which reflects the "unconscious nature of collective phenomena," is concerned with the resolution of unwanted contradictions. The basic structure, according to which the several parts are interrelated, is composed of a set of binary oppositions ("life and death," "us and them," "nature and culture," to name but a few) which are mediated (i.e., the conflict between them is resolved) by a third term. This 'middle term' does not belong strictly or solely to either of the polar opposites but, nonetheless, partakes in the nature and function of each, while, at the same time, gathering up, merging and transporting both the opposites into a more comprehensive realm of meaning.

We must also bear in mind one corollary to these notions: namely, that a myth, viewed in terms of its most extensive definition, consists of the collection of all the variations contained in the different versions. Hence, in order to arrive at an adequate understanding of the central meaning of the myth, the analyst must take into account all the versions at his disposal. The implication of [illegible] methodological presupposition is that no one version can be [illegible]d to be truest, most original or most authoritative. In [illegible] fact that each version of a myth gives expression to the [illegible] meaning of the entire mythology, each form must be c[illegible] 'true' in its own terms.

To preview our argument briefly wi[illegible]he application of the Lévi-Straussian approach to the [illegible] Churning of the Ocean: granted that the various pers[illegible] situations in the myth do appear to stand with each [illegible]ations of bi-polar opposition, none of the components represents either of the extremities unambiguously. The quality or identity of each pole is reflected obliquely in (or, better still, is interchangeable with) its opposite. For example, the *Devas* and *Asuras* (gods and demons) "although distinct and opposite in operation, are in essence consubstantial, their distinction being a matter not of essence but of orientation, revolution or transformation. . ." (Coomaraswamy, 1935: 373). The Devas, though generally benevolent in their relationship with mankind, given the right conditions, will act malevolently and 'demonically'.

The Asuras, though normally fearsome and destructive (representing, as they do, the powers of darkness and death), given the necessary prerequisites, will manifest themselves as friendly and supportive of gods, as well as men. The Devas and Asuras coexist in a relationship that is not only oppositional and, at the same time, complementary, but also, from the standpoint of the Godhead, consubstantial and interchangeable.

Furthermore, the god Viṣṇu, who in Lévi-Straussian language appears to function as the principle of mediation, (and, at the same time, as the great magician, the master of magical power [*mahāmāyin*] who is capable of assuming any mode of manifestation he chooses), is not only supportive of both the parties in conflict (the Devas *and* the Asuras), but *is* both the parties as well. In a word, Viṣṇu is the omnipresent superintendent of the Churning of the Ocean who identifies himself not only with both the extreme and the middle positions, but with all other positions on the continuum. At various moments during the story, Viṣṇu manifests himself as being both the One and the Many, the principle which simultaneously unifies the polarities and polarizes the unity.

With this fact in view, we will be arguing explicitly that the meanings expressed in this myth (and perhaps many other Hindu myths and legends as well) are far too complex and multivalent to be analyzed adequately with reference to a simple polar opposition combined with a final synthesis. The confirmation of our argument will be exemplified in the ambivalent relationship obtaining between the Devas and Asuras, and in the uniform—*cum*—multiform appearances of Viṣṇu.

### *A Survey of the Sources*

One important consideration which should be kept in mind is that, although the Churning of the Ocean myth *per se* does not appear anywhere in the pre-epic literature,[6] it does contain numerous

[6] A. K. Coomaraswamy does seem to imply, in his essay on "Angels and Titans. An Essay on Vedic Ontology," [JAOS 55, 4 (1935), 373-419] that the act of churning the milk of the Soma plant within the context of the Soma rites, may have served as a model for the composers of the epic and purāṇic versions of the myth. S. A. Dange asserts outright, in his *Legends in the Mahābhārata* (Delhi: Motilal Banarsidass, 1969, 239-86, 360-61) that "The idea of the Churning of the Ocean is not a new one and can be traced in the Vedic literature, as we note in Vedic passages, where Soma, spoken as *amṛta*, is said to be rising up to the heaven from the 'Samudra' which is the name of the Soma vessel. . . The legend of the churning as it is given in the MBh., thus, seems to have its roots in Vedic

mythic themes which are to be found in the earlier phases of the tradition.[7] The myth appears somewhat unexpectedly and in a rather highly developed form in the early portions of both the *Rāmāyaṇa* and the *Mahābhārata* and in more highly embellished forms in numerous *purāṇas*.

Because of its brevity and sparseness of detail we have selected the version of the myth contained in the *Rāmāyaṇa* (*Bāla-kāṇḍa* 45, 14-31) as the paradigmatic model for purposes of this analysis. The myth in the *Rāmāyaṇa* is related to Śrī Rāma and his brother Lakṣmaṇa by the venerable sage Viśvāmitra, within the brief compass of eighteen verses. This version contains a narration of the selection of the Mt. Mandara and the cosmic serpent Vāsuki as the churning implements, the production of the dreadful poison from the serpent's mouth, Śiva's gracious act of drinking the poison and retaining it in his throat, the production of the precious gifts from the ocean, and the recovery of the nectar of life by the gods through Viṣṇu's assumption of the guise of a beguiling maiden. The elements which are unique to this version of the myth are the rejection of the *Apsarases* by both gods and demons and the acceptance by the gods of Varuṇī or Surā, the Goddess of Wine, together with her rejection by the demons.[8]

The version in the *Mahābhārata* is couched within the context of the eternal warfare (*saṁgrāma*) between the gods (*Devas*, *Ādityas*) and the Titans or antigods (*Asuras*, *Daityas*, *Dānavas*). Purportedly, the story is related by Sauti in order to account for the appearance of the sacred horse, *Uccaiḥśravas* and the origin of solar and lunar eclipses resulting from the consumption of the elixir by the demon, Rāhu (the 'Seizer').

---

literature, especially in the sacrificial ritual of the pressing of the Soma." (p. 279) He goes on to support his interpretation by noticing formal similarities between the pressing stones and Mt. Mandara, between the juice of the Soma plant and 'the various fluids dripping into the ocean from the mountain Mandara'.

[7] Mention should be made of the references to the tortoise incarnation of Prajāpati in ŚB VII 5.1.5-6 and of Kaśyapa, 'Tortoise,' a venerable Ṛṣi in the Rig Veda (IX 114.2) and the patronymic title of a priestly family (AB VII.27). The tortoise form of manifestation is intimately related to both Prajāpati and Viṣṇu in the Atharva Veda and the late Vedic literature. In the ŚB reference cited above, it is said that, "since tortoise (*kūrma*) is identical with Kaśyapa, therefore, men say: all beings are the children of the tortoise [i.e., Kaśyapa]. Now this *kūrmaḥ* is the same as yonder sun."

[8] Hence the origin of the names of the two groups of supernatural beings: *Suras* (gods, who "possess wine") and *Asuras* (demons, who are "without wine".)

In the *Viṣṇu Purāṇa*, the story is told in order to account for the appearance of *Śrī* and of Viṣṇu's choice of her as his divine consort. This account (probably the latest version to develop along with that in the *Śrībhāgavatam*) emphasizes the fact that the gods and demons "entered into an alliance" and jointly undertook the acquisition of the beverage of immortality. But the theme of the quest for the nectar is all but lost in this version because of the overriding stress placed upon the epiphany and praise of Śrīdevī, the female consort of Viṣṇu.

We derive no significant new information from the *Matsya Purāṇa* account of the myth, except that the demons who were killed on the battlefield by the gods were resuscitated with the *saṃjīvinī* lore ("enlivening, rejuvenating"), perhaps a kind of herb of immortality, by Śukra, the son of the fire-priest, Bhṛgu and father of Varuṇī or Surā, wife of Varuṇa. The *Mahābhārata* and *Matsya* versions possess so many details in common it seems likely that either both versions were derived from a single common source or that one of them (most probably the M*atsya*) was composed in imitation of the other.[9]

Finally, in the *Śrībhāgavatam*, there appears a most highly embellished version after which follows immediately an effusive adjulation of Mahāviṣṇu by Brahmā, Śiva and the other celestials. Once again, the acquisition of the elixir is the central focus of the story, with the episodes of Viṣṇu taking on the form of a beautiful maiden (*mohinī*) and the theft of the nectar by the demon Rāhu appended (as in the MBh.) to the principal narrative.

The *Mahābhārata* [10] version, to which we will make frequent reference, will be designated as variant one; the expanded version from the *Viṣṇu Purāṇa* [11] will be termed variant two; the *Matsya Purāṇa* [12]

---

[9] This claim, shared by V. M. Bedekar, is presented in an essay entitled, "The Legend of the Churning of the Ocean in the Epics and Purāṇas, A Comparative Study," *Purāṇa* IX (February, 1967), 7-61.

[10] *Śrīmadmahābhārata*, critically edited by V. S. Sukthankar, 19 vols. Poona: Bhandarkar Oriental Research Institute, 1933-66, Vol. 1 (English translation by P. C. Roy, 12 vols., Calcutta: Oriental Publishing Company) [The *Ādi-parvan* of a new English translation of the Critical Edition with copious notes by J. A. B. van Buitenen was published in 1973 by the University of Chicago Press].

[11] *Viṣṇumahāpurāṇa*, Gorakpur: Gītā Press [English translation by H. H. Wilson London: J. Murray, 1840].

[12] *Matsyapurāṇa* (ASS no. 54) Poona: Ānandāśram Press, 1907. [English translation by a Taluqbar of Oudh, in the *Sacred Books of the Hindus*. Vol. XVII, pt. 172, Allahabad: Pāṇini Office, 1916].

form, variant three; and the *Bhāgavata Purāṇa* [13] form, variant four.[14]

*The Rāmāyaṇa Version: The Mythic Paradigm*

We realize that the decision to restrict the focus of this paper to the analysis of a single myth places certain limitations upon our ability to test adequately Lévi-Strauss' approach to the structural analysis of myths. We feel justified in doing so, however, on the basis of the fact that Lévi-Strauss himself concentrates on one myth (though in two different versions) in "The Story of Asdiwal". He also asserts in the "Overture" to *Le Cru et le Cuit* that he will be studying a single Bororo myth (which he calls "the reference myth") as "an extended transformation of other myths which have originated either in the same society or in other near and distant societies." We, therefore, will adopt a similar view that the myth of the Churning of the Ocean is "a more or less extended transformation of other myths," resulting from both an exclusion and inclusion of elements from those other myths according to the needs of the mythographer.

Because of its brevity and simplicity, we have chosen to use the form of the story recorded in the *Rāmāyaṇa* [15] as the paradigmatic or 'control' version. We have chosen this version as the model, not because we feel it to be earlier, truer or more authoritative than the others, but because it is this version which manifests most clearly and dramatically the central underlying *structure* and *message* of the myth.

The account of the Churning of the Ocean in the *Rāmāyaṇa* is set within the context of a long narration by the sage Viśvāmitra in which he relates the story of the death of the sons of King Sagara, the descent of the Ganges and the origins of the city of Viśāla. The sage discards all irrelevant details and relates the story in such a cryptic manner that he seems to be drawing directly upon a visual representa-

---

[13] *Śrīmadbhāgavatam* with commentary of Raghavānanda Muni, edited by M. B. Sankaranarayana Sastri [Sree Ravi Varma Sanskrit Series, no. 2] Trichur, 1949. [English translation by J. M. Sanyal, Calcutta: Oriental Pub. Co., 1964-65].

[14] According to a lengthy footnote in H. H. Wilson's translation of the *Viṣṇu Purāṇa* (p. 77-78), this myth is briefly alluded to in the *Śiva*, *Liṅga* and *Kūrma Purāṇas*. The *Vāyu* and *Padma* (*Uttara-kāṇḍa*) present accounts which are almost identical to the one in the *Viṣṇu Purāṇa*, as do the *Agni* and *Śrībhāgavatam*. The version in the *Harivaṁśa* (v. 12834) is brief and obscure and is explained by the commentor, Nīlakaṇṭha, as an allegory in which the churning typifies ascetic penance and the ambrosia is final liberation.

[15] *Śrīmadvālmikirāmāyaṇa*. Crit. Ed. by J. M. Mehta *et al.* (Baroda: Oriental Institute, 1960). [English Translation by H. P. Shastri, London: Shanti Sadan, 1953].

tion of the event. He relates the story to Rāma and his brother, Lakṣmaṇa, as he had received it from Indra, as follows: during the Kṛta or Satya Yuga (the Cosmic Era of Perfection and Truth) Diti (supernatural personification of boundary or limit) gave birth to a powerful Daitya, a demon or titan. Aditi (= boundless, unlimited), mother of the gods and the embodiment of Infinity, gave birth to Devarata (= delighting in the gods, pious) who was distinguished for his great heroic valor (*vīrya*) and righteousness (*sudharmika*). These two supernatural beings desired to become immortal (*amṛta* = non-dying), incorruptible, and free from disease, old age and death. After consultation they decided to churn *Kṣīroda* (the Ocean of Milk) in hopes of obtaining from it the water (*rasa*) of immortality. Employing the divine serpent Vāsuki ('possessor of treasures' or 'one who clothes all things') as the churning rope and Mt. Mandara (= steady, unmoving), as the churning rod, they commenced churning.

After churning for a thousand years, Vāsuki began to gnash the rocks of the mountain with his teeth and to vomit venom from his one-thousand mouths, thus creating a scene which resembled in appearance the holocaust (*pralaya*) which portends the end of the World Aeon. From this venom developed the awful poison [16] (*halāhala*, *kālakūṭa*) which spread throughout the world, threatening the existence of men, gods and even the demons themselves.

The gods sought refuge at the feet of Lord Viṣṇu, who in turn, invoked Śiva-Mahādeva: "O Lord, thou art the *chief* of the gods, and should accept whatever is produced *first* from the churning of the Ocean. Kindly receive the poison as thy gift, the tribute of the *first-fruits*" [emphasis added] The Lord Śiva, moved by the words of Lord Viṣṇu and grieved by the plight of the gods, "drank the dreadful poison, *as if it were nectar* (*amṛta*) and returned to his abode on Mt. Kailāsa." [emphasis added].

As the gods and demons resumed the churning, the churning rod began to sink into the waters of the Cosmic Ocean. In response to their cries of anguish, Viṣṇu assumed the form (*avatāra*) of a tortoise (*kūrma*),[17] entered the waters and supported the mountain on his

[16] According to Monier-Williams' *Sanskrit Dictionary*, a deadly poison made from a plant, the seed of which resembles a cow's teat.

[17] Concerning the role of the tortoise in Hindu mythology and folklore from earliest times to the present, consult J. J. Meyer, *Trilogie altindischer Mächte und Fest der Vegetation* (Zürich-Leipzig, 1937, III), pp. 221ff.; S. Kramrisch, *The Hindu Temple*. (Calcutta: University of Calcutta, 1947), pp. 111-13; and J. Gonda, *Aspects*

back. Taking hold of the peak with both hands, he churned the Ocean while standing between the Devas and Asuras.[18] After another thousand years had passed, numerous articles of great value [19] (*ratnas*) emerged from the milky-white ocean: first, Dhanvantari, the physician of the gods and author of the Āyur-veda, holding a staff and a lump of clay (*loṣṭa*) in his hands; then, the Apsarases by the thousands (*ap* = water; (*sara* = flowing within), who were rejected by both the Devas and Asuras and, therefore, remained without a lord (or, conversely, belonged to all creatures). They are known until this day as *Sādhāraṇās* (= harlots). Then in succession, there appeared Varuṇī or Surā (lit. 'wine') the wife of Varuṇa, who was accepted by the Ādityas but was rejected by the Daityas;[20] *Uccaiḥśravas* (= 'great noise' or 'lofty praise'), the celestial horse and prototype of the equine race;[21] the magical jewel *Kaustubha*, which Viṣṇu chose as an embodiment of his consort Śrī-Lakṣmī, and finally the water of immortality (*rasāmṛtam*).[22]

---

*of Early Viṣṇuism*. (Utrecht, 1954), pp. 126-29, together with *Die Religionen Indiens*, (Stuttgart: W. Kohlhammer Verlag, 1960), I, *Veda und älterer Hindusmus*, 89ff. by the same author.

[18] A panoramic bas-relief representing this scene is to be found in the eastern gallery, southern half of the main shrine at Angkor Wāt dating from the early 12th century. Consult H. Zimmer's *Art of Indian Asia* (New York: Pantheon Books, 1955), plates 548-51, for an excellent reproduction of the bas-relief. (See also B. P. Groslier *Angkor, Art and Civilization* (London: Thames and Hudson, 1962), plate 42.

[19] There is a popular Sanskrit stanza, customarily chanted in the context of the marriage rite, which enumerates 14 precious objects. This list of 14 objects includes the 12 standard jewels, occurring frequently in the purāṇas, plus the bow (*Śārṅga*) and conch-shell (*Śaṅkha*) of Hari. Given the apparent Vaiṣṇava bias of this myth, it is a wonder that these primary symbols of Viṣṇu do not appear in the traditional lists. The Sanskrit stanza reads as follows: *lakṣmīḥ kaustubha pārijātakasurā dhanvantariścandramāḥ gāvaḥ kāmadughā sureśvaragajo rambhādidevāṅganāḥ / aśvaḥ saptamukho viṣaṁ haridhanuḥ śaṅkho'mṛtam cāmbudheḥ ratnānīha caturdaśa pratidinaṁ kurvantu vo maṅgalaṁ / /.*

[20] And, the text adds: "Those who accepted her were called *suras* (gods) and those who rejected her were called *asuras* (demons)."

[21] E. W. Hopkins speaks of the celestial horse as "the divine ever-youthful horse, produced at the churning of the ocean and famous only as the white roaring charger of the sea. What can that be save the roaring breakers?" *Epic Mythology* (Strassburg: Verlag Von Karl J. Trübner, 1915), p. 125. Cf. MBh. I.20.1ff.; I.17.3; 18.35f; V.102.12; VI.34.27; VII.196.30.

[22] The etymology of the term *amṛta* is a much debated issue. The most credible suggestion is the following: *A* = non and *mṛta* = death. The term may be distantly related to the Greek term *ambrosia*. In Hindu mythology, the word 'immortality', which is the customary translation of *amṛta*, does not mean eternal life as it does in the Judeo-Christian tradition, but simply a long life filled with prosperity, health, many progeny and general well-being. Consult F. Edgerton's ar-

The truce between the gods and demons was short-lived. Immediately after obtaining the elixir, the eternal antagonists fell to fighting once again for absolute lordship over the powers of life and death. In order to distract the Daityas, Viṣṇu employed his *māyā* (magical power of illusion) to take the form of a charming maiden, *Mohinī* (= beguiling, deluding) and retrieved the nectar from the Asuras. The text concludes with the statement: "Those who opposed the imperishable (*akṣara*) Viṣṇu were destroyed by him. In this battle, the gods slew countless Daityas. Indra, after slaying the Asuras, became king of the gods and with the assistance of the Ṛṣis, began to rule with felicity (*mudita*).

*Relevant Variations from the Other Versions*

Lévi-Strauss contends (1963: 218-19) that different versions of the same myth, different myths from the same cultural tradition, or even myths taken from different cultures communicate the same message, (even when the specific contents of the myths differ radically), provided the component parts of each of the myths in question are interrelated according to the same principle of coherence. If this proposition be true, then all the relevant variants of a single myth must be taken into consideration with a view toward formulating an adequate analysis of the 'reference myth'. We shall pause briefly to note some of the relevant variations found in the other accounts of the myth of the Churning of the Ocean, before proceeding to an analysis of the myth proper.

1. After the Devas had failed in their efforts to uproot the mighty Mandara, the cosmic serpent, Vāsuki, in response to the command of Nārāyaṇa-Viṣṇu, pulled up the mountain and Indra, the leader of the divine armies, established it upon the back of the Cosmic Tortoise (*Kūrma* = Viṣṇu in his amphibian incarnation but here identified as *Akūpāra*, the king of the Tortoises). [MBh.]
2. After some disagreement as to who would hold the head of Vāsuki, the Asuras were granted the honor by Viṣṇu, in response

ticle, "The Fountain of Youth," *JAOS*, XXVI, no. 1, (1905), 1-67 and Murray Fowler "A Note on ἄμβροτος", *Classical Philology* XXXVII, (January, 1942), 77-79. The latter study contends that the Greek ἄμβροτος and the Sanskrit *amṛta* may be distantly related etymologically. Be that as it may, both words are used to designate that which liberates from the bonds of death or provides abundant life in the world of the living.

to their claim to possess a pre-eminence of birth and deeds. What they had anticipated would be a position of advantage over the Devas turned out to be one of disadvantage. The rapid raising and lowering of the hood of Vāsuki created clouds of fire and smoke, [MBh.] substances which, at one and the same time, distressed the Asuras and reinvigorated the Devas. [Bhāg. P., V.P.] In the MBh. version, the Devas report to Brahmā that both they and the Daityas have become exhausted by their labors and that without the assistance of Nārāyaṇa they cannot succeed.

3. Viṣṇu is presented as existing in three different guises and performing three separate roles simultaneously: (a) as the Sacred Tortoise supporting the churning rod; (b) as the controller of the churning rope and rod and the actual churner; and (c) as the superintendent of the entire procedure, seated atop Mt. Mandara. [V.P.]
4. The Devas and Asuras cast into the Cosmic Ocean various varieties of medicinal creepers, herbs, and grasses (*oṣadhis*, *bheṣajas*) in order to augment the healing powers of the waters. [V.P., Bhāg. P.]. The juices of the herbs and saps of the tree flowed into the water of the Ocean. With the milk (*payasā*) of these juices (*rasānāṁ*) that possessed the power of elixir, together with the residue of molten gold, the Devas achieved Immortality. By adding sap to the Ocean, the waters were transformed into milk; by churning the Ocean, the milk was transformed into butter (*ghee*, *soma*). [MBh.]
5. Indra, as leader of armies of the celestials, extinguished the conflagration created by the churning of the Ocean, established Mt. Mandara on the back of the tortoise, led the defensive attack against the Asuras, [V.P.] killed various demons (Bala, Bali, Namuci) [Bhāg. P.], and finally, as a reward for these heroic accomplishments, was established as king of the gods [MBh., Rām., V.P.]
6. After being presented with various hymns of adoration by the choirs of heaven, Śrī, the goddess of prosperity and welfare, took up her position on the breast of Hari (= Viṣṇu) and cast her glances (i.e., bestowed prosperity) upon the gods, while Viṣṇu turned his back upon the Daityas, led by Vipracitti (= inspired mind) and, thereby, denied them access to the goddess of prosperity. [V.P.]

7. The Daityas slain by the gods in battle were restored to life by Śukra, son of Bhṛgu, with the *Samjīvinī* or herb of immortality which the latter had discovered. [Mat. P.]
8. The Ocean was churned as a result of Viṣṇu's desire to play (*līlā*, *krīḍa*) in its waters. [Bhāg. P.]
9. The world was renewed throughout the divine and human spheres (both spiritually and physically); prosperity, longevity and general well-being were established throughout the cosmos as a result of the acquisition of the Elixir of Immortality, the defeat of the demons, and the reestablishment of divine rule in heaven. [V.P.]

*Preliminary Considerations*

Even a cursory reading of the myth gives rise to numerous provocative questions. A few of the more obvious questions are these: where would this tale be placed most appropriately within a typology of myths? Is it a cosmogonic myth [23] and, if so, in what terms is the world said to have been produced or evolved? [24] If not a cosmogonic myth, then is it a myth concerning the quest for Immortality on the order of the Gilgamesh Epic or the legend of Ponce de Leon's search

[23] Jeannine Auboyer claims that this myth performs a cosmogonic function. When the churning staff becomes dislodged, falling into the waters, most of the versions present Viṣṇu as ascending from the base of the mountain to its peak, whereon is the seat of Brahmā, the creator god. This ascent of Viṣṇu, she contends, is a representation of his traversing the three levels of the cosmos. This view is borne out vividly in Khmer iconography in Cambodia which pictures Viṣṇu as present within all three spheres of the cosmos at the same moment. *Le Trône et son symbolisme dans l'Inde ancienne*. (Paris: Presses Universitaires de France 1949), 96ff. Dr. S. A. Dange also argues for a cosmogonic function of this story: "The phase of the ocean—still and serene before the vigorous movements of churning—hiding the gems in its depths—looks very much similar to the state of the streams of waters that are held captive (and hence are to be released) with all the luminaries kept hidden by some demon. The stirring of the ocean is symbolic of the beginning of the act of creation. The mountain Mandara, reminding us of the Vedic 'adri' or 'giri' stands also as a symbol of creation and resembles the first lotus stalk that comes out of the primeval waters. The tortoise and Vāsuki are also symbols of creations. Vāsuki, as also the mountain Mandara, does not signify any particular entity; it is the world serpent signifying the creating spirit like the tortoise." (*Legends in the Mahābhārata*. Delhi: Motilal Banarsidass, 1969, p. 279).

[24] The claim could be defended that the world already existed and provided the setting for the Churning of the Ocean, on the basis of a statement made by the Vedic Ṛṣis to the effect that, "the gods appeared later on—after the creation of the world. Who can know, therefore, out of what it has evolved?" (RV X.129. 12).

for the Fountain of Youth? What was the original core of the myth (viz. Warfare between Devas and Asuras, Churning of the Ocean, Quest for Immortality)? Can it be argued convincingly that the myth developed around a single primal meaning and, if so, is that original meaning accessible to the analyst?

Again, given the fact that it is the nectar of life that is being sought, why, according to certain versions, is the poison the initial substance to appear? If this myth was composed in glorification of Viṣṇu, as it seems to have been, how did Śiva come to play such a crucial role in the myth and precisely what is the nature of his role? For what reason do the gods falter and find it necessary to resort to Viṣṇu for guidance and support? Why did Viṣṇu himself, who is lacking in neither wisdom nor power, find it necessary or desirable to resort in the end to subterfuge and deceit in order to retrieve the elixir from the Asuras—a goal which he, no doubt, should have been able to accomplish through the powers of Divine Sovereignty? Finally, given the apparent Vaiṣṇava orientation of the myth, why are many of the versions told primarily to account for the establishment of Indra as the King of the Gods and, if Viṣṇu is the All-god, according to this myth, what is the relationship between Indra and Viṣṇu in the economy of Divine Sovereignty?

While we cannot hope to address ourselves to all these queries in a study of such limited scope, we will attempt to discover plausible solutions to certain of the problems presented by this myth and, thereby, uncover the organizing principles on which the framework (and hence, the message) of the myth is established.

*Analysis of the Myth*

Every myth, regardless of cultural origin or nature of contents, represents a set of structural units or 'mythemes' which may be pictured in the form of a bilateral chart. This chart provides a visual representation of the pattern on the basis of which the units of the myth are grouped together according to their exhibition of certain common features to form 'gross constituent units'. These 'gross constituent units' are not particular entities standing in isolation from each other but 'bundles of such relations' which alone "can be put to use and combined so as to produce a meaning." (Lévi-Strauss, 1963: 210-11). It is these aggregates of relations which display the underlying structure of the myth in all its variants and which, taken together, freight the meaning of the myth.

CHART 1

*'Gross Elements' in the Myth of the Churning of the Ocean*

| I<br>*Crisis Event* | II<br>*Disastrous Result* | III<br>*Remedial Action* | IV<br>*Fortunate Result* |
|---|---|---|---|
| *Rām.*: Primordial conflict between gods (*Ādityas*) and demons (*Daityas*) and temporary truce for purpose of churning of Ocean for elixir | Churning of Ocean produces dreadful poison which threatens to engulf the cosmos | Śiva swallows poison to save world from destruction | Churning is resumed and treasures, including the nectar (*amṛta*), are produced |
| Gods are unable to uproot mountain and set it on its base | Mountain begins to sink into the Ocean | Viṣṇu appears in form of a tortoise and supports mountain | Viṣṇu churns Ocean standing between gods and demons |
| Demons steal nectar from gods for their own evil purposes | Resumption of warfare | Viṣṇu appears in form of divine maiden and steals nectar from the demons | Viṣṇu destroys demons and restores nectar to the gods |
| *MBh.* (Var. 1): Gods and their attendants unable to uproot mountain | | Ananta uproots Mt. Mandara, Indra places it on back of tortoise where gods had failed to do so | Churning of Ocean is resumed |
| Gods exhausted from churning, repair to Viṣṇu for refreshment | | Viṣṇu refreshes gods by mere glance of eyes | |
| Gods weakened from heat and fatigue | | Gods refreshed by cascades of flowers sent down from heaven | Churning is resumed |
| Poison produced from mouths of Vāsuki or from churning as gods pull on the serpent | | Śiva in *mantra*-form drinks poison, holds it in his throat | |

| I<br>*Crisis Event* | II<br>*Disastrous Result* | III<br>*Remedial Action* | IV<br>*Fortunate Result* |
|---|---|---|---|
| The creatures are threatened by falling rocks and trees and fires created by pervasive friction | Cosmos endangered with return to chaos | Indra extinguishes fires with celestial showers | Celestial rains transform water of Ocean into milk and then into butter which is the golden nectar |
| Demons claim the nectar for themselves | | Viṣṇu through *māyā* takes form of celestial maiden and deludes demons | Demons lose control of senses and hand *amṛta* over to Mohinī, divine rule is reestablished |
| A Dānava, Rāhu, steals nectar and drinks it | | Sun and moon alert Viṣṇu of danger of losing nectar to Dānavas once again | Viṣṇu decapitates Rāhu to keep him from swallowing the nectar |
| Demons again try to take nectar by force | Horrendous battle between gods and demons ensues | Viṣṇu intervenes with his celestial discus (*sudarśana*) | The gods win the day |
| *Viṣṇu Pur.* (Var. 2):<br>Demons shorn of glory by flames from hood of serpent; gods refreshed by same | | Śrī placed on Viṣṇu's breast and gazed upon the gods | Viṣṇu with Śrī on chest turns away from demons denying them access to goddess of prosperity |
| Daityas steal *amṛta* from Dhanvantari | | Viṣṇu takes female form and charms the demons | Gods defeat demons, Indra crowned as king of gods, world is renewed |
| *Matsya Pur.* (Var. 3):<br>The quest for elixir thwarted by mutual antagonism between gods and demons | Daityas slain by gods, thereby threatening quest for elixir with failure | Daityas restored to life by Śukra with herb of rejuvenation (*saṁjīvinī*) | Churning is resumed and carried to successful end |

| I<br>*Crisis Event* | II<br>*Disastrous Result* | III<br>*Remedial Action* | IV<br>*Fortunate Result* |
|---|---|---|---|
| *Bhāg. Pur.* (Var. 4): | | | |
| Demons demand front of Vāsuki, leaving gods with hindpart | Reversal of natural order | | Demons scorched by fire from serpent's mouths, while the gods are refreshed |
| Gods and demons exhausted from carrying mountain; it sinks into Ocean; they become weak and despondent | | Viṣṇu places mountain on back of Garuḍa who places it upon back of Ananta; he encourages and reinvigorates gods and demons | |
| Marine life agitated, world threatened by conflagration, poison produced | Cosmos threatened with destruction | | Śiva vows to drink poison to please Viṣṇu and Umā |
| Demons argue over who is to partake of nectar first | | Viṣṇu distributes nectar to gods and deludes demons into forgetting it<br>Demons denied *amṛta* because of disloyalty to Nārāyaṇa | |
| Renewed battle between gods and demons | | Indra slays various demons in battle and gives victory to gods | Viṣṇu dissolves conflict by his appearance<br>Śiva himself is deluded by Mohinī and sings Viṣṇu's praises |

We note in passing Lévi-Strauss' claim that "the only method we can suggest at this stage is to proceed tentatively, by trial and error, using as a check the principles which serve as a basis for any kind of structural analysis: economy of explanation; unity of solution; and ability to reconstruct the whole from a fragment, as well as later stages from previous ones." (*Ibid.*, 211) We will return at a later point in the paper to offer additional critical observations concerning this *modus operandi*.

Even a casual perusal of the myth of the Churning of the Ocean will awaken the mind of the reader to the existence of a number of consistently repetitive patterns, which represent to a limited extent Lévi Strauss' 'gross constituent units'. (Consult the chart on pages 186-188.)

Reading vertically from left to right, the elements in Column I present a certain crisis-event arising from a conflict between two opposing forces, a dangerous shifting of power onto the demonic side for the manipulation of the instruments of churning, or a failure of strength or cunning on the divine side. The units of material in Column II present the catastrophic effects resulting from the crisis and the demand for some kind of redemptive action to compensate for the misfortune. The components in Column III represent such a salutary action performed by a deity (most often, Viṣṇu, but sometimes Śiva or Indra) which serves to rectify the disequilibrium of forces appearing in Column II. The data in Column IV presents either the deeds which the agent is enabled to perform by the activities in Column II or the felicitious state of affairs which ultimately brings all lines of conflict into a state of (at least, temporary) resolution.

A careful study of the chart will indicate that each *persona* in the story undergoes every *typical* experience in the scenario and the relationships between the several parties across lines of opposition and synthesis give expression to the overall structure of the myth. As Lévi-Strauss himself remarks in his essay entitled, "Overture," "the structure of myths can be revealed through a musical score" (1964, 15).

The setting for the Churning of the Ocean is established by the arrangement of a temporary truce in the eternal warfare between the gods and the demons.[25] Although the two groups of forces manage to

---

[25] One of the strikingly persistent features of Hindu ideology is the identification of right and life with light, wrong and death with darkness. In the Vedas the gods and hosts (*gaṇas*) are luminous, while the demons are generally darkness.

establish a 'functional' cessation of their eternal conflict, in the knowledge that without doing so "the amelioration of your lot is impossible," [Bhāg. Pur. VIII. 6], they resume the fighting almost immediately after the appearance of the elixir. Indeed, they come into conflict even earlier, as shown in variant 4 [Bhāg. Pur.], exemplified in the debate as to which of the groups is to be allotted the prestigious station at the forepart of the serpent. It is as though the formation of a permanent armistice between the gods and demons were contrary to Universal Law.[26]

The ambiguity of the relationship between the Devas and Asuras is hinted at in this myth but is not elaborated. If we look to the earlier Vedic literature for additional information concerning this matter, we find that the Devas and Asuras, from earliest times, are represented as being, not only arch-enemies engaged in an eternal conflict of cosmic proportions, but also as two groups of beings who are related to each other on the most intimate terms.

Perhaps a brief survey of the Vedic cosmogony would serve to illuminate more fully the nature of the relationship between the two groups of celestials. As the accompanying chart illustrates (page 191), according to the Vedic cosmogony, the world was brought into being when the Primal Unity (*tad ekam*: RV X 129.2), 'breathing without wind' and 'creating energies from its austerities', projected its own essence into the phenomenal world of names and forms (*nāmarūpa*). Within the finite realm, *Tad Ekam* is invoked by many names: Agni (RV III 3.11), Soma (IX 10.7) or Varuṇa, who separates Heaven and Earth and props apart the two halves of the cosmos by means of a pillar of enormous proportions (X 55.1; 113.5). With the 'breathing by its own power', the state of 'neither non-being

---

This system of correspondences is generally considered to be most peculiar to the Iranians and Persians but given its persistence in the Indian context nothing could be more thoroughly Indic. The fire-priest, Bhṛgu, proclaims, "Untruth is a form of darkness and by darkness one is brought to hell; veiled in darkness one sees not the light of heaven. It has been said that light is heaven, darkness is hell" (MBh. XII. 183, 2-3, Crit. Ed.).

[26] It is also not unreasonable to view the counterbalancing pull of the churning rope and rod as a kind of tug-of-war, a contest for the booty of *amṛta* and that, as such, this act of Churning the Ocean of Milk is an instance of warfare sublimated into the form of a sportive contest. In fact, in many cultures of the world, games of competition frequently serve as a vicarious substitution for actual military conflict. J. Huizinga provides a most learned discussion of the custom of treating warfare as a game of competition and of viewing various sorts of competitive sports as 'muted warfare', in his classical work, *Homo Ludens. A Study of the Play-Element in Culture* (Boston: The Beacon Press, 1950), 89-104.

(*asat*) nor being (*sat*)' came to an end through a primal beginning. This originative power by means of its inner incandescence (*tapas*) procreated itself into multiple forms of life. Thus, the original unity was broken, divided into two parts (Being and non-Being, Heaven and Earth, etc.) and subdivided again to form the realm of multiplicity.

Viewing the cosmogony at a glance, the separation of Being and non-Being, or of Heaven and Earth ('twin brother and sister' I. 62.7), into distinct realms of existence is the initial cosmogonic act. From this primal pair, all the other beings (both mobile and immobile) sprang into existence within a realm defined as Two-in-One or the Disunified-Unity.[27]

CHART 2

*Structural Framework of Vedic Cosmogony*

| | |
|---|---|
| *TAD EKAM* = That One<br>(Prajāpati, Tvaṣṭṛ, Brahman) | |
| SAT (= Being) | ASAT (= non-Being) |
| Aditi (= 'the limitless') | Diti (= 'limiting force')<br>(Danu) |
| Ādityas | Daityas<br>(Dānavas) |
| Devas (gods, angels) | Asuras (demons, titans) |
| Indra (= chief of Ādityas) | Vṛtra (= chief of the Daityas) |

The Devas and Asuras are said to have come into being subsequent to the cosmos. Together they represent the cosmogonic elaboration of the primal bifurcation of the original unity into 'fields' of power, function and status which are distinct and oppositional and, at the same time, complementary aspects of the same reality.

Vedic sages present the relationship between the gods and demons in a most paradoxical fashion.[28] On the one hand, the two groups of

[27] As Stella Kramrisch has remarked in her provocative essay, "Two: Its Significance in the Ṛgveda," E. Bender (ed.) *Indological Studies* in Honor of W. Norman Brown, (New Haven: American Oriental Society, 1962), 109-36. "Two is the number of the pairs of opposites. Two is the number of the relation of the One to itself. Two is the number that unites while it separates. . . It is charged with the tension of the opposites. Two is the principle of the manifest cosmos which is patterned by the dialectic of the Two. . . Two inheres in One. When this, however, becomes manifest, there is separation, opposition, comparison, measure. . . The texture of the cosmos and the tissue of life are woven out of polarity, tension and homology, inherent in two. . ."

[28] The ambiguous relationship between the Devas and Asuras in Vedic literature has received a most extensive study by A. K. Coomaraswamy in his essay,

celestials are pictured as being entrenched in an eternal warfare for control over the universe or, on occasion, for some lesser good. They stand in distinct ('functional' but not 'essential') opposition to one another, with the Devas representing the powers of Life and Light and the Asuras, the powers of Death and Darkness. The story of the primordial battle between Indra (the chief of the Ādityas) and Vṛtra (the chief of the Daityas) is recapitulated time and time again in brahmanical myths and rituals. But the Devas and Asuras are presented as being not only ancient rivals in eternal combat but, also, as close kinsmen. They are said to be half-brothers, by virtue of the fact that they were born of different mothers (the Ādityas or Devas sprang from Aditi, the personification of the 'Boundless', and the Daityas or Asuras the manifestation of 'limit' or 'boundary'), but of the same father, Prajāpati (ŚB I 2.4.8ff.). Because of this common lineage, they are consanguine relations, if not consubstantial entities (Coomaraswamy, 1935: 373ff.), and, as such, represent the primal reality as a united polarity and a polarized unity.

As one scholar has noted, "One has the impression that Vedic doctrine is at pains to establish a double perspective: although, as an immediate reality, and as the world appears to our eyes, the Devas and the gods [sic] are irreconcilably different by nature and condemned to fight one another, at the beginning of time, on the other hand, that is to say before the Creation or before the world took its present form, they were consubstantial." (Eliade, 1965: 88-89) The concept of the consubstantiality of the forces of divinity and demonism, coupled with the idea of sibling rivalry provides the leitmotif for much of Indian thought in brahmanical and Hindu literature. This same ambiguity is often expressed in the form of certain bi-polar divinities (e.g., Indra-Vṛtra,[29] Agni-Soma,[30] Mitra-

---

"Angel and Titan. An Essay in Vedic Ontology," JAOS, LV, (1935), 373-419, and in "The Darker Side of the Dawn," [Smithsonian Miscellaneous Collections, 94, no. 1] Washington, D.C., 1935. Cf. M. Eliade *Mephistopheles and the Androgyne*, (New York: Sheed and Ward, 1965), 88-93.

[29] In both Vedic and purāṇic literature, the cosmic snake Vṛtra son of Diti and the prototypical Asura begs Indra to repress the urge to kill him and to be satisfied with maiming him out of respect for their blood relationship through Prajāpati. In the purāṇic accounts of the Indra-Vṛtra struggle, Vṛtra, quite paradoxically, is said to be a brahman and Indra is roundly condemned for committing brahmanicide, the most heinous of all sins. Cf. W. Norman Brown, "Theories of Creation in the Rig Veda," JAOS, LXXXV, 1 (1965), 23-34, and ŚB I.6.3. 1-17.

[30] In the Vedas, Agni, the principle of light on all three levels of the cosmos, is invoked as the "Asura priest" (RV VII.30.3) and is said to be consubstantial

Varuṇa,[31] and Rudra-Śiva[32]), who are invoked together because of certain common traits or functions which the pairs of gods possess in common.

The myth of the Churning of the Ocean, in particular, recapitulates this identity-*cum*-disidentity between the Devas and Asuras by means of the polar opposition between (1) righthand side versus lefthand side, (2) forepart of serpent versus hindpart of serpent, and (3) high birth and valorous deeds versus low birth and lack of valorous deeds. Taking into view this particular 'bundle of relations', we interpret the myth as being concerned with recapitulating the theme of the paradoxical relationship between the two groups of supernaturals. The bard asks his listeners to accept the fact that the gods and demons exist together in a relationship which is characterized, at once, by both contrariety and complementarity—and, as suggested previously, by consubstantiality.

This is the first significant set of 'binary oppositions' which is exhibited in terms of conflict-within-temporary-resolution. In a general sense this is the basic set of opposites on which the dialectical movement of the story is established, the other polarities being nothing more than structural extensions or narrative elaborations of the original paradigm.

The story affirms that the relationship between the gods and demons within the frame of this story is one of ambivalent and tenuous alliance—exemplified in the fragile truce followed by fresh outbreaks of conflict. The gods, who are weak and undependable in the beginning but who prevail against their demonic adversaries in the end, on the one hand, and the demons, who seem to dominate the gods in the beginning but ultimately fall into defeat because of their stupidity and avarice, on the other, are descendents of the same lineage.

---

with the serpent, Ahi Budhnya, the embodiment of subterranean darkness and homologous with Vṛtra. In one place Agni is called a "fierce serpent" (RV I.79.1).

[31] Consult two earlier studies of Mitra-Varuṇa in Hermann Güntert, *Der arische Weltkönig und Heiland* (Halle: M. Niemeyer, 1923), 97ff.; Georges Dumézil, *Mitra-Varuṇa. Essai sur deux représentations indo-européennes de la souveraineté* (Paris: Gallimard, 1948) and a more recent study of Mitra by Jan Gonda, *The Vedic God Mitra* [Orientalia Rheno-Traiectina, vol. XIII] (Leiden: E. J. Brill, 1972), for an elaboration of this set of polarities.

[32] See E. Arbman, *Rudra. Untersuchungen zum altindischen Glauben und Kultus* (Uppsala Universitets Årsskrift, 1922) and this writer's doctoral thesis, *Visions of Terror and Bliss: A Study of Rudra-Śiva in Pre-purāṇic Hinduism.* University of Chicago, 1970.

*Major Points of Crisis*

This same ambiguity between the forces of good and evil, life and death is reiterated by means of what we will call the four 'crisis points' in the story. Those crisis points are: (1) the debate over which group of celestials deserves to hold the forepart of the serpent; (2) the production of deadly poison in the very process of churning for the Nectar of Immortality; (3) the summons to Śiva, the God of Death, to save the world from being annihilated by the cosmic poison; and, finally, (4) the theft of the *amṛta* by the Asuras followed by Viṣṇu's act of taking the delusive form of a charming maiden (*mohinī*) for the purpose of retrieving the nectar for the benefit of the Devas.

Each crisis appears as a paradoxical and unexpected frustration to the movement of the narrative and a threat to the successful conclusion of the enterprise. In each instance, the conflict between opposing forces blocks the natural flow of power for the creation or preservation of Life. Viṣṇu (or some other embodiment of Absolute Divinity) enters the arena of conflict as a kind of *deus ex machina*, in order to mediate the conflict between the polarized forces or to reopen the channels of power by restoring a state of balance between the two sides.

(i) *Renewed Conflict Between Gods and Demons.* In all versions of the story, the demons are stationed at the head of the cosmic snake and the gods at the tail. This situation stands contrary to our expectations and contrary to the logic of Hindu symbolism. As the demons themselves declare in the *Bhāgavata Purāṇa*, the forepart is the auspicious and the hindpart is the inauspicious portion of the snake. Much the same sort of ambivalence is said to obtain here as between the lefthand and righthand side of anything. At any rate, the demons persuade the supervisor (Viṣṇu, Kṛṣṇa, etc.) that the superiority (i.e., priority) of their birth and the pre-eminence of their deeds—both are virtues normally reserved for brahmans only—entitle them to hold the head of Vāsuki. This transference of the demons, in the 'auspicious' direction at the forward position of the serpent, should have given them the advantage over their adversaries, but it did not. Instead of thriving in that position they are choked and fatigued by the billowing clouds of black smoke and fire which shot from the serpent's one thousand mouths. Meanwhile, the gods are refreshed by those same clouds.

The rules of logic are transgressed and normal human expectations are frustrated in two instances. According to the rules of the game,

Viṣṇu, as Absolute Sovereign, should have placed the gods in front (the front part being the 'first', or 'foremost' portion = *agrāṁśa*) and the demons in the rear (*paścāḍbhāga*). After this initial reversal, we would expect the demons to thrive and the gods to suffer, but the reverse is the case again. One contradictory situation is replaced by another and one set of oppositions is transposed into another, thus leaving us, as Lévi-Strauss has claimed, with "a second set of binary opposites which stands in contradiction to native theory".

(ii) *Appearance of the Poison.* It should begin to be clear by now that the central themes of the myth are developed through a dialectical movement, set within the conflict between polar opposites, the conflict itself reversing the normal and natural position of the polarities. The sacred becomes profanized and the profane is sacralized. The negative and positive forces are reversed, transposed or transmuted, and, in turn, another set of contradictions is projected. It is precisely this apparent refusal of the Hindu mythographer to allow the opposites to flow together into a final resolution and his belief that each set of polarities which defines their relationship can only give rise to another set of contraries that places this myth beyond the jurisdiction of Lévi-Strauss' approach.

The next set of oppositions is exhibited in the production of the deadly poison. The gods and demons have jointly entered into a cooperative effort to secure the Elixir of Immortality (*amṛta*), which is capable of "removing decrepitude and death and all other ills." [Bhāg. Pur. IX 9.12] In their quest for the elixir of life, they unexpectedly have churned up the elixir of death. Their efforts to secure abundance of life and prosperity for all supernatural creatures have, in the end, threatened the entire cosmos with extinction.

(iii) *Śiva Rescues the Cosmos by Swallowing the Poison.* This is one of the most interesting and puzzling 'moments' in the entire myth. Confronted by the threat of world-annihilation, the gods retreat to Brahmā and thence to Śiva in search of an escape from the menace of death. This turn of events is riddled with internal contradictions which can be explained only by reference to some principle or figure who is situated both within and beyond the conflict and who is, for that reason, capable of setting things straight. The *Rāmāyaṇa* says: "Śrī Viṣṇu smilingly addressed the bearer of the trident, Śrī Mahādeva, saying: 'O Lord, thou art the chief (*parama*) of the gods and should not you, therefore, accept what is first (*pūrvaka*) produced by the churning of the Ocean. Receive the poison (*viṣa*) as the gift (*dānāṃ*), the first (*prathama*) offering (*nivedana*)." Śiva accepted the beaker of poison and drank the poison. But rather than allowing the deadly substance to flow into his stomach, he retained it in his throat, the effects of which turned his neck blue-black (*nīlakaṇṭha*).[33]

The contradictions in this section are legion. Śiva-Mahādeva, who is called Rudra in the Vedas, is designated in Hindu mythology as the Lord of Death (*bhairava*, *mahākāla*). By means of this mode of manifestation (*mūrti*) he functions as both the bringer and remover of Death. In his horrifying and death-dealing guise, he is invoked as *Hara* (= the Remover) and is juxtaposed with Viṣṇu as *Hari* (= the Life-force or Sustainer). He is *Bhairava* (= the Terrible One) and *Mahākāla* (= Time as Destroyer) who destroys all living things at the termination of the World Age. It is, therefore, paradoxical that this agent of death and destruction should be summoned by Brahmā and Viṣṇu (both of them traditional representatives of the Life-force according to *Tri-mūrti* ideology) to save the world from annihilation.

This strange and unexpected turn of events might be explained in the terms of the overall myth by referring to the fact that Viṣṇu is the wielder of magical power (*māyin*) of cosmic proportions. Thus, he succeeds in deluding even Śiva-Mahādeva, the Great God, by convincing the Lord of Death that the poisonous substance (which threatens the cosmos with death) was, in fact, the Elixir (i.e., *ghee* or *soma*) for which the celestials had been churning.

But, within this paradox resides an even more troublesome problem: namely, that the dreaded poison, the prototypical embodiment of decay, disease and death, should be identified as the first 'treasure' (*ratna*) to emerge from the churning of the Ocean of Milk (*kṣīroda*). The ambiguous nature of this substance is emphasized by Viṣṇu's punning upon the various terms for 'first', 'foremost' and 'choicest'. In this regard, he refers to the poison as the "first fruit" of the churning and to Śiva as the "first god" (both in a chronological and a statutory sense) among the gods.

[33] Hence Śiva's much revered epithet, "Śitikaṇṭha" or "Nīlakaṇṭha". In the drama *Kumārasaṁbhava* (II.61; VI.81) Brahmadeva reports to the gods that only Śiva, the black-necked, who possessed the courage and grace to drink the virulent poison, has the power to release the Apsarases from the demon, Taraka. It is noteworthy that Śiva held the poison in his throat so that it might not enter his stomach. His stomach is the cosmic dwelling place of all the creatures. If he had allowed the poison to travel to the stomach, he would have inadvertently destroyed the very creatures he had intended to save in the first place. Structurally, the throat stands midway between the mouth and the stomach, thereby signifying that this act is a form of mediation.

In the normal process of churning butter, it is the choicest and richest portion, the pure butter, that emerges first of all; the residue or dross will be derived after the best part has been removed. But, paradoxically, in this story the substance which should have come last has appeared first and that which should have been discarded as 'leftovers' is offered to the chief of the gods as Elixir.

There is a long-standing tradition, extending back to the time of the Vedas, that the remainder or residue (*ucchiṣṭa*) of the sacrificial offering is to be praised as the choicest and most favorable portion (*bhāga*) of the oblation and as that portion which brings immortality (*amṛta*). In the Vedas, Rudra, the precursor of Śiva, feared by all the other gods and always kept at arm's length by them, is presented with the *ucchiṣṭa* as his special tribute. The *ucchiṣṭa* is designated as the prime portion (being both first-produced and choicest) of the offering and given to Rudra in hope of placating his wrath and gaining his pleasure.[34]

It is common knowledge that Prajāpati, chief of the gods in the Brāhmaṇas, traditionally receives the first (*pūrvaka*, *prathama*) offering. In the ŚB (VI 1.3.16) *Mahān-deva* (= *Mahādeva*) is identified with Prajāpati. So, by extension, Śiva-Mahādeva is "the enjoyer of the first oblation in the sacrifice." [35]

Furthermore, the remnant of the offering is praised highly in one hymn of the *Atharva Veda* (XI. 7) as being the foundation of the world and the "All in All".[36] It is upon *ucchiṣṭa* that 'name and form' (*nāmarūpa* = the phenomental world), the heavens and earth, Indra and Agni, death and life and even Prajāpati himself are established.[37]

---

[34] In ŚB I.7.3. when Rudra demands his share, the gods give him the last oblation under the euphemistic name of Agni Sviṣṭakṛt. "The Maker of Good Offering," Rudra's most 'auspicious' (*śānta*) name. Cf. ŚB I.2.5.17: ". . . for rubbish means cattle and well-stocked with cattle, he thereby makes it."

[35] Recall that the gods' favorite repast in the Vedic sacrifice is clarified butter (*ghee*) and that one of the offerings given to the serpents in the *sarpabali* sacrifice during the month of *śravaṇa* is milk (*kṣīra*). Cf. M. Winternitz, "Der Sarpabali, ein Altindischer Schlangenkult", *Mitteilung der Anthropologische Gesellschaft in Wien*, XVIII (1888), 250.

[36] Paul Deussen, in his *Allgemeine Geschichte der Philosophie* (Leipzig: F. A. Brockhaus, 1894), I.1.305-10, argues that *ucchiṣṭa* does not designate the 'remnant of the offering' in this Vedic hymn as many scholars have claimed but the 'residium in general', the 'remainder that we get after subtracting from the universe all the forms of world-phenomena.' In other words, the remainder, in mystical terms, is the subtle, unqualified Spiritual Essence, or *élan vital*, perhaps *amṛta* or, the "Existing One without a second" about which so many of the Hindu sages speak.

[37] We should also note in passing that Śeṣa (= Vāsuki) the mythical thousand-headed serpent regarded as the emblem of eternity or infinity (= *Ananta*) who

In the *Bhagavad Gītā* Kṛṣṇa proclaims to Arjuna that whoever partakes of the leftovers of the sacrifice with purity of mind and heart is freed from sin, but those who neglect the sacrifice and eat only for their own benefit, will incur great evil.[38] And, elsewhere in the *Mahābhārata* the sage declares in no uncertain terms that "he that eateth the *vighasa* (of the sacrifice) is regarded as eating *amṛta*. What remaineth in a sacrifice after dedication to the gods and ancestors is regarded as *amṛta* and what remaineth after feeding the guest is called *vighasa*, as it is equivalent to ambrosia itself."

The dialectical tension which obtains in this situation should be clearer by now. Viṣṇu offers the poison to Śiva and praises him as 'chief of the gods', hence the only proper recipient of the first-fruits of the sacrifice. He urges Śiva to receive it as his special oblation and as 'the first (= both original and supreme) tribute'. The final words in this portion of the text confirm our original impression that this deadly substance, when viewed from the standpoint of God's transformative power (*māyā*), is Śiva's favorite repast. The transformative power of the sacrifice is declared in a most dramatic fashion in the concluding words of the sage, "... the Blessed Lord Śiva, moved by the distress of the gods and *the words of Viṣṇu*, drank the dreadful poison, *as if it were nectar* (*amṛta*) and returned to his dwelling on Kailāsa." [39] (emphasis added) [Rām. I. 45. 23-24]

(iv) Finally, the fourth moment of crisis, which serves both to convey the dialectical movement of the myth and to threaten to halt its progression altogether, arises with a renewal of conflict between the gods and demons over the question of the final possession

---

serves in this story as the churning cord and elsewhere as the couch and canopy of Viṣṇu while he sleeps between the World Ages and (and, therefore, is homologous with Viṣṇu himself), is itself the embodiment of the 'remainder,' 'residue' or 'leavings' of the cosmogony. This explains why Śeṣa is, at once, the source of life as the Cosmic Ocean and the agent of death as producer of the cosmic poison. For the 'leftovers' are both poison and elixir, a potion of death and a medicine of life, depending upon the state being of him who partakes of it.

[38] *yajña śiṣṭ'āśinaḥ santo mucyante sarva-kilbiṣaiḥ/ bhuñjate te tv aghaṁ pāpā ye pacanty ātmakāraṇāt* / / (III.13).

[39] This relative value and effect of the poison with its power to bring life or death to its recipient is given exquisite poetic expression in Puṣpadanta's *Mahimnastava* or *The Greatness of Śiva*. (W. Norman Brown, Ed. and Trans., Poona: American Institute of Indian Studies, 1965), stanza 14. The relevant stanza reads, "The stain which you received when you swallowed the poison, O three-eyed one, while you were swayed by compassion for the Devas and Asuras, who feared the sudden destruction of the universe, that stain on your throat, paradoxically, does not fail to produce beauty. Even disfigurement commands praise for one engaged in removing a danger to the world."

of the Elixir of Immortality. In the *Rāmāyaṇa* and *Mahābhārata* versions, the two sides dissolve the truce by engaging in a horrendous battle. In the *Viṣṇu Purāṇa* version the indignant Daityas forcibly seize the beaker of Elixir from the hand of Dhanvantari. All the versions portray Viṣṇu as assuming the guise of a charming young maiden (*mohinī*=distracting, deluding) by means of his bewitching power of *māyā*, and with his amorous gestures he 'courted the asuras' (MBh.), 'beguiled and deluded them' (V.P.) and, finally, 'retrieved the nectar from the adversaries of the gods'. (Rām.)

This denouement of the myth in Viṣṇu's retrieval of the nectar from the demonic powers and his bestowal of the precious beverage as a gift upon the gods is puzzling on numerous counts. Why, for instance, were the Devas unable to overcome the Asuras with their own resources and, as the result of their impotence, why did they find it necessary to resort to Viṣṇu once again for aid? Again, why, having lost the Elixir to the Asuras, did the gods, represented in the person of Viṣṇu, choose to resort to acts of deceit and subterfuge in order to recover it?

In the first place, the resolution of the conflict between the Devas and Asuras is always tenuous and temporary. The two sides will continue to engage in combat as long as the cosmos itself endures. A permanent armistice, we can surmise, would dissolve the universe into a state of perfect stasis or chaos. *Secondly, according to the myth, in the end the opposites are not transcended or merged. The conflict is not resolved but is merely halted by the achievement of victory (complete, though temporary) for the gods.*

In symbolic terms, light triumphs over darkness and life ultimately is discovered to be the sovereign ruler over death. The two groups which stood in 'functional' but not 'essential' opposition at the beginning remain in the same state in the end. The gods gain the upper hand through the agency of Viṣṇu and, thereby, bring the conflict to a temporary halt. They have won the battle, but the war continues. Both gods and demons live on to fight another day.[40]

Again, as the *Mahāmāyin*, Viṣṇu serves as the source from which

---

[40] In this regard, there is a most interesting incident recorded in the Vedas in which the Devas ask, "Is there not some means whereby we might defeat the Asuras once and for all and never have to fight them again?" Prajāpati appears and informs the gods that the way to achieve total victory over the Asuras leads through the performance of the Soma rite. According to this text, the gods perform the ritual in strict adherence to the rules and win a final victory over the Asuras. (ŚB I.2.4.8ff.).

all crystallizations of power (i.e., Devas and Asuras) emerge and the point around which they gravitate. By wielding his *māyā* he may assume any form that he chooses. Rightly understood, the Devas and Asuras are nothing more than specialized manifestations of the essence of Viṣṇu into the many forms of *māyā*. While he does perform the function of mediator of the polarities (i.e., Devas and Demons, Life and Death, etc.) in apparent conformity to the Lévi-Straussian model, he fractures that pattern defined as 'polar opposition followed by resolution and synthesis.' He does so by assuming whatever mode of manifestation he deems appropriate. Hence, the Devas and Asuras are *not* different by nature; that is the reason for their conflict. They are merely two facets of a single reality in conflict over the acquisition and utilization of power (*śakti*). They are alike in nature but different in function. At the same time, they are opposed—by definition, the demons (*Asuras*) are the creatures who oppose the gods (*Suras*). The relationship is characterized by functional and structural, but not *essential*, opposition. They are opposed structurally, and only structurally.

At the same time, Viṣṇu is not only totally involved *in*, but also identified *with*, the affairs of the terrestrial and celestial orders. This capacity to exist in and operate at two levels of reality simultaneously, without confusing them with each other, enables Viṣṇu to promote the quest for *amṛta* by modes of action which, from the viewpoint of social ethics, is morally reprehensible.

A cursory reading of the myth of the Churning of the Ocean would seem to indicate that the myth is concerned to express the opposition between life and death, good and evil, strength and weakness and the ultimate (but temporary and conditional) triumph of the gods over the demons. The scheme of opposition might be expressed according to the following sets of dichotomies:

| | |
|---|---|
| Gods | Demons |
| Life | Death |
| Cooperative effort | Conflict |
| Amṛta (= Life) | Poison (*kālakūṭa*) |
| Soma (= *Amṛta*) | Agni (universal conflagration) |

The dramatic tension upon which the entire narrative is established is the opposition-*cum*-cooperation between the powerful and effective gods (who weaken and falter in the beginning but prevail in the end)

CHART 3

*Basic Outline or 'Structure' of the Myth Without Regard to Choice of Version*

| *Crisis Event* | *Unfortunate Consequence* | *Salutory Effort* | *Fortunate Result* |
|---|---|---|---|
| 1. Perpetual warfare between gods and demons (*devāsura-saṁgrāma*) | 1. No hope of improving their lot | 1. Viṣṇu or Brahmā urges gods and demons to make truce | 1. Co-operative effort between gods and demons in quest of Elixir of Immortality |
| 2. Weakness or failure of strength of gods and demons | 2. Gods' inability to establish mountain on base or to continue churning | 2. Viṣṇu or Indra establishes the mountain upon back of tortoise | 2. Gods are reinvigorated and enabled to continue quest for *amṛta* |
| 3. Production of dreadful poison (*halāhala*, *kālakūṭa*) | 3. Cosmos is threatened with disaster | 3. Śiva-Mahādeva swallows poison and holds it in throat | 3. World is saved from de-struction and churning is resumed |
| 4. Demons attack the gods and steal the elixir | 4. Renewed warfare and threat of loss of *amṛta* to demonic forces | 4. Viṣṇu takes the form of a beguiling maiden (*Mohinī*) through his *māyā* | 4. Gods recover the *amṛta*, Indra is established as king of the gods, and the world is re-newed |

and the powerful but ineffective demons (who seem to dominate in the beginning but collapse in the end). The *amṛta* is the sacred substance which will provide health, wealth and liberation from death. The serpent and the sacred mountain are the instruments employed to acquire the precious Elixir and the guiding power of various divine mediators—Viṣṇu, Indra, and Śiva—serves to conduct the enterprise toward a successful termination.

The dramatic and dialectical tension of the story resides in the four principal points of conflict between the polar opposites. These four points of crisis, which both promote movements of the enterprise toward a successful completion and threaten it with failure at each moment, are represented in the accompanying chart (page 201). The chart displays the basic 'structure' of the myth without regard for choice of version. At each of the four points of conflict, the normal flow of creative and redemptive power is interrupted and the anticipated goal of the action seems doomed to failure. A third, so-called 'outside' party is summoned to mediate the conflict between the two parties and to restore things to their natural course. Viṣṇu and Indra, representatives of passive (legalistic) and active (martial) sovereignty respectively, act as mediators at points one and four. Śiva mediates at point two and Viṣṇu alone at point three.

But, given the fact that this myth seems to have been composed in glorification of the power and majesty of Viṣṇu and given the dictates of the logic of Hindu religious thought that all forms of divinity are mutually interchangeable and ultimately resolvable into an Absolute Divine Entity (e.g., the Brahman of Vedānta), the various deities—Indra, Śiva, Nara, Nārāyaṇa—are nothing more than the many modes of manifestation of Viṣṇu. It is, therefore, in the person and activity of Viṣṇu that all the opposing forces are gathered together, unified, refragmented and, finally, projected another time to play out their respective roles. Viṣṇu is the beginning, middle and end of the story. He is the writer, director, actor and audience of the drama. Or, in metaphysical terms, he is the material, efficient and final cause of the entire process of cosmic evolution.

## *Conclusion*

As we remarked at the beginning of this paper, although it may appear that the myth of the Churning of the Ocean conforms to Lévi-Strauss' theory about the nature and function of myths, a closer analysis of the story has shown that this is not the case. While the various elements do, in fact, appear to be organized according to a certain scheme of polar opposition, we are convinced that, to the extent that the polarities are opposed in the first place or that they are mediated or resolved in the last place, the procedure which the ancient Indian bard employs in promoting this scheme is far too complex and multivalent to be dealt with in terms of simple polar opposition and ultimate mediation.

One way of demonstrating that Lévi-Strauss' approach to the study of myths is not applicable to this Hindu story (and, perhaps, by extension, many other Hindu tales as well) would be to show that the story of the Churning of the Ocean *is not a myth* in Lévi-Straussian terms.

Lévi-Strauss argues in his essay, "The Science of the Concrete" (1966: 30-33) that myths and rituals are analogous to 'bricolage' in that they begin with an original state of asymmetry (e.g., a distinction between 'sacred' and 'profane') and in the course of things issue into a state of symmetry, with the ritual process resulting "in a particular type of equilibrium between the two sides". Games, on the other hand, are established upon a pre-ordained structural symmetry (i.e., both sides, theoretically, start with an equal chance of winning) and, in the course of activity, engender an asymmetry, by ending "in the establishment of a difference between individual players or teams where originally there was no indication of inequality." At the end of the game they are distinguished into winners and losers. In other words, myths and rituals produce a *conjunctive* effect by a process of merging things which earlier had appeared to exist in separate categories. Games, on the contrary, produce a *disjunctive* result by differentiating between apparently identical or related items and separating them into distinct categories.

The story of the Churning of the Ocean *departs* from this model in three remarkable ways: (1) the participating parties do not exist in a state of symmetry in the beginning; (2) they do not emerge into a state of symmetry in the end; and, (3) there is no sign of a mediation or resolution of opposites in the end but rather the separation of things into different categories.

We shall elaborate these points one at a time. First, the story begins, at best, with an 'artificial' or 'functional' symmetry between the gods and demons as exemplified in the establishment of a truce between the two groups of forces for the purpose of Churning the Ocean. But asymmetry is expressed in a number of ways. The Vedic sages declare that the birth of the demons preceded that of the gods. As the elder brothers of the gods, the demons should occupy a position which is superior (genealogically, ritually and symbolically) to that of the gods. The demons lay claim to such a superior status on the basis of their 'high birth' and 'pre-eminent deeds.' But the *real*, as contrasted to the attested or theoretical, superiority of the divine forces is verified at the denouement of the narrative with the final victory of the gods over the demons. The asymmetrical relationship which seemed to favor the demons in the beginning, shifts over to the benefit of the gods in the end.

Second, if the company of gods and demons stand with each other in a state of opposition at the beginning of the story, they are allowed to continue in that state in the end. That is, to the extent that the two forces are opposed to one another in the first place, their opposition is stated and left to be dealt with on its own terms. Viṣṇu is the Great Magician, who both mediates and projects the sets of opposites by assuming various disguises according to his pleasure, without ever bringing those polarities into a state of resolution or harmony. Once again, it should be noted that while Viṣṇu does appear to function as a divine mediator his most crucial role (in this story, at least) is that of the Great Magician (*Mahāmāyin*) who projects himself into all manner of forms for his own delight and for the edification of the creatures. He does not effect the mediation of the opposites into a higher unity but provides for the complete (though temporary) victory of one group over the other. But the question remains: in what sense is the victory of the gods *complete*, given the fact that even though in possession of the Elixir, the gods must continue combating the demon armies as long as the universe endures?

One conclusion which might be drawn from this entire discussion is this: while the gods and demons *appear* to exist in a state of polar opposition, they do not. The apparent rather than real character of the polarizing of the gods and demons in Hindu mythology is demonstrated by the practice of interchanging and transposing their respective roles and characters to fit the meaning to be expressed in the story. We might refer in this regard to the paradoxical assertion in epic and purāṇic mythology that Indra (the chief of the Ādityas) and Rāma (the embodiment of Dharma) both are said to be guilty of the sin of brahminicide in the killing of Vṛtra (chief of the Daityas) and Rāvaṇa (chief of the Dānavas), respectively. That which is normally considered to be 'high' is brought 'low'; that which is considered 'low' is elevated. The sacred is profanized and the profane is sacralized. Therefore, since there is no *real* opposition in the beginning or middle of the narrative, there is no real resolution in the end. *There is no need for resolution of opposition where there is no real opposition in the first place.*

Thirdly, at the point of the denouement of the story, the groups of forces which have played the roles of adversaries at numerous moments in the story undergo a 'relative-absolute', i.e., functional, extension of the oppositional nature of their relationship. There is no sign of the resolution of bi-polar opposition within a third mediating term, but rather the separation of the two groups into different categories and the eventual triumph of one party over the other. Though the demons claim superiority over the gods, it is the latter who always prevail. It is inconceivable that the game of their divine-demonic warfare could ever end in a 'tie'; much less a victory for the demons. The demons are asphixiated by the fumes; the gods are resuscitated. Viṣṇu obtains the Kaustubha jewel representing his consort Śrī-Lakṣmī which is blue-black in color; Śiva receives the oblation of the poison (also black in color) which he drinks as if it were the Elixir. The gods obtain the Elixir; the demons lose it. The original 'functional' symmetry is transmuted, in the end, into a 'functional' asymmetry. Thus, this myth stands in a disanalogous relationship with the Lévi-Straussian model at every point along the way.

In order for a structural approach to the analysis of myth to be able to account for the full range of oppositions, complementations, and transpositions in the myth of the Churning of the Ocean, the terms of the method would have to undergo considerable refinement. One such refinement which we might suggest is the supplementing of the notion of the 'conflict of opposites' with that of the 'conflict of similars'. The implications of the latter analytical model is that those phenomena (e.g., the gods and demons, or the poison and the *amṛta*) which express the meaning of the myth in terms of bi-polarity are not real oppositions in the first place but rather interchangeable terms employed to describe a single, multifaceted reality. In this story, one entity is seen giving rise to the other out of its own essence. For example, the poison which is produced from the Ocean of Milk (the vessel containing the Elixir) and stands in 'functional' or 'expressive' opposition to the *amṛta*, is transmuted into the *amṛta* (or revealed as being *in essence* Elixir) when appropriated by divinity. Even so, the blue-black stone (Kaustubha) which adorns Viṣṇu's chest is an object of rare beauty and an embodiment of marvelous powers when worn by Viṣṇu and a reservoir of darkness, misfortune and even death when worn by an unworthy agent. Finally, Śiva, the one who removes Life by bringing Death, as an expression of the transformative power of his grace (*prasāda*), removes Death in order to provide Life.[41]

In conclusion, we would assert that, in reality, the story of the Churning of the Ocean is no myth at all, in Lévi-Straussian terms, but a ritual in mythical form or rather *a mythic-ritual played out as a game*. To be more specific, this tale is the Soma ritual celebrated by means of a *narrative performance*, with the various structural components of the story taking the place of the sacrificial paraphernalia of the rite. Structurally speaking, this story manifests an original asymmetry which Lévi-Strauss associates with myth, ritual and 'bricolage'. But, at the same time, it manifests an 'engendered asymmetry' which produces a disjunctive effect at the end—elements which he claims are characteristic of games. In keeping with the ritual paradigm, the elements of the story are found existing in a state of asymmetry in the beginning and periodically in temporary symmetry during the interval of the churning. But, unlike the ritual pattern and more in keeping with the game pattern, the denouement issues into a state of asymmetry with the gods winning a decisive (though temporary) victory over the demons. Though this is a story which functions as the vicarious performance of a ritual, one would expect, on the basis of Lévi-Strauss' model, that it would produce a conjunctive effect, with both sides coming into a state of union, communion or at least harmony. But, in this case, the opposite is true.

We feel compelled, therefore, in light of the intractability of this story of the Churning of the Ocean, when analyzed from the Lévi-Straussian perspective, to conclude that the 'Indian Mind' (at least, as exemplified in this story) operates on the basis of a set of intellectual principles which differ fundamentally from those of the 'Savage Mind'. If Lévi-Strauss is correct in his reading of the similarities and differences between the Savage or mythological mind and the modern

[41] Viṣṇu's universality is expressed in grandiloquent terms in the Thvear Kdei inscription found on the right pier of the great temple at Angkor Wāt in Cambodia. It reads as follows, "Victorious is Viṣṇu whose four arms bear the discus, the earth, the conch and the club which are like the four guardians of the four cardinal points." Quoted in B. Groslier, *Angkor, Art and Civilization* (London: Hudson and Thames, 1962), p. 62.

or scientific mind, then, once again, we find that the 'Indian Mind' falls into an area that is betwixt and between the two prototypical mentalities. The mind of the Indian mythographer partakes of the characteristics of each of the other two models, but does not conform naturally with either.

## BIBLIOGRAPHICAL REFERENCES

Coomaraswamy, A. K. 1935. "Angel and Titan. An Essay in Vedic Ontology". *Journal of American Oriental Society.* LV (1935): 373-419.

Eliade, Mircea. 1965. *Mephistopheles and the Androgyne. Studies in Religious Myth and Symbol.* New York: Sheed and Ward.

Leach, Edmund. 1970. *Claude Lévi-Strauss.* (New York: The Viking Press).

Lévi-Strauss, Claude. 1963. *Structural Anthropology.* (New York: Basic Books, Inc.)

——. 1964. *Le cru et le cuit.* (Paris: Librarie Plon).

——. 1966. *The Savage Mind.* (Chicago: The University of Chicago Press).

O'Flaherty, Wendy. *The Origins of Evil in Hindu Mythology.* Forthcoming. I am indebted to her formulation of the concept of the relationship between the Devas and the Asuras.

# THE BURNING OF THE FOREST MYTH

Alf Hiltebeitel

Recent interest in the *Mahābhārata* has resulted in several varieties of interpretation which have polarized over a number of major controversies, among them, most prominently, being whether to view the epic primarily as "myth" or "history," and whether to rely on (or emphasize) the reconstituted Critical Text (the Poona Edition of the Bhandarkar Oriental Research Institue) or an unprejudiced use of "all the variants" in the "Vulgate". Clearly, fundamental issues are raised by these alternatives, making it important to indicate where the leading names in epic research stand on them.

As to myth and history, few would deny that the most fruitful recent research has come from those who have stressed a mythic background—whether Indo-European (Stig Wikander, Georges Dumézil [1]) or Purāṇic (Madeleine Biardeau [2])—to the main narrative. This is not to say that "myth" and "history" should be allowed to stand as categories that automatically eclipse the third category of *epic*, which elsewhere I have sought to argue is a sui generis category in its own right.[3] It is rather to say that the epic story is itself closely integrated with, and strongly influenced by, a mythology (or mythologies). But even if some of the main results of these scholars' comparisons are accepted, it will still be legitimate to seek for elements of the story that seem to have historical provenance. Such quests for the historical core have always produced varied results, the most sustained effort being that of Walter Ruben.[4] They have also been an

---

[1] See, most importantly, Wikander, "Pāṇḍava-sagen och Mahābhāratas mytiska forutsattningar," *Religion och Bibel*, IV (1947), 27-39, and Dumézil, *Mythe et épopée*, Vol. I: *L'Idéologie des trois fonctions dans les épopées des peuples indo-européens* (Paris, 1968).

[2] See especially Biardeau, Comptes-rendus of "Conferénces de Mlle. Madeleine Biardeau," *Annuaire de l'École Pratique des Hautes Études*, Section des Sciences Religieuses, 77 (1969-70), pp. 168-73; 78 (1970-71), pp. 151-61; 79 (1971-72), pp. 139-46 [henceforth *EPHE*], and "Études de mythologie hindoue: Cosmogonies purāṇiques," Parts 1-3, *Bulletin de l'École Française d'Extrême Orient*, 54 (1968), pp. 19-45; 55 (1969), pp. 59-105; and 58 (1971), pp. 17-89 [henceforth EMH 1-3].

[3] See the opening chapter of my forthcoming book, *The Ritual of Battle: Kṛṣṇa in the Mahābhārata* (Ithaca: Cornell University Press, 1976).

[4] Ruben, *Krishna: Konkordanz und Kommentar der Motive seines Heldenlebens* Istanbul, 1944), *passim.*

almost universal concern of Indian authors.[5] And, J. A. B. van Buitenen, whose new and invaluable translation of the first book (*Ādiparvan*) of the *Mahābhārata* will make the digestion of this essay much easier for its readers, even while expressing skepticism on the historicity of the main story, thinks that the latter has been mythicized only secondarily and often gratuitously, and that certain portions of the story reflect specific historical events and socio-political conditions.[6]

Secondly, on the matter of how to use the Critical Edition, the situation is perhaps more fluid. Van Buitenen takes his stand upon it and has apparently made a convert of Dumézil.[7] Biardeau argues from the structuralist standpoint that no text should be regarded as privileged.[8]

While no comprehensive solution to either of these problems is within our grasp, it will be worth showing what is at stake by way of an example. One episode which brings these issues to a head perhaps better than any other is the Burning of the Khāṇḍava Forest, which ends the *Ādiparvan* of the *Mahābhārata*.

Yudhiṣṭhira and his brothers have set up their rule over a forested tract of land to the west of Hāstinapura, the seat of their cousins the Kauravas. As the episode begins, the reign is described as peaceful and prosperous, with new heirs in abundance after the births of Draupadī's five sons (one with each of the Pāṇḍavas) and the birth of Abhimanyu, the son of Arjuna and Kṛṣṇa's sister Subhadrā. It is, in fact, the birth of this sixth prince, the Pāṇḍavas' eventual sole heir, that has brought Kṛṣṇa Vāsudeva to Indraprastha to perform the child's birth rites (1:213, 63-64 [9]). The epic will present us with few if any moments more suitable for a scene of ease and pleasure, and

[5] See especially Tadpatrikar, "The Kṛṣṇa Problem," *Annals of the Bhandarkar Oriental Research Institute* 10 (1929), pp. 269-343 and, with the notable exception of D. C. Sircar's own contribution, the essays in Sircar, ed., *The Bhārata War and the Purāṇic Genealogies* (Calcutta, 1969).

[6] van Buitenen, trans. and ed., *The Mahābhārata*, I: *The Book of the Beginning* (Chicago, 1973), Introduction, pp. 8-13; and see below.

[7] See Dumézil's change in tone from *Mythe et épopée*, I (especially pp. 34, 74-76) to *Mythe et épopée*, II: *Types épiques indo-européens: un héros, un sorcier, un roi* (Paris, 1971), in the latter not only promising in the future to suppress the "grief" formulated in Vol. I, but thanking van Buitenen for pointing out that his remarks on the Critical Edition were "unfair".

[8] See especially Biardeau, "The Story of Arjuna Kārtavīrya Without Reconstruction," *Purāṇa* 12,2 (1970), 286-303.

[9] All my citations are from the Poona Critical Edition, whose Notes and Appendices supply variants and interpolations.

that is what we now find. Arjuna and Kṛṣṇa, at the former's urging, decide to go with a party of friends—in particular, women—to sport beside the banks of the Yamunā (214, 14-25). The women dance, sing, laugh, quarrel, and drink wine, and Draupadī and Subhadrā are given special mention: "drunk with wine (*madotkaṭe*), they gave away their valuable gems and ornaments to the other women" (22). The singularity of this episode has drawn some comment, but it seems contrived to link it with later love scenes concerning Kṛṣṇa.[10] He himself is not a main figure of feminine attention, and, in fact, as the revelry wears on, he and Arjuna betray a rather retiring disposition, removing themselves to a nearby charming spot in the forest where they engage each other in private conversation.

### A. *The Central Narrative and the "Background Myth"*

In terms of wider developments, the picnic seems to be a contrivance to get Arjuna and Kṛṣṇa to this secluded spot,[11] for it is here that they are approached by a strange looking brahman of gold complexion, yellowish brown beard, radiant and splendid (214, 30-32). It is Agni in disguise. Thus begins one of the oddest and most grisly segments of the epic, the burning of the Khāṇḍava forest.

This forest is the home of a Pannaga (a variety of Nāga) named Takṣaka whose friend, Indra, protects the forest with his control of rainfall. It is Agni's wish, however, to consume all the forest's creatures. But he cannot do this unless—and these are his two requests of Arjuna and Kṛṣṇa—Indra is prevented from dousing his flames, and unless the creatures are barred from fleeing the forest. Why is Agni so grim and ruthless? A story given in full only in the Northern recension, and either shortened or "entirely missing" in various

---

[10] Edward Washburn Hopkins, *The Great Epic of India, Its Character and Origin* (1901; repr. Calcutta, 1969), p. 376, writes: "Getting drunk at a picnic . . . is not proper conduct for an exemplary Hindu lady. . . . Such shocking behaviour belongs to the revelry of the *Harivaṁśa*. . . . It is not a moral episode of the fifth century B.C." Cf. William Archer, *The Loves of Krishna* (New York, n.d.), p. 22.

[11] Charlotte Vaudeville, "Aspects du mythe de Kṛṣṇa-Gopāla dans l'Inde ancienne," *Mélanges d'Indianisme à la mémoire de Louis Renou* (Paris, 1968), p. 755, n. 2, tries to connect the two episodes by viewing the first as a springtime festival and the second as a legend based upon it. But this is only partially convincing. Though one could perhaps see the arrival of the hot days (*uṣṇāni*; 214,14) reflected in the burning legend, the identification of Arjuna-Phalguna with Balarāma, the "dieu-blanc" of "springtime," is contrived.

Southern texts, provides the answer.[12] Naturally this "background myth" is missing from the Critical Edition.

A certain king Śvetaki had worn out his priests by excessive sacrificing, and when finally he wished to perform a ceremony lasting a hundred years, they told him: "Go to the presence of Rudra. Surely he will sacrifice for you" (*Ādiparvan*, Appendix I, No. 118, line 39). Much annoyed, Śvetaki went to Mount Kailāsa, performed terrible austerities, and at last obtained the sight of Śiva (l.49). But Śiva would agree to assist at the the sacrifice only if Śvetaki poured a steady stream of clarified butter into the fire (i.e., into Agni) for twelve years (ll. 62-63). Śvetaki achieved this, and, when he again came before the god, Śiva fulfilled his promise not by himself—"assisting at sacrifices is for brahmans," he said (l. 71)—but in the person of the erratic and irrascible brahman Durvāsas ("Ill-clad"), who, as Śiva put it, was "my own portion on earth" (*mamāṁśastu kṣititale*: l. 73). The twelve years of being surfeited on butter, however, had taken their toll on Agni's energy (*tejas*). But, from Brahmā Agni learned that the terrible Khāṇḍava forest, which he had formerly reduced to ashes, had since become an abode of enemies of the gods (ll. 105-6). By consuming the fat of these creatures, said Brahmā, "You will be reestablished in (your own) nature" (*prakṛtistho bhaviṣyasi*; l. 108). Hearing this, Agni went quickly to Khāṇḍava and, aided by Vāyu, the Wind (l. 113), began to blaze forth. But the initial efforts—seven of them (l. 123)—were thwarted by elephants and Nāgas who doused his flames with water from their trunks and hoods (ll. 116-23). Discouraged, Agni returned to Brahmā, and this time was told that the help he would need to consume the forest was now available in the person of "those two ancient divinities (*pūrvadevau*) Nara and Nārāyaṇa who have arrived in the human world to carry out the work of the gods" (ll. 130-31). This is what has brought Agni-the-brahman before Arjuna and Kṛṣṇa. As one can see, much will depend on how one takes this "background myth."

We now return to the Critical text. Arjuna asks for the equipment to fulfill Agni's requests, and Agni, with the collusion of Varuṇa, supplies the heroic pair with their most illustrious arms: Arjuna with the bow Gāṇḍiva plus two inexhaustible quivers and a chariot (216, 2-20), and Kṛṣṇa with the discus (*cakra*) and mace (216, 21-25).[13]

[12] See n. to 1:215,11, *Ādiparvan*, p. 841.

[13] One may note that it is the *cakra* which makes Kṛṣṇa "superior in battle

The two are thus ready to "fight with all the gods and Asuras, let alone a single Indra" (216, 27), and to contain the forest's inhabitants. And Agni now puts forth his "form of fiery splendor" (*taijasaṁ rūpam*) . . . like that at the end of the yuga," ablaze with "seven flames" (216, 31-32).

The great slaughter begins. Agni burns creatures of all classes—birds, animals, fish, reptiles (217, 9)—and the noise is deafening like that heard at the churning of the ocean (217, 13). On that occasion, too, there was a conflagration, which Indra managed to drown out (1:16, 23-25). Now the gods come before Indra and ask whether the time has come for the destruction of the worlds (*saṃkṣayaḥ . . . lokānām*; 217, 16). Seeking to protect the forest and its creatures, Indra covers the sky "with great cloud-masses of various forms" (*mahatā meghajālena nānārūpeṇa*; 18), but their water is prevented from reaching the ground by the heat of the fire (20) and by Arjuna's arrows (218, 1)! This contest between Indra and Arjuna, between father and son (see 218, 46), continues with the advantage going first to the one, then to the other.[14] With Indra thus neutralized, the list of creatures who oppose Arjuna and Kṛṣṇa is now extended to include the Garuḍas, Uragas, Suras (Gods), Gandarvas, Yakṣas, Rākṣasas, and Pannagas (19-25)—all of whom Arjuna defeats; and the Daityas and Dānavas, who are dispelled by Kṛṣṇa (26).

But the gods are still capable of striking a menacing pose in opposition to the two heroes. Indra first raises his *vajra*, and then all the rest raise their characteristic weapons or emblems in an intriguing array.[15] But when they make a rush, all are routed (41) except Indra, who continues the fight, testing Arjuna further by hurling great stones and mountain peaks, all easily dispersed by the hero. Meanwhile, Kṛṣṇa moves about like Time or Death (*kāla*; 219,6; cf. *Bhagavad Gītā* 11, 32), cutting up creatures with his *cakra*; indeed, "the form of that soul of all creatures became very terrible then" (*babhūva rūpamatyugraṁ sarvabhūtātmanastadā*; 8). At last, Indra ceases

---

to men and even gods, as well as Rakṣas, Piśācas, Daityas, and Nāgas" (216,23); it is presumed that he did not have this weapon in his defeat of Kaṁsa or in his earlier childhood exploits.

[14] Indra helps Aśvasena, Takṣaka's child, to escape (218,4-12); Arjuna is able to dispel Indra's clouds (218,15-16).

[15] Some of the gods' weapons are interesting: Yama—*kāladaṇḍa*, "Staff of Death (or Time)"; Aśvins—*auṣadhīrdīpyamānās*, "resplendent (van Buitenen: "phosphorescent") plants": for healings and rejuvenations in battle? (218,29-38). See also below, n. 35.

his opposition and, pleased (*prītaḥ*) with Arjuna and Kṛṣṇa's prowess, applauds them (11). A deep incorporeal voice then tells him that his friend Takṣaka has not been slain, and that his two foes are, in fact, the gods and ancient ṛṣis Nara and Nārāyaṇa (12-16); and, leaving the conflagration to burn on unimpeded, Indra departs with the other gods in train.

The narrative now tells about the "six" survivors (219, 40)[16]: the Asura Maya, strangely the brother of Namuci,[17] whom Arjuna spares (219, 35-39); Takṣaka's son Aśvasena (see above n. 14); and four fledgling Śārṅgaka ("Horned") birds, all conversant about scripture (*brahmavādinaḥ*; 220, 17), whose father, a brahman-turned-bird so as to beget offspring as quickly as possible, had earlier bargained with Agni for their release (220, 22-32).

Finally, when all else has been burnt, Agni reveals his identity to Arjuna (225, 6), and Indra and the Maruts descend (*avatīrya*; 225, 7) from the atmosphere to grant boons to Arjuna and Kṛṣṇa. Arjuna asks that he might always have Indra's weapons, and these Indra promises for a time "when the blessed Mahādeva will be pleased with you" (225, 10)—pointing toward the Kirāta episode in which Arjuna will obtain Śiva's favor by wrestling with the god while the latter is in a woodsman disguise. Kṛṣṇa asks for "eternal friendship (or affection) with Arjuna" (*prītīm pārthena śāśvatīm*; 225, 13). Indra, Agni, and the Maruts then ascend to heaven, leaving Arjuna, Kṛṣṇa, and the Asura Maya by the banks of the river (225, 19), this being the close of the *Ādiparvan*.

### B. *Clearing a Forest*

There has been no shortage of comment on these scenes, and, in some respects, much of the testimony forms a coherent picture. The younger Adolf Holtzmann sees Agni here as the "Führer der brahmanischen Kultur bei ihrem Vordringen nach Osten," [18] and similarly—although presumably with a different historical background

[16] Actually, there are seven; the birds' mother also escapes (224,17ff.).

[17] Unlike Maya, Namuci has a rich and ancient mythology; see Maurice Bloomfield, "The Story of Indra and Namuci: Contributions to the History of the Veda," Part 1, *Journal of the American Oriental Society* 15 (1893), 152-63, and Georges Dumézil, *The Destiny of the Warrior*, Alf Hiltebeitel trans. (Chicago, 1970), pp. 29-39 and *passim*. It seems likely that the intent is to lend prestige to Maya by this association.

[18] Holtzmann, *Das Mahābhārata und seine Theile*, Vol. I: *Die Neunzehn Bücher des Mahābhārata* (Kiel, 1893), pp. 44-45.

in mind—C. V. Vaidya sees a slash and burn form of land cultivation here, interpreted as a dedication to Agni.[19] Holtzmann also suggests that the forest was probably a retreat for Natives (= Asuras) in their resistance to "die anrückenden Arier"; [20] and Irawati Karve attempts to give further precision to the notion of a mythologized conquest: the Nāgas and the Birds are forest clans whom the Aryan "conquering settlers" Kṛṣṇa and Arjuna liquidated.[21]

Now, most recently, van Buitenen has brought some political and geographical precision into the picture. The forest burning scene transpires after several earlier episodes have resulted in important conflicts and alliances. First, as youths the Kaurava and Pāṇḍava cousins pay their guru's fee to Droṇa, their instructor in military arts, by presenting him, at his request, with the northern half of the land of Pāñcāla (with its capital Ahicchattrā), after wresting it from King Drupada, who is thus reduced to the southern half of the kingdom (with its new capital Kāmpilya) across the Ganges, on the river's southern bank. Secondly, the Pāṇḍavas have married Drupada's daughter Kṛṣṇā Draupadī, forming an alliance with her family and land. And thirdly, they have consolidated an alliance with the Vṛṣṇis, the people of Kṛṣṇa Vāsudeva. Although the *Mahābhārata* never says so, this bond would presumably go back to the marriage of Kuntī, a Vṛṣṇi princess, and Pāṇḍu; in any case, at Draupadī's Svayaṁvara (the "self-choice" marriage rite which finally results in the bride's marriage to Pāṇḍu's five sons) Kṛṣṇa arrives and strikes up an intimate friendship with the six newlyweds, and then later marries off his own sister Subhadrā to Arjuna. The implications of this alliance with the Vṛṣṇis are not made fully clear until the *Sabhāparvan*, the epic's second book; but Kṛṣṇa's people have at some point, and certainly before the marriage to Draupadī and Subhadrā, been forced to flee from their homeland around Mathurā,[22] on the

---

[19] Vaidya, *The Mahābhārata: A Criticism* (Delhi, 1966), p. 99.

[20] Holtzmann, "Indra nach den Vorstellungen des Mahābhārata," *Zeitschrift der Deutschen Morgenländischen Gesellschaft* 32 (1878), p. 314.

[21] Karve, *Yuganta: The End of an Epoch* (Poona, 1969), p. 141; see also pp. 141-42 on various forests having the connotation "sweetness" (Khāṇḍava = "Sugar Candy"). On this intriguing connection, in particular as it concerns products from the flowers and leaves of the Madhuka tree, see also Georges Dumézil, *The Destiny of a King*, Alf Hiltebeitel trans. (Chicago, 1973), pp. 70-84 and 144, n. 28.

[22] The epic does not actually tell us when Kṛṣṇa and his folk left Mathurā for Dvārakā, but it is there that Kṛṣṇa *returns* after the wedding to Draupadī (1:199, 51). He is also certainly at Dvārakā by the time Arjuna visits this city and abducts Subhadrā. When Kṛṣṇa finally describes the events that led to the flight from

Yamunā river (in the territory neighboring South Pāñcāla to the West). At the time of the burning of the forest, they have dwelt for some time in Dvārakā, on the coast of today's Gujarat; but Kṛṣṇa still harbors designs of vengeance [23] against Jarāsaṅdha of Magadha, whose kingdom lies down the Yamunā and Ganges from Mathurā, and his army marshal Śiśupāla. Now, according to van Buitenen, it is not surprising that Kṛṣṇa and Balarāma appear at Draupadī's Svayaṁvara to ally themselves with the Pāṇḍavas; "they were hardly in a position to ignore the Pāñcāla hegemony across their river to the Ganges"; [24] they were, in other words, "securing their left flank." [25] Moreover:

> The oval figure beginning at Hāstinapura, continued through Ahicchattrā and Kāmpilya, and reversed through Mathurā of the Vṛṣṇis, must if it is to return to its source, once more intersect the river Yamunā. It is at this approximate spot that we find Indraprastha, the city founded by the Pāṇḍavas in the Khāṇḍava Tract given them by Hāstinapura after the alliance with Pāñcāla. It is surely Kuru country, but it is Vṛṣṇi riverside, and it is the Vṛṣṇi diplomat Kṛṣṇa who helps them to clear the area and establish themselves. A triangle of alliances has been forced by Kṛṣṇa, from Indraprastha to Mathurā to Kāmpilya, and the security of Mathurā is secured by the marriage bond of Indraprastha with Kāmpilya. In the process Kṛṣṇa has also wound up with the balance of power: if war is to break out, Indraprastha, Mathurā and Kāmpilya can jointly converge on Hāstinapura; or Indraprastha on Hāstinapura, and Mathurā on Kāmpilya; and so on.[26]

There are, of course, some problems with this historical reconstruc-

Mathurā, he does not correlate them with the affairs of the Pāṇḍavas; all that is said is that the flight occurred after Jarāsaṅdha was enraged by the deaths of his son-in-law Kaṁsa and his two most illustrious warriors Haṁsa and Ḍibhaka (2:13,33-46).

[23] Van Buitenen speaks of a desire to control the Yamunā-Ganges river basins: *Book of the Beginning*, "Introduction," pp. 10-11. But there is a different problem once we locate Kṛṣṇa in distant Dvārakā (see n. 22). I would only note that Kṛṣṇa's concern as a Vṛṣṇi, or descendant of Yadu, for the justness of Yudhiṣṭhira's claim to rule the "center of the earth" (*avanīm madhyamām*; 2:13,7) squares with an "old" injunction laid down by king Yayāti that whereas the line of his youngest son Pūru (in which the Kurus and Pāṇḍavas descend) should occupy the center, the line of Yadu will be reduced to outlying lands and always be *arājyabhākta*, with "no share in the kingdom" (1:79,7); see Dumézil, *Destiny of a King*, p. 16.

[24] Van Buitenen, *Book of the Beginning*, p. 10.

[25] *Ibid.*, p. 11.

[26] *Idem*; see also van Buitenen, "On the Structure of the Sabhāparvan of the *Mahābhārata*," *India Maior*: *Congratulatory Volume Presented to J. Gonda*, edited by J. Ensink and P. Gaeffke (E. J. Brill, 1972), p. 69.

tion, in particular concerning the nature of Kṛṣṇa's and the Vṛṣṇis' interest in the Khāṇḍava Tract, not to mention the down-river areas to the east, now that they are in Gujarat (see nn. 22 and 23). Nor does the epic ever give us any reason to suppose some potential enmity between (Southern) Pāñcāla and the Vṛṣṇis. But, certainly, of all the efforts to find real *events* behind the burning of the forest, van Buitenen's are the most well thought out and plausible. Nonetheless, what all these historicizations have in common is the assumption that the essence of the story lies simply in its result: the forest is cleared, civilization marches on. But look at the differences in the types of civilization that the story is presumed to reflect: a slash and burn subsistence, the Āryans in their push to the east (despite the fact that Khāṇḍava is west of Hāstinapura), and the settled, citied conditions of inter-"clan" geo-politics.

As soon as one puts these historical assumptions face to face with the story itself, certain difficulties arise. The most obvious has been raised by Holtzmann and Hopkins, and while the immediate problem does not emerge from van Buitenen's interpretation, the latter also does not account for the real anomalies which it presents. If Agni, Arjuna, and Kṛṣṇa represent, in some manner, the *ārya*, it is striking that they oppose not just Nāgas and Birds but the "Āryan" gods. Holtzmann and Hopkins attempt to counter this difficulty, as the former puts it, by supposing that the "old saga" would have had Agni on the side of the gods, burning down the forest at their command, and that the new version, in which Arjuna and Kṛṣṇa are superior to the gods, "ist eine unsinnige Übertreibung zu Gunsten der vergötterten Kṛṣṇa." [27]

C. *The Symbolism: Initiations, Allegories, Levels of Narrative Tradition*

There is a point where all of these conquest and land-opening hypotheses should be tested. The symbolism and theology of the story should make sense. But without positing some interpolation and some *inversion* of the text, the "Āryan" opposition to the "Āryan" gods is unintelligible. Such gratuitous rearranging of the text as Holtzmann's, however, is not the only alternative. Rather, two other interpretations suggest themselves as quite plausible. First, as a sort of narrative thread, the episode has an initiatory character,

---

[27] Holtzmann, *Mahābhārata und seine Theile*, II, p. 45; cf. E. W. Hopkins, "The Bhārata and the Great Bhārata," *American Journal of Philology* 19 (1898), p. 15.

one that stands out all the more clearly if we read it as it is presented in the Critical Edition, without the "background myth." It is here that Arjuna and Kṛṣṇa receive their most characteristic weapons, and it is here that their identity as Nara and Nārāyaṇa propels them into action for the first time as figures who carry out the gods' work on earth. There is an initiatory character to the scene where the gods stand before Arjuna and Kṛṣṇa with their weapons upraised. And, more particularly, Arjuna's contest with Indra shows an initiatory pattern: a sort of mock battle in which the god is finally "pleased" with his human son, "descends" (at the same point that Agni reveals himself to Arjuna) to grant favors, and, in doing so anticipates the second initiatory test of Arjuna by Śiva.

The battle itself between a god, lord of this world, and a human also reminds one of the attack by Mara, lord of this world, and his hosts upon Gotama on the eve of the latter's enlightenment: one of the Buddha's final tests. Arjuna, especially in his connection with Kṛṣṇa and in the dual identity of the pair as Nara-Nārāyaṇa (e.g., 1:219, 15) or "the two Kṛṣṇas" (e.g., 1:214, 32; 219, 3), is as much the ascetic hero, even a sort of saviour, as he is the warrior hero. And this is not the only instance where related or even identical folklores have descended upon Arjuna and the Buddha. Aside from the general symbolic connections of each with Indra,[28] there are intriguing common points concerning their marriages. Both, of course, marry at a Svayaṁvara and succeed (Arjuna in winning Draupadī) at drawing a great bow. But more than this, first, whereas the Buddha's wife is named variously Gopā and Yaśodharā (= "Fame Bearer"),[29] Arjuna's second wife Subhadrā is consistently introduced by the epithet *yaśasvinī* ("possessed of fame"; 1:213, 6 and 18, in the latter verse twice). And secondly, when Arjuna introduces his second wife to his first, he attempts to soothe Draupadī's jealousy in the following manner: "Hurriedly, Arjuna had Subhadrā, who was wearing a red silk skirt, change into a cow maid's dress" (*gopālikāvapuḥ*; 1:213, 16: van Buitenen translation). This double convergence of names, epithets, and aspects is most intriguing. Whatever the associations with cowherdesses might mean (Subhadrā being Kṛṣṇa's sister!) the connections with *yaśas* ("fame, glory") is significant. Yaśodharā's main role will be to give the Buddha the one son, Rāhula, through

[28] See Alfred Foucher, *The Life of the Buddha*, Simone Brangier Boas trans. (Middletown, Ct., 1963), p. 30 (births from their mothers' sides).

[29] See *ibid.*, p. 60.

whom Siddhārtha and his father's "royal" line will be able to continue, and then end in the renunciation of both father and son to the life of ascetic abstinence. Similarly, the main role of Subhadrā *yaśasvinī* will be to give Arjuna the one son, Abhimanyu, through whom the Pāṇḍava and Kuru line will be able to continue, and this only after Abhimanyu has died in battle and his son Parikṣit, stillborn, miraculously revived by Kṛṣṇa.[30] Both women are thus "bearers of the fame" of their husbands' lineages, and with instructive inversions: the Buddha's lineage henceforth "spiritual" rather than biological thanks to the double renunciation of father and son, the Pāṇḍavas' lineage biological thanks to the "spiritual" power of Kṛṣṇa who can raise the stillborn child through an "act of truth" [31] by citing, among other things, the "true" fact that he "never brought about hostility with Vijaya [Arjuna]" (14:68, 21). Now it was an "eternal friendship (or affection) with Arjuna" (1:225, 19), granted to Kṛṣṇa by Indra at the end of the burning of the Khāṇḍava forest, that—in the skein of epic events—presumably made this act of truth possible.

But if we regard the initiatory themes as fundamental, the only approach to make sense of the episode as a whole, with all its variants, is Biardeau's. The theme of initiation is itself incorporated: Indra's opposition to Arjuna is only apparent, a test for Arjuna who must be capable of his divinely appointed task.[32] The "background myth," however, is Biardeau's master key. And although the Critical Edition shows us that it is not found in every recension, some of the myth's main themes—in particular, the symbolism by which Biardeau interprets it: that of the *pralaya*, or "dissolution"—are found throughout the text. Indeed, we have purposefully cited much of the *pralaya* imagery already.[33]

Following Biardeau's analysis,[34] Agni's plight is the result of a sacrifice gone wrong and instigated by Śiva, who aids king Śvetaki in

[30] See the discussion of this episode in my article, "The *Mahābhārata* and Hindu Eschatology," *History of Religions Journal* 12,2 (1972), pp. 131-33.

[31] On this concept, citing both Buddhist and Hindu sources, see W. Norman Brown, "Duty as Truth in Ancient India," *Proceedings of the American Philosophical Society* 116,3 (1972), pp. 252-68, and p. 252, n. 1 for bibliography. For fuller discussion of Kṛṣṇa's act of truth, see my *Ritual of Battle*.

[32] Biardeau, *EPHE* 79, p. 140.

[33] See above: e.g., Agni's "seven flames" (216,32) like the seven suns at the *pralaya*; the burning of creatures of all varieties; the great clouds (217,18); Kṛṣṇa as Kāla (219,6), etc.; on the *pralaya* myth, see Biardeau's works (cited above, n. 2), especially EMH, 3.

[34] *EPHE* 79, pp. 140-41.

his egotistical and antidharmic project by pushing him to an excessive sacrifice. Śiva's connection with Agni, the sacrificial fire gone awry, is thus analogous to his own role as Destroyer in the pralaya, where he takes on the character of the fire that exceeds its limits and burns the three worlds. Against this background a full symbolism emerges. Agni's sickness significes the pitiful state of *dharma* and of the brahmans, and the need for "une restauration du bon ordre socio-cosmique." Śiva's intervention indicates that this restoration can take place only through a disaster. Kṛṣṇa, with Arjuna here, thus fulfills his role as *avatāra*: restoring dharma and renewing the world order. Moreover, Biardeau offers an intriguing explanation of the significance of the identities of the survivors: Takṣaka, the "Façonneur," is a "figure du démiurge" [35] Aśvasena ("Army of Horses") is a "nom qui semblerait désigner le fonction royale"; Maya, who will soon build the Pāṇḍavas an illusion-producing palace, "fait voir en lui la Māyā" which permits the empirical world to be recreated and to subsist; and, surprisingly most crucial, the four Śārṅgaka birds represent the four Vedas.[36] On the whole, this interpretation is convincing, the only weak point being a reliance on the names of the first two snakes, whose actual roles do not suggest the identities which they supposedly symbolize. But the case of the birds seems too clear to be dismissed. Thus the escapees, as a group, seem to symbolize the ingredients indispensible, after the pralaya, for a new Creation.

Biardeau also views this episode as prophetic: "L'incendie de la forêt Khāṇḍava est ainsi une nouvelle figure . . . de la guerre de destruction à venir." [37] But in what sense? Here, we feel her own success raises a difficulty. If her interpretation is correct, the story emerges in outline as a very carefully constructed allegory of the pralaya and *sṛṣṭi*. In our view, however, this cannot be said of the Kuru-Pāṇḍava war, the war of destruction to come. The latter presents far more than a mere allegory of the pralaya. Rather, if we are to link the forest-burning episode with the rest of the epic drama, it would seem that its initiatory character is more basic than its

[35] Cf. E. W. Hopkins, *Epic Mythology* (1915; repr. New York, 1969), p. 29.

[36] Not only are the four birds *brahmavādinaḥ* (220,17), but they obtain Agni's favor by chanting hymns to him in a pseudo-Vedic manner (223,7-19); and one in particular, Droṇa, is credited by the gratified Agni with being a ṛṣi and a speaker of brahman (223,21). The birds' clever mother, however, receives no mention (see above, n. 16).

[37] *EPHE* 79, pp. 140-41.

"prophetic" one.[38] We might say that Arjuna and Kṛṣṇa—Nara and Nārāyaṇa—are initiated here into their *capacity* to destroy and "re-create," but without symbolizing, in any direct way, an anticipation of the *fashion* in which they will do so in the great battle. Moreover, it is possible to see conflicting roles for Śiva, on whom the pralaya interpretation rests: in the "background myth" he instigates the sacrifice and the transformation of Agni into the "yuga-ending" fire with which he is identified; but in the "initiatory" scene in which the gods raise their weapons against Arjuna and Kṛṣṇa, Śiva is among the gods who are protecting the forest from Agni.[39]

If one works from the Critical Edition and takes the view that the "background myth" is an interpolation, one might thus see Śiva's "initiatory" role, however minor, as his basic or even "original" one in the episode. Otherwise, Śiva appears as both the cause of the conflagration (even symbolically identical with the destructive Agni), and also opposed to it. But the important point against extending Biardeau's interpretation of this episode to an interpretation of the epic as a whole is that there is no such opposition by Śiva, or for that matter by the rest of the gods, to Arjuna and Kṛṣṇa in the epic war. It is only in the rather vague sense that all "destructions" or "dissolutions" are one that we may speak of the burning of Khāṇḍava forest as a prefiguration of the war of destruction to come.

Much thus depends on how one regards this material which the Critical Edition judges to be interpolated. If we follow the synchronic approach of Biardeau, we see a definite coherence to the passage; but from a diachronic perspective it is a coherence that seems to result from a reshaping of the story to bring it into accord with the cosmology and mythology of the pralaya. On the other hand, if we take the reconstituted Critical text as it stands, pralaya imagery is present; but the main thrust, and the most consistent means to connect the scene with the rest of the epic, concerns a sort of initiatory test with ascetic overtones. One is thus encouraged to look further into the Nara-Nārāyaṇa mythology which seemingly pervades this first

[38] See for a more detailed analysis of the symbolism shaping the *Mahābhārata* war, including a discussion of Biardeau's treatment of it, my "*Mahābhārata* and Hindu Eschatology," especially pp. 102-105.

[39] 1:218,31: he raises a *vicakra* (Monier-Williams: "wheelless," "having no discus" or "no wheels"); vars. *tricakra*, *triśūla*, *vicitra* (?), *śūla*, and *pināka*; van Buitenen settles for "Trident."

joint action of Arjuna and Kṛṣṇa. It is a knotty problem which future research will hopefully begin to unravel.[40]

It is also noteworthy that the interpolated material bears a certain relationship to, and consistency with, other material which, thanks to the Critical Edition, we now know to be "late." It will be recalled from the interpolated "background myth" that Śiva agrees to assist at King Śvetaki's adharmic sacrifice through his brahman surrogate, the ascetic Durvāsas. Now it is this same Durvāsas who, with ten thousand disciples (what we might well call his Śaiva "sect") appears in a clearly interpolated passage (*Āraṇyakaparvan*, App. I, No. 25) as a mere foil of Kṛṣṇa.[41] On the occasion of a visit by Durvāsas to Hāstinapura while the Pāṇḍavas are in exile in the forest, Duryodhana goes all out to gratify the *muni* and is finally granted a boon. He asks Durvāsas and his followers to appear before the Pāṇḍavas in the forest at a time when their meal is finished and Draupadī has just laid down to rest. At such a moment he should demand food for himself and his horde. When Durvāsas arrives at the Pāṇḍavas' retreat and demands food, Draupadī is at a loss. What can she do but pray to Kṛṣṇa (lines 73-88)! Her words express the humble piety of the troubled soul turned to its divine saviour, with the conclusion: "With you as protector, O lord of gods, in every distress there is no fear, as formerly I was set free from Duḥśāsana in the *sabhā*" (lines 86-87). Leaving Rukmiṇī's bed (line 92), Kṛṣṇa comes immediately, and, after some frivolities at the anxious Draupadī's expense, takes some "vegetable and rice" (105) left over from the meal and miraculously causes it to enter Durvāsas and his attendants' stomachs so that they can eat no more. Thinking they might arouse the Pāṇḍavas'

---

[40] Van Buitenen has yet to elaborate on a statement that "Arjuna and Kṛṣṇa . . . are meaningfully said to be the ancient hero pair of Nara and Nārāyaṇa, who, it would appear, are old champions of a rhapsodic tradition drawn into the *Mahābhārata*" (*Book of the Beginning*, p. xxi; see also p. 435, n. to 1.0). If this means that Arjuna and Kṛṣṇa are only secondarily connected with the mythology of Indra and Viṣṇu, and Arjuna only secondarily connected with the Pāṇḍavas and the trifunctional array of gods whom they incarnate as a whole, I think there may be some problems. For a different approach to Nara-Nārāyaṇa, also rather tentative, see Biardeau, EMH, 1, pp. 33-37; 2, pp. 68-80; and 3, pp. 48-56.

[41] This is not to say that everything concerning Durvāsas is necessarily interpolated; it is he who, after testing Kuntī, grants her the ever-so-important mantra that allows her to call down gods to father her children (1:104,4-7). It is interesting to note that this contribution by a "portion" (or a "portion"-to-be) of Śiva to the birth of the Pāṇḍavas is balanced by the contribution of Vyāsa, an incarnation of Viṣṇu-Nārāyaṇa (12:334,11 and 337,4), to the birth of the hundred Kauravas (1:107)—very neatly the opposite of what one would expect.

wrath by having to refuse their meal, Durvāsas decides the wisest course is to leave. And he adds: "I fear still more, O brahmans, from men who take refuge at the feet of Hari" (121).

V.S. Sukthankar has caught much of the tone and significance of this interpolated passage:

> With this story disappears one of the very few episodes . . . in which Śrī Kṛṣṇa is represented as hearing from a distance, as it were by clairaudience or divine omniscience, the prayers of his distressed devotees and as either coming instantly to help them in person or providing invisibly the means of their rescue or safety. The other episode I had in mind . . . [is] the disrobing of Draupadī . . . They undoubtedly represent a later phase of Kṛṣṇa worship.[42]

One must agree, noting not only that the one interpolation recalls the other, but that the "phase" seems to involve a sectarian outlook. Along with a debasement of Durvāsas and his horde of followers, the implications of such a shift in tone seem to include a diminution in the stature of Draupadī consistent with her characterizations in other interpolations. Kṛṣṇa leaves the bed of his consort Rukmiṇī, whom still another interpolation makes into the incarnation of Śrī (see 1:61, 5 and note 566*). And Draupadī is divested of her independence, a representative of submissive bhakti rather than of the mysteriously imperious dignity which she incarnates elsewhere as the *true* embodiment of Śrī on earth.

All this is not to say that the Critical Edition is to be followed blindly. Very often material limited to one recension throws real light on a passage or episode. Indeed, such is the case with the "background myth" discussed by Biardeau. But there are instances where the Critical Edition allows us to see that interpolated material seems to have a synchronism of its own, one which sets the material involved apart from what can pretty safely be called true epic. At this point, the "background myth" of the Khāṇḍava episode looks like a transitional case. There is nothing of the gratuitous piety and sectarianism that marks the other interpolations just cited. But there are inconsistencies in the characterization of Śiva which point us in the direction of regarding the pralaya symbolism as a clever and thoroughgoing reshaping of an initiation scenario. It would be nice if it were possible to make this notion more precise, but that must await further elucidation of the Nara-Nārāyaṇa problem. For the moment,

---

[42] Sukthankar, ed., *Āraṇyakaparvan* (Critical Edition), "Introduction," p. xiii n. 1.

we may note a remark by van Buitenen: "It is debatable how far this account of *The Burning of the Khāṇḍava Forest* belongs to the central story, but surely it is an ancient story, and part of the cycle of the heroes of the epic."[43] It would seem that if it is originally from some extra-epic source, it has been linked to the rest of the story first by its initiatory content, and secondarily through the symbolism of the pralaya. Yet this does not necessarily imply a temporal order of development. As pointed out earlier, the type of initiation which the heroes undergo is an ascetic one, and one which thereby implies an initiation into the capacity for world destruction.[44] A "trial by Fire," that is, by an agent of world destruction, is thus entirely fitting, even more so as it is concerned with the pair Nara-Nārāyaṇa.[45] Accordingly, even if the "background myth" is late, the pralaya theme is probably essential. Indeed, it would seem most likely that this theme, which is woven through the narrative as it is presented in the Critical text, has been amplified by the "background myth" and worked into a full allegory by incorporating into the main story the sub-episode concerning the four precocious Śārṅgaka birds.[46] One might thus propose that whereas the initiatory content provides a

---

[43] Van Buitenen, *Book of the Beginning*, p. 13.

[44] It becomes a commonplace in the Indian tradition that the ascetic has power to create and destroy "worlds". Creation of worlds can be traced at least to *Bṛhad-Āraṇyaka Up.* 1,4,15-16 (out of the *loka* of the Self one creates, *sṛjate*, whatever he desires, i.e., *lokas* for other classes of beings), and perhaps to *Śatapatha Brāhmaṇa* 6,2,2,7, on which see Jan Gonda, *Loka: World and Heaven in the Veda* (Amsterdam, 1966), pp. 139, 143-44. "Breaking through spheres" (*maṇḍalāni bhittvā*) on the way to the ultimate abode of Viṣṇu occurs in an interesting passage in *Maitrāyaṇīya Up.* 6,38. Cf. also the "levelling" or "clearing" of Buddha-fields (e.g., *Lotus Sūtra*, chap. 11), and the passage of *kuṇḍalinī* through the tantric *cakras*. All these instances reflect stages and powers of meditation.

[45] A basic motif is met in stories of heroes (e.g., Viśvāmitra: *Mbh.* 1:65,20ff.) whose ascetic heat, *tapas*, menaces the throne of the god of *this* world (i.e., Indra), Arjuna and Kṛṣṇa's halfhearted opponent in the forest burning scene (cf. also, again, the Buddha and Mara). As a theological power, creation and destruction of worlds is of course attributed to Śiva, Viṣṇu, and Kṛṣṇa (see *Bhagavad Gītā* 11, 19-32 and Biardeau, EMH, 3, pp. 52-54), and it is notable that Vyāsa once explains that the identity which Kṛṣṇa and Arjuna share, as Nara-Nārāyaṇa, is due to Nara being born from Nārāyaṇa's *tapas* (7:172,80). One might well think of Kṛṣṇa's invitation to Arjuna to "be the mere instrument" (*Gītā* 11,33) of destruction at Kuru-*kṣetra*(!) in this connection. On Arjuna-Nara's destructive capacity, see also *Mbh.* 5:94 (Dambhodbhava episode).

[46] One must agree with van Buitenen that the Śārṅgaka bird story, which clearly breaks up the narrative and has its own folkloric tone, "can hardly be original" (*Book of the Beginning*, p. 1).

narrative link with the rest of the epic, the pralaya symbolism supplies a thematic link that continued to serve as a base for further elaborations. Such reflections, of course, neither confirm nor undermine the geo-political considerations raised by van Buitenen, or for that matter by others. They only indicate that the story itself can begin to make sense as story, whether or not it also makes sense as history.

# CONTRIBUTORS

BARDWELL L. SMITH is the John W. Nason Professor of Asian Studies at Carleton College, Northfield, Minnesota. He has also served as Dean of the College, 1967-72. He has received his B.A., B.D., M.A. and Ph.D. from Yale University and was a member of the Yale University Council, 1969-74. During 1972-73 he did research at the School of Oriental and African Studies, University of London, on a grant from the American Council of Learned Societies. He has edited a number of books, among them: *The Two Wheels of Dhamma: Essays on the Theravada Tradition in India and Ceylon* (American Academy of Religion, 1972); *Tradition and Change in Theravada Buddhism: Essays on Ceylon and Thailand in the 19th and 20th Centuries* (Leiden: E. J. Brill, 1973); and *Unsui: A Diary of Zen Monastic Life* (Honolulu: University Press of Hawaii, 1973).

NORVIN J. HEIN is presently Professor of Comparative Religion at Yale Divinity School. His undergraduate work was at the College of Wooster and his B.D. and Ph.D. (1951) were at Yale. Prior to his appointment at Yale he taught English for four years at Ewing Christian College, Allahabad, India. He is the author of the bibliographical guide, "Hinduism," in Charles J. Adams, *A Reader's Guide to the Great Religions* (New York: Free Press Macmillan, 1965), now undergoing a new edition; and of the book, *The Miracle Plays of Mathura* (Delhi: Oxford University Press 1973); and of various articles in *Die Religion in Geschichte und Gegenwart*, 3rd edition. At present, he is working on the adaptation of the Upanishad material in the *Bhagavadgītā*'s teaching on meditation.

JOSEPH T. O'CONNELL is Assistant Professor of Religious Studies at St. Michael's College in the University of Toronto, where since 1968 (excluding one year for research in Bangladesh) he has taught comparative courses in religion with a concentration upon the Hindu tradition. He has published in the *Journal of the American Oriental Society*, the *Ecumenist*, and the *International Journal*. His research includes a doctoral dissertation on Bengali Vaiṣṇavism and current projects in Bengali Islam, e.g., an anthology of Muslim writings in Bengali and a textual study of the *Satī Maynā o Lor-Candrānī*.

WALTER G. NEEVEL, Jr. is Assistant Professor of Philosophy and Religious Studies at the University of Wisconsin, Milwaukee. He has previously taught at the University of Virginia and at Boston University. More recently, he has been a Research Assistant at the Center for the Study of World Religions, Harvard University. His doctoral dissertation at Harvard, in the field of History of Religion, is entitled "The Pāñcarātrika Vedānta of Yāmunācārya". His previous publications are "Rāmānuja on Bhakti and Prapatti," in *The Journal of Religious Studies* (Patiala, India), 1971; and *Ethnic and Universal Religions* (Delhi: Motilal Banarsidass, forthcoming), a partial English translation of Gustav Mensching's *Die Religion*, on which he collaborated with Hans J. Klimkeit.

CYRUS R. PANGBORN is Professor of Religion and Chairman of the Department in Douglass College, Rutgers—The State University, New Brunswick, N.J. A graduate of Kansas Wesleyan and Yale Divinity School, he received his Ph.D. in Religion from Columbia University in 1951 and taught at the State University of Iowa until called to Rutgers in 1954. His interests in Hinduism and Zoroastrianism have been shaped by studies in India as a Fulbright Research Scholar (1962-63) and as a Fellow of the K. R. Cama Oriental Institute in 1971. He has contributed to the *AAUP Bulletin*, the *Journal of Bible and Religion* (now entitled *Journal of the American Academy of Religion*), *Christian Century*, *Prabuddha Bharati*, and *Contributions to Asian Studies* (ed. by K. Ishwaran).

MIRA REYM BINFORD is with the Department of South Asian Studies, University of Wisconsin. Born in Poland, she has lived in India for six years and Bangladesh for six months writing and researching documentary films, doing research on educational and family planning films, and currently making several films with Michael Camerini for the "Civilization of South Asia Film Project" (*Pilgrimage to Ramdevra*, *Pilgrimage to Kashi*, *Chittirai Festival of Madurai*, *Four Hindu Sadhus*, *Village and City*, and *Bangladesh: A Nation's Search for Identity*). At present, she is doing graduate work in South Asian Studies and Communication. Her research interests involve the use of film in cross-cultural communication, comprehension of the film medium in non-literate societies, and traditional modes of 'mass' communication and their adaptation to new ideas. Her publications include the following: *Films for the Study of India*, 1970; *Family Planning Films*, 1971 (both are critically annotated catalogues).

ELEANOR ZELLIOT is Associate Professor of History at Carleton College, where she has been since 1969. Prior to that, she taught at the University of Minnesota (1966-69) to which she remains affiliated as a researcher for the South Asia Historical Atlas project which is centered there. Her undergraduate work was at William Penn College, her M.A. at Bryn Mawr, and her Ph.D. (1969) at the University of Pennsylvania. Over the years she has spent more than two years in India, mainly in Maharashtra where her research interests lie. She has held offices in both the American Institute of Indian Studies and the Association for Asian Studies. Her publications include the following: "Buddhism and Politics in Maharashtra," in Donald E. Smith (ed.), *South Asian Politics and Religion* (Princeton: Princeton University Press, 1966); "Background of the Mahar Buddhist Conversion," in Robert Sakai (ed.), *Studies on Asia, 1966* (Lincoln: University of Nebraska Press, 1966); "Learning the Use of Political Means: The Mahars of Maharashtra," in Rajni Kothari (ed.), *Caste in Indian Politics* (New Delhi: Allied Publishers, 1970); "The Nineteenth Century Background of the Mahar and non-Brahman Movements in Maharashtra," *The Indian Economic and Social History Review*, Vol. VII (No. 3), 1970; "Literary Images of the Indian City," in Richard G. Fox (ed.), *Urban India: Society, Space and Image* (Durham: Duke University Press, 1971); "Gandhi and Ambedkar: A Study in Leadership," in J. Michael Mahar (ed.), *The Untouchable in Contemporary India* (Tucson: University of Arizona Press, 1972); also, "Bibliography on Untouchability," in the same work on Eknāth, a 16th century Maharashtrian saint-poet.

J. BRUCE LONG has been a member of the Asian Studies Department at Cornell University since 1972. He received his M.A. in Theology and Literature (1963) and his Ph.D. in History of Religions (with a specialization in Sanskrit and Indian Studies) in 1970 from the Divinity School of the University of Chicago. Following a year of research in Madras, under a grant from the American Institute of Indian Studies, he taught for four years (1968-72) at Haverford College, Pennsylvania. Among his publications are the following: *Judaism and the Christian Seminary Curriculum*, ed. (Chicago: Loyola University Press, 1966); "Shiva and Dionysos—Visions of Terror and Bliss," *Numen*, XVIII, 1971; "Festival of Repentance: A Study of Mahāśivarātri," *Journal of the Oriental Institute*, Baroda, XXII, 1972; "Death as Necessity and Gift in Hindu Epic Mythology," in *Encounters with*

*Death and Dying*, ed. by Frank E. Reynolds; and "A Critical Introduction: in Sri Aurobindo's *The Synthesis of Yoga*, American Edition, 1974.

ALF HILTEBEITEL is Assistant Professor of the History of Religion at George Washington University, where he has taught since 1968. His publications include articles in the *History of Religions Journal* and the *Journal of Asian Studies*. Also, he has translated two books by Georges Dumézil: *The Destiny of the Warrior* and *The Destiny of a King* (Chicago: University of Chicago Press, 1970 and 1973). His doctoral dissertation is being prepared for publication under the title *The Ritual of Battle: Kṛṣṇa and the Mahābhārata*. His present interests involve further research into Indian epics and comparative epic mythology.

# INDEX